GOVERNMENT AND THE RAILWAYS
IN NINETEENTH-CENTURY
BRITAIN

STUDIES IN POLITICAL HISTORY

Editor: Michael Hurst

Fellow of St John's College, Oxford

CHIEF WHIP: The Political Life and Times of Aretas Akers-Douglas 1st Viscount Chilston by Eric Alexander 3rd Viscount Chilston.

GUIZOT: Aspects of French History 1787–1874 by Douglas Johnson.

MARGINAL PRYNNE: 1660–1669 by William M. Lamont.

LAND AND POWER: British and Allied Policy on Germany's Frontiers 1916–1919 by H. I. Nelson.

THE LANGUAGE OF POLITICS in the Age of Wilkes and Burke by James T. Boulton.

THE ENGLISH FACE OF MACHIAVELLI: A Changing Interpretation 1500–1700 by Felix Raab.

BEFORE THE SOCIALISTS: Studies in Labour and Politics 1861–1881 by Royden Harrison.

THE LAWS OF WAR IN THE LATE MIDDLE AGES by M. H. Keen.

GOVERNMENT AND THE RAILWAYS IN NINETEENTH-CENTURY BRITAIN by Henry Parris.

THE ENGLISH MILITIA IN THE EIGHTEENTH CENTURY: The Story of a Political Issue 1660–1802 by J. R. Western.

SALISBURY AND THE MEDITERRANEAN 1886–1896 by C. J. Lowe.

GOVERNMENT AND THE RAILWAYS

in

Nineteenth-Century Britain

by

HENRY PARRIS

Lecturer in Politics
in the University of Durham

LONDON: Routledge & Kegan Paul
TORONTO: University of Toronto Press
1965

First published 1965
in Great Britain by
Routledge & Kegan Paul Ltd
and in Canada by
University of Toronto Press

Printed in Great Britain by
R. & R. Clark Ltd, Edinburgh

CONTENTS

PLATES

Note: Plates I–VII and VIII (a) and (c) are from the
Illustrated London News; Plate VIII (b) is reproduced by
courtesy of the Institution of Royal Engineers, Chatham;
Plate VIII (d), by courtesy of the National Portrait
Gallery.

PREFACE

RAILWAYS, declared *The Times* in 1884,

> have become an Empire within the Empire. . . . The experience of forty years has brought conclusive proof of the grave initial mistake made in the relations between the State and the railways. It would have been well if large powers of State interference had been insisted upon from the very first. As this was not done, it remains only to create them now that the need for them has been amply demonstrated. . . . State interference is not safely to be dispensed with in face of the gigantic forces which railway enterprise has called into being.

Long before those words were written, railways had indeed raised problems for almost every department of British government. The Post Office had to arrange for the carriage of mails by train. The Foreign and Colonial Offices were interested in railway development overseas. The Home Office was quick to realise the value of railways in the preservation of public order.[1] The Admiralty watched all projects that might hinder navigation. Robert Stephenson's design for the Britannia Bridge, for example, was radically modified as a result of Admiralty objections.[2] The Army authorities exercised a similar scrutiny. Their hostility was probably the most important factor in the suspension of work on the Channel Tunnel in 1882.[3]

All these departments, however, were merely extending their existing functions to the new system of transport. What *The Times* had in mind was a new function; the regulation of railways by the government on behalf of the public. The growth of

[1] F. C. Mather, 'The Railways, the Electric Telegraph, and Public Order during the Chartist Period, 1837–48', *History*, xxxviii (1953) 40–53; and the same author's *Public Order in the Age of the Chartists*, Manchester Univ. Press (1959).

[2] S. Smiles, *Lives of the Engineers. iii: George and Robert Stephenson*, London (1862), 421.

[3] C. H. Ellis, *British Railway History, 1877–1947*, Allen & Unwin (1959), 70.

that function in nineteenth-century Britain forms the theme of this book. To discharge it new agencies were set up of which the most important was the Railway Department of the Board of Trade, the origin of the present Ministry of Transport. What were its powers and in what spirit were they exercised? Who worked in it and what sort of men were they? What did they know about railways? Were they mere theorists trying to push their ideas down the throats of practical railwaymen? Or were they practical men themselves? What did the Inspecting Officers look for when deciding whether new lines were safe enough to open for passenger traffic? How did they conduct accident enquiries? What was the attitude of the companies towards the Department's recommendations? Were they implemented willingly, or grudgingly, or not at all? What was the Department's rôle in the development of such devices as signalling, or block working? In short, how much influence did the Department have on British railways in the nineteenth century?

Just as government regulation influenced railways, so did the railways influence government. Failure to recognise this truism mars some previous discussions of the subject. Older authors[1] tended to regard the state as something that was—or ought to be—above the activities of social and economic life (e.g. railway enterprise) and endowed with sufficient power to influence those activities in any desired manner. If, therefore, the state did not do what such historians thought it should have done, they were inclined to explain the failure in terms of the short-sightedness, or the cowardice, or even the treachery of statesmen. Admittedly, their railway policies had their shortcomings. But to understand them, it is necessary to consider, not only the character of the statesmen responsible, but also the political system in which they functioned. Nineteenth-century British statesmen worked always within the limits of what Parliament would stand, and among the most important facts of Parliamentary life was the strength of the interests represented there. Prominent among them, especially from the 'forties to the 'eighties, was the railway interest. The conflicting aims of the companies prevented it achieving very much positively to

---

[1] E.g. G. Cohn, *Untersuchungen über die englische Eisenbahnpolitik*, 3 vols., Leipzig (1874–83); and E. Cleveland-Stevens, *English Railways: their Development and their Relation to the State*, Routledge (1915).

promote the welfare of railways in general; but as a negative force, united in opposition to measures of regulation, it was to be reckoned with.

The delegation to the Board of Trade of powers over the companies raised novel problems, and novel means had to be devised for their solution. The Railway Department was a microcosm of the process whereby British government adjusted itself to the new needs of an industrial society. Hence a study of it throws light on many aspects of public administration. Was recruitment of civil servants by patronage so bad in practice as it sounds in principle? How far does modern administrative law stem from the nineteenth century? A general trend in nineteenth-century administration was the supersession of boards by ministerial departments; why? These are a few of the topics raised by the experience of the Railway Department. It also offers a new view of some well-known characters. The nineteenth-century statesman carrying Bills through Parliament, or corresponding with colleagues about matters of high policy, is a familiar figure. But what of the gestation of those Bills in the Department, long before their first reading? And after receiving the Royal Assent, what of their implementation? What filled up a minister's days in the office, and what were his relations with his subordinates there? Such question are usually ignored by political historians and biographers. This book seeks to supply some of the answers.

I would like to acknowledge the obligations which I owe, for access to the records on which this study is based, to Her Majesty, the Queen, for the Melbourne Papers; the Earl of Clarendon, and the Bodleian Library, for the Clarendon Papers; the Public Record Office, for departmental records and the Russell and Cardwell Papers; the British Museum, for the Ripon, Gladstone, Peel, Pasley, and Aberdeen Papers; the Scottish Record Office, for the Dalhousie Papers; the National Trust, for the Disraeli Papers at Hughenden; British Transport Historical Records; the House of Lords Record Office; and the Inspecting Officers of Railways at the Ministry of Transport. I am grateful to the editors of *Public Administration* and the *Bulletin of the Institute of Historical Research* for permission to use material which has already appeared in their pages. I must also acknowledge my indebtedness to the Trustees of the Houblon-

Norman Fund for a generous grant towards the expense of research: and to the Rt. Hon. Harold Wilson C.B.E., M.P., who allowed me to read his unpublished study of government regulation of railways.

This book is a revised version of a thesis accepted by the University of Leicester for the degree of Ph.D. I should like to thank Professors A. J. Brown and Maurice Beresford for their help during the early stages of its academic career; and Professor Jack Simmons, whose encouragement and sympathy, as supervisor, were not less valuable than his advice and guidance. In its present form, it owes much to the friendly criticism of a number of people who have read it at various stages: Professor H. J. Hanham, Professor Edward Hughes, Mr. Michael Hurst, Mr. R. M. Robbins, and the late Mr. T. S. Lascelles. My friends Graham and Mary Higgins have laboured to remove some at least of the infelicities of style, while Mr. Colin Franklin, of Routledge, has been most helpful, not least in suggesting the title. I am grateful to them all. Finally, I must thank my wife for her help and support at every stage in the writing of this book.

HENRY PARRIS

CONVENTIONS AND ABBREVIATIONS USED IN THE TEXT

IN quotations, words are given in their modern spelling; the use of capital letters has been made to conform with modern practice; punctuation marks have been added where needed to bring out the sense more clearly; words omitted are indicated thus . . .; words added or altered are enclosed in square brackets.

The word 'Board' normally means the Board of Trade; the word 'Department' normally means the Railway Department of the Board of Trade.

The ampersand (&) has been used in the titles of railway companies: e.g. 'Manchester & Birmingham'.

ABBREVIATIONS

(a) General

Add. MS.	British Museum: Additional Manuscript.
BT	Public Record Office: Board of Trade Papers.
BTHR	British Transport Historical Records.
C.J.	House of Commons Journals.
Cleveland-Stevens	E. Cleveland-Stevens, *English Railways: their Development and their Relation to the State*, Routledge (1915).
Cohn	G. Cohn, *Untersuchungen über die englische Eisenbahnpolitik*, 3 vols., Leipzig (1874–83).
Dir.	Directory.
D.N.B.	Dictionary of National Biography.
Hansard	Hansard's Parliamentary Debates: Third Series: (quoted by volume and column number).
L.J.	House of Lords Journals.
MacDermot	E. T. MacDermot, *History of the Great Western Railway*, 2 vols.: vol. 1 bound in 2 parts, G.W.R. (1927–1931).
MT	Public Records Office: Board of Trade Railway Department Papers, subsequently transferred to the Ministry of Transport.

P.P.	Parliamentary Papers.
P.R.O.	Public Record Office.
Rolt	L. T. C. Rolt, *Red for Danger*, Bodley Head (1955).
S.R.O.	Scottish Record Office.

(b) *Titles of Railway Companies*

G.E.	Great Eastern.
G.J.	Grand Junction.
G.N.	Great Northern.
G.N.E.	Great North of England.
G.W.	Great Western.
L.B.S.C.	London, Brighton & South Coast.
L.C.D.	London, Chatham & Dover.
L.N.W.	London & North Western.
L.S.W.	London & South Western.
L. & Y.	Lancashire & Yorkshire.
M. & L.	Manchester & Leeds.
M.S.L.	Manchester, Sheffield & Lincolnshire.
N.B.	North British.
N.E.	North Eastern.
O.W.W.	Oxford, Worcester & Wolverhampton.
R.	(added to the abbreviated title of any company) Railway.
S.E.	South Eastern.
Y.N.B.	York, Newcastle & Berwick.
Y.N.M.	York & North Midland.

THE NEED FOR
GOVERNMENT ACTION

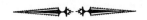

GOVERNMENT regulation of railways in Great Britain dates from 1840, when the Board of Trade Railway Department was set up. The middle decades of the nineteenth century seem to many in retrospect the very heyday of *laissez-faire*. Why was such a step taken at such a time? The answer is to be found in the development which had already taken place prior to that date.

In one sense, railways in Britain were already old. In the early seventeenth century, there was a wagon-way laid with rails to take coal from pits near Nottingham down to the Trent. In 1606, a railway was used to carry coal from Broseley in Shropshire to the banks of the Severn. Eight years later, there was one in Northumberland running between coal pits and salt pans near the mouth of the River Blyth. Since that date, there has been a continuous history of railways in north-east England. There, in 1676, the practice was to lay

> rails of timber from the colliery down to the river, exactly straight and parallel; and bulky carts are made with four rowlets fitting these rails; whereby the carriage is so easy that one horse will draw down four or five chaldron of coals, and it is an immense benefit to the coal merchants.[1]

In the early eighteenth century, coals were

> loaded . . . into a great machine, called a wagon, which by the means of an artificial road, called a wagon-way, goes with the

[1] R. North, *Life of the Rt. Hon. Francis North* (1742), quoted in C. E. Lee, *Evolution of Railways*, Tothill (2nd ed. 1943), 28.

help of but one horse, and carries two chaldron or more at a time; and this sometimes three or four miles to the nearest river or water-carriage.[1]

By this time, and probably in the seventeenth century too, much capital was invested to secure a level road. In 1725, near Tanfield in County Durham, there was a wagon-way

> over valleys filled with earth, 100 foot high, 300 foot broad at bottom: other valleys as large have a stone bridge laid across; in other places hills are cut through for half a mile together . . . [with] frames of timber laid for five miles to the river side.[2]

One such stone bridge was the Tanfield Arch, which still stands today.

These early railways had many features in common with their modern counterparts. They were specially designed for the traffic they had to carry, with elaborate engineering works where the nature of the country required them. Though the rails were of wood, they rested on transverse sleepers like a modern line. The rolling stock was specialised also. It is highly probable that the distinguishing feature from the earliest times was the flanged wheel, although the earliest positive evidence of its use in this country dates from 1734. In this case, the wheels were of iron, and it appears that the practice of covering wooden rails with plates of iron came in at about the same period. Cast-iron rails were certainly in use at Coalbrookdale in Shropshire in the second half of the eighteenth century.

These early lines were built by private agreement with the land-owners. In 1758, a further step was taken when an Act of Parliament was obtained, which authorised the construction of a railway from Middleton colliery to Leeds. During the Canal Age, many railways were authorised in this way as feeders to canals, the first being constructed under an Act of 1776, to link the Caldon Low quarries to Froghall wharf on the Trent and Mersey canal.

Canal proprietors might allow the public to use their lines on payment of a toll. But the first public railway in its own right was the Surrey Iron Railway, authorised by Act of Parliament in 1801, and opened in 1803. It linked Croydon with the

---

[1] D. Defoe, *Complete English Tradesman* (1726), quoted in Lee, op. cit., 28.
[2] W. Stukeley, *Itinerarium Curiosum*, quoted in Lee, op. cit., 31.

Thames at Wandsworth. A separate company carried the line on from Croydon to Merstham in 1805. This, like all the railways mentioned so far, carried goods only. The first passenger traffic was on the Swansea & Oystermouth from 1807.

None of these lines, of course, used mechanical power. The steam locomotive, invented by Cugnot, and developed by Murdock, was put on the rail by Richard Trevithick. It first ran on the Penydarren tramroad near Merthyr Tydfil in 1804. Four years later, Trevithick demonstrated another engine on a circular track near Euston; he was a mechanical genius but lacked the business acumen to develop his ideas further. The first commercially successful locomotive was built by Matthew Murray and John Blenkinsop and started work on the Middleton colliery line near Leeds in 1812. It was driven by means of a cogged wheel engaging in a track rail laid beside the ordinary track. The purpose of this was to increase the tractive effort whilst keeping down the weight of the engine so as to minimise the wear and tear on cast-iron rails. This refinement soon proved unnecessary.

The main centre of development in locomotive design in the years that followed was the north-east coalfield. George Stephenson's work was part of this development; he built his first engine there in 1814. Another important step taken about the same time in that district was the use of wrought-iron in place of cast-iron for rails. The former material had been tried at various places, especially in Scotland. Its greater durability was recognised, but its cost was too high for general use. In 1820, however, John Birkinshaw patented a new method of rolling which made it possible to produce a greater length of rail from a given quantity of material. The new rails were first used at Bedlington and their success led to the general introduction of wrought-iron for the permanent way.

The Stockton & Darlington Railway (opened in 1825) brought together most of the strands of development over more than two centuries. It was a specialised track laid over a specially engineered route. It had specialised rolling stock and locomotive power. It provided public services, though only for goods traffic. In its early years, passengers still travelled by coaches adapted for use on the rails, drawn by horses, and not operated by the company. Outside its immediate locality,

Stockton & Darlington aroused little interest at the time. In the next county, only a few months before it opened, the *Yorkshire Gazette* devoted a leader to railways without mentioning it. When it did open, the same paper thought the event worth only eight lines.[1] In 1830, most men 'still imagined that a railway was a purely industrial machine of local significance . . . [and] regarded it much as people of our own time regard ropeways, telpherage and belt-conveyors'.[2] It was not until the opening of the Liverpool & Manchester Railway in 1830, where passengers enjoyed from the first a regular service of trains drawn by locomotives and operated by the company, that the public sensed the dawn of a new age.

Thus in 1840 British railways, which had existed for almost two and a half centuries, were in another sense only ten years old. To put it in another way, the elements were old, but the compound excitingly new.

The clearest way to indicate the newness of railways in August, 1840, when the Board of Trade Railway Department began work, is to show how rudimentary was the railway network. The early lines had been built independently of one another. Often they were envisaged as subsidiary to water transport. The earliest wagon-ways carried coal from the pit-head to the nearest river. On a larger scale, the Stockton & Darlington carried the produce of a coalfield to the sea. Its rôle was still secondary. In 1840, railways conceived as entities complete in themselves, or intended to function with other railways, were still exceptional. The lines in existence, moreover, were only just beginning to link up with one another. It was possible to take a train from Newcastle to Carlisle at one end of England, or from Bodmin to Wadebridge at the other. But there were few long-distance through routes.

Of those few, London was already the centre, although its first line—a section of the London & Greenwich—had opened only in 1836. The Londoner had the choice of two main-line termini south of the Thames, and three north. From Nine Elms, he could travel to Southampton by the newly opened London & South Western. From London Bridge, he could as yet go only as far as Greenwich or Croydon; the lines to

---

[1] *Yorkshire Gazette*, 5 Feb. and 1 Oct. 1825.
[2] C. H. Ellis, *British Railway History, 1830-1876*, Allen & Unwin (1954), 22.

Brighton and Dover were still unfinished. On the other side of the river, the Eastern Counties had made great promises, but was in fact open from its terminus at Shoreditch only to Brentwood. Paddington was the gateway to Reading; the other terminus of the Great Western, however, was not Bristol, as ultimately planned, but Faringdon Road, a small station in the depth of a remote countryside. Only Euston offered the traveller a wide choice of destinations.

Euston was the starting-point of the London & Birmingham Railway, which had been open two years. It passed through Rugby and Coventry, and had one branch (owned by an independent company) to Aylesbury. At Birmingham, the traveller could change to the Grand Junction and go on, by way of Stafford and the still insignificant Crewe, to the point where it joined the Liverpool & Manchester. Most passengers terminated their journeys in one or other of those towns. Those wishing to go farther north could go as far as Lancaster by way of Wigan and Preston. Any further extension of the route was highly problematic.

Euston was also the Londoner's station for the Midlands and north-east. From Rugby, on the London & Birmingham, he could go by way of the Midland Counties, to Leicester (junction with the Leicester & Swannington), Nottingham, or Derby. At Hampton Junction, beyond Coventry, or at Birmingham itself, he could transfer to the Birmingham & Derby Railway. By whichever route the traveller reached Derby, he could go on to Leeds by the North Midland, with an independently owned branch to Sheffield. At Normanton, there was a junction with the newly-completed York & North Midland—all of these lines had been opened since 1837. The York & North Midland crossed the Leeds & Selby, which had been open since 1834. Beyond York, a company was building a line to Darlington and had powers to carry it to Newcastle. But the prospect of an East Coast route to Scotland, like that of the West Coast route, was uncertain and remote. The prospect of two routes was visionary. Two commissioners, Lt.-Col. Sir Frederic Smith, R.E., and Professor Peter Barlow, of the Royal Military Academy, Woolwich, were making a survey for the Treasury to show which of the two contemplated routes to Scotland was preferable. In fact, both were to be completed within ten years. But few seriously contemplated such a possibility in 1840.

The northern extremities of what eventually became the main routes to Scotland were only two of the obvious gaps in the rail network of 1840. England, south of the G.W.R. and west of the L.S.W., had only the minute Bodmin & Wadebridge. Between London and the Humber there were no railways whatever. Wales and Scotland had no main lines. Although the commercial results of the lines so far open had in general been encouraging, economic conditions were so depressed in 1840 as to create great difficulties for those companies which were still building. Promotion of new lines was at a standstill and districts still unprovided for could entertain few rational hopes of being soon supplied.

Nor was the locomotive by any means completely established. There were still lines worked by horses, such as the Surrey Iron Railway, The Stratford & Moreton, and the Whitby & Pickering. The Canterbury & Whitstable, after struggling with its solitary engine for ten years, actually gave up using it, and reverted to working by horse power, gravity, and a stationary engine. Elsewhere, stationary engines supplemented locomotives. Even from Euston, trains were drawn up by cable to Chalk Farm. Where locomotives alone were used, they were often very unreliable. In this respect, the G.W.R. went through the worst difficulties. Brunel designed most of its early engines with unfortunate results. When the first section of the line opened in June, 1838, only one of the ten locomotives was dependable. Breakdowns occurred almost daily. The company gave up working to time-table, and in August, 1840, announced only the times at which trains would leave the termini, not venturing to prophesy when they would arrive at any particular station. The first engine of improved design, the work of Daniel Gooch, was delivered in March, 1840, and things began to get better. Time-tables were not restored, however, until December, 1840.

Unreliable engines and frequent breakdowns were partly, but not wholly, responsible for the haphazard methods of operation. In September and October, 1838, G.W. drivers were liable to meet an experimental train which the company had given the freedom of its rails. At least two accidents ensued, one of them fatal. It was quite usual on that line also, prior to November, 1840, to put down-trains on the upline, and vice versa, when the proper line was for any reason not available. On one occasion, Babbage, the mathematician, was about to set out by special train from Paddington on the wrong line but deferred his departure when he heard an engine coming. It was another special, of which the station staff had no knowledge. When trains were late, it was quite usual to send out an engine on the same line, at the risk of collision, to search for the missing train and assist it in case of need.

The trains had very little braking power. Continuous brakes had, of course, still to be invented. Brake-vans were coming into use, with a guard to operate the brake. The fireman might have one on the tender. But some trains still ran without any brakes, and on the longer trains, the amount of braking power was rarely increased in proportion. Signals were usually given by means of a flag or lamp held in the hand. Fixed signals were coming into use on the main lines; between March, 1840, and February, 1841, for example, on the G.W.R. The first signal box had been put up in 1839 at the junction of the London & Greenwich and London & Croydon, but was no more than a shelter for the signalman. The electric telegraph had been tried experimentally as an aid to railway operation prior to 1840; but no company was using it systematically for that purpose in August of that year. Nor was there any means of communication between the guard and the driver while the train was in motion—except, indeed, on those lines where traffic was so slow that railway servants clambered from coach to coach, collecting tickets along the moving train.

Hence, railway travelling was potentially very dangerous. The actual number of accidents attributable to management prior to 1840 was small. But the equipment and mode of operation was such that serious accidents could be expected anywhere at any time. What were the prospects of improvement? The orthodox economics of the age relied on competition as the motive force making for improved service by entrepreneurs to the public. But in the case of railways it could not be relied on. For all their imperfections, railways had already by 1840 shown their superiority to other forms of transport. Thoughtful men already saw that competition would do little to make railway companies provide better services. On the contrary, the prospect was that they would become more and more monopolistic as time went on.

It was this fear of railway monopoly that led directly to the first Railway Regulation Act and the beginning of the Board of Trade's jurisdiction over railways. In 1839, traders petitioned the House of Commons, complaining of the monopolistic policy pursued by the London & Birmingham Railway. In consequence, a Select Committee was appointed.[1] The committee saw that the development of railways was already such that the ordinary assumptions as to the relation between economics and politics no longer applied. Indeed, inasmuch as railway companies had been granted special powers, and subjected to special restrictions, by Parliament, they never had been on the same footing as other business enterprises. Parliament had supposed, however, that once free access to the lines had been secured for carriers, and the tolls payable by those carriers to companies fixed, free competition would secure the best and cheapest service in the interest of the public.

These expectations had not been realised. Competition from road transport was already almost dead. Competition from canals was still sometimes effective, but the committee was 'aware that instances are not infrequent where companies and large capitalists, instead of competing with each other . . . have combined, and entered into agreements, whereby the public have suffered'.[2]

As to competition on any given line by rival carriers:

> it does not appear to have been the intention of Parliament to give to a railway company the complete monopoly of the means of communication upon their line. . . . The intention of Parliament . . . cannot, however, be carried into effect . . . any person with the mere authority to place an engine and carriage on a railway would be, practically, unable to supply his engine with water, or to take up and set down passengers . . . and, indeed, would be placed in such a disadvantageous situation, that all competition with the company would be rendered impossible.[3]

More fundamentally, even if such competition were possible, it was not desirable, since:

[1] Hansard, **xlvi,** 1220; Cleveland-Stevens, 71.
[2] P.P. 1840, xiii, 175.   [3] P.P. 1839, x, 132.

the safety of the public also requires that upon every railway there should be one system of management. . . . On this account it is necessary that the company should possess a complete control . . . although they should thereby acquire an entire monopoly. [Therefore] it becomes most important that they should be so controlled as to secure the public as far as possible from any abuse which might arise under this irresponsible authority.[1]

Where companies were sole carriers, legal maximum tolls were ineffective in restricting charges. Indeed, a company might increase its income, under monopoly conditions, by raising fares, and reducing the numbers of passengers carried. On at least one railway—the Leeds & Selby—this had already happened.[2]

The committee were clear that the solution lay in public regulation. They reported that 'control should be placed in the hands of the executive government, and it might be expedient to vest it in a Board to be annexed to the Board of Trade'. 'The absence of any effectual check from the absence of free competition on their respective lines . . . [makes] it advisable to subject this monopoly to some general superintendence and control . . . [which] will be most advantageously entrusted to some department of the executive government.'[3]

Such was the problem in Great Britain in 1840. It was unique since few other countries had anything that could be called a railway system at all, and none had reached a comparable stage of development. In this, as in other aspects of railway development, Great Britain was the pioneer. The development of public regulation in the three countries—U.S.A., Belgium, and France—which, together with Great Britain, then led the world in railway development, shows this.

Lardner, writing in 1850 as a champion of public regulation, compared Great Britain unfavourably with the U.S.A. 'Railways in America', he wrote, 'have been generally constructed, as in England, by joint-stock companies, with which, however, the state interferes much more largely than in England.'[4] This

---

[1] Ibid., 132–3. [2] P.P. 1840, xiii, 105.
[3] P.P. 1839, x, 139, and 1840, xii, 173.
[4] D. Lardner, *Railway Economy*, London (1850), 411–12.

interference was limited to legal provisions of various kinds, of which he gives the following examples:

1. Legal maximum dividends.
2. Division of dividends above a certain limit between the company and the state.
3. Limitation in time of privileges conferred on companies.
4. Periodical revision of legal maximum rates.
5. Dividends above a certain limit to be taxed.
6. Dividends to be limited to 10 per cent after a preliminary period of ten years, under the penalty of a reduction in maximum rates.
7. Reservation of powers to revise Acts by the state.[1]

Lardner himself admits, speaking of the last of these devices, 'In no case, however, has this clause been yet brought into practical operation, and it is generally regarded as the mere theoretical expression of the unlimited sovereignty of the state'.[2] Historians of American railways have held that the attempt at regulation through legal provisions alone was not effective, for 'although the states were in a position to exert such control over the railroads as they chose . . . the control which was actually exercised was slight'.[3]

There was, on the other hand, no administrative regulation of railways in the United States in 1840. When the first state commission was set up in New Hampshire four years later, it was constituted 'after the English model'.[4] Problems of railway regulation bedevilled American politics long after this early period—particularly in the Middle West after the Civil War. The agitation eventually led to the intervention of the Federal government, as distinct from the States, and the creation of the Inter-State Commerce Commission in 1887.

In France the history of railways may be traced back to the eighteenth century,[5] and, at that period, it would not have been patently foolish to prophesy that French railways would keep pace in their development with those in Great Britain. In fact,

---

[1] Lardner, op. cit., 411–12.   [2] Ibid., 412.

[3] E. R. Johnson and T. W. Van Metre, *Principles of Railroad Transportation*, Appleton (1916), 468.

[4] W. Z. Ripley, *Railroads, Rates and Regulations*, London (1913), 627.

[5] For a valuable account of early French railway history in an unexpected context, see P. J. Wexler, *Formation du vocabulaire des chemins de fer en France, 1778–1842*, Geneva and Lille (1955), 1–40.

however, they made little headway. When the question became a matter of public debate in 1832, there was one essential difference between the situation in the two countries. In France there was already a department of central government to handle all questions relating to the new form of transport. For ten years relationships between the state and the railways were debated in Parliament and elsewhere. There were those who held that the state alone should build the lines, while others argued that they should be left entirely to private enterprise. But on both sides there was a lack of capital. Some form of partnership was needed, for 'without a considerable measure of state control and some state assistance, France could not hope to create a railway system appropriate to her economic and political requirements. Gradually discussion narrowed itself down to the form and amount of state assistance. No government was prepared to carry the financial responsibility of a complete state system.'[1]

In 1840, only nine lines were open, with a total length of 160½ miles.[2] The Select Committee of 1844 were told that 'the construction of railways in France has been delayed by the want of enterprise on the part of private capitalists, and by the uncertainty which has prevailed as to the extent to which the government and legislature would adopt the Belgian system of taking the construction and working of the railways . . . into the hands of the State'.[3] This was settled only in 1842, on the basis of a partnership between government and private enterprise. The scheme then laid down took two decades to complete.

At first sight, Belgium seems to have offered the complete vindication of state railways in the world of 1840. The question of private versus public enterprise was fully debated in Parliament in 1833 and 1834. The choice was a real one, inasmuch as there was private capital available, had that alternative been preferred. However, it was decided that the railways should be built by the state so that the newly independent nation should deflect the course of international trade which might otherwise pass through Holland. The programme adopted in 1834 was planned to meet national needs and was carried out in ten

[1] J. H. Clapham, *Economic Development of France & Germany*, (4th ed., 1936), C.U.P., 145.
[2] P.P. 1844, xi, 624. [3] Ibid.

years. It achieved its aim of raising the prestige of the new nation, and hastening its economic development. The Belgian example was highly praised by those who favoured greater public regulation in Britain.

In the year 1840, however, the example of Belgium was not encouraging to believers in the principle of government enterprise. Fares had been raised in the previous year. This measure had proved unproductive and extremely unpopular, and they were cut again in 1842.[1] Nor had the goods traffic been much more successful. At first the government acted as general carriers, collecting and distributing the goods as well as carrying them on the rail. But this 'proved a complete failure, causing general dissatisfaction, and involving the government in a loss. Finally, in 1841, a tariff was adopted, which confines the function of the railway administration to transporting the goods along the railway.'[2] Collection and distribution were left to private carriers. It is not surprising to learn that 'as financial speculations . . . the Belgian railways have hitherto been unsuccessful', paying only $2\frac{1}{2}$ per cent.[3]

A few references to foreign railways occur in Hansard and Parliamentary Papers prior to the setting up of the Railway Department; but there was no systematic public enquiry into the subject. Nor does it appear that the results of such an enquiry would have been helpful. The American situation was similar, in that there had already been a considerable development of railways under private enterprise. But, in public regulation, they had no example for Britain to follow. They were, indeed, to learn from Britain. France already had a department of government competent to take charge of railways. Her problem was to encourage rather than to control. The Belgian model came too late, for by 1840 British railway development had already gone too far to be planned in that manner. In any case, the results up till that time were not such as to recommend the system to the average Member of Parliament. The problem was a native one, and the solution devised was a characteristically native one also.

Not less insular was the reaction of the law to the new form of transport. By 1840, the law of railways already consisted of three elements: statutory provisions, case law, and the Acts of

[1] P.P. 1844, xi, 622.   [2] Ibid., 623.   [3] Ibid.

the companies themselves. Of these, the first was the least important. An Act of 1832 had imposed a passenger duty, analogous to that already levied on stage-coaches.[1] Another, of 1838, gave the Postmaster General powers relating to the carriage of mails on railways.[2] A Highways Act of 1839, amending an earlier one, dealt with the question of level crossings.[3] Thus, statute law had recognised the existence of railways; but it had scarcely begun to define their legal status. For case law, the main source of information is a series of reports,[4] not the least significant thing about which is the date—1840—when they began to appear, for it suggests that lawyers were just then becoming aware of railway law as a distinct branch of their subject. These reports will show how far older doctrines and remedies of law and equity had been applied to the new railways. The companies' own Acts can speak for themselves. As loquacious as the statutes were taciturn, they set out, often at interminable length, the powers and duties of the companies they had brought into being.

The provisions of the law were often ineffective in practice. For example, the enactment of maximum tolls and fares did not secure charges as low as the public felt they had a right to expect. The right to all comers to run engines over a company's lines did not lead to competition between carriers. But the reasons why such provisions had not worked out were technical rather than legal. There was in addition by 1840 a widespread popular belief that railway companies were abusing their powers and evading their obligations, and that they should be called to account in the courts. But who was to do it? English law had no place for a Public Prosecutor. The Attorney-General occasionally appeared in cases of public interest, but as a rule the traditional view prevailed that the law could be enforced through the agency of common informers, grand juries, and interested parties. The idea of enforcement by administrative means outside the courts was only just beginning to take root.[5] One of the main motives in the setting up of the Railway

---

[1] 2 & 3 Will. IV, c. 120.
[2] 1 & 2 Vict., c. 98.   [3] 2 & 3 Vict., c. 45.
[4] H. Nicholl *et al.*, *Cases Relating to Railways & Canals*, 7 vols., London (1840–55).
[5] See below, pp. 204–6.

Department was the growing belief that such enforcement was necessary, because the existing machinery of the law made no adequate provision for it.

For example, the Liverpool & Manchester Act, 1826, provided for a reduction in the company's charges if it paid a dividend of more than 10 per cent.[1] Here, at the very dawn of the Railway Age, was enacted the principle of revision of rates which was to exercise the ingenuity of so many men during the remainder of the century. It is very much the check which Morrison, a decade later, wished to make universal; and which Lardner, in 1850, admired in certain American states.[2] It should not be dismissed out of hand merely because it was never operative; neither was Gladstone's attempt to deal with the problem in the Act of 1844.[3] What is noteworthy here is that the Act made no provision for enforcing the revision of charges. The very next section lays down that the dividends and revised tolls shall be declared to the Clerks of the Peace in neighbouring counties and published in local papers. This implies that enforcement was the concern of local Justices, but no procedure is clearly indicated.

Such vagueness was characteristic of early railway Acts. Since it was often difficult or impossible to enforce them, it is not surprising that they were often evaded, or ignored. In 1842, for example, in the course of a dispute between the Grand Junction and the Manchester & Birmingham companies, it was alleged by the former that the passenger carriages of the latter were heavier than its Act permitted. On enquiring into the subject, it was found

> that a clause requiring that no carriage should be used upon the railway whose weight, *inclusive of its load*, should exceed four tons, had been copied from the original Act of the Liverpool & Manchester Railway into almost all subsequent railway Acts, but that this clause has been completely disregarded in practice.[4]

Among the offending companies was the Grand Junction itself. To Lord Ripon, then President of the Board of Trade, it

[1] 7 Geo. IV, c. xlix (Local and Personal), s. 128.
[2] See above, pp. 9–10; and below, pp. 22–3.
[3] See below, p. 56, and H. Pollins, 'Finances of the Liverpool & Manchester Railway', in *Economic History Review*, 2nd ser., V (1952–3), 93–4.
[4] P.P. 1843, xlvii, 19.

seemed 'absurd that the law should have been evaded or set aside'.[1] Since, however, the extra weight of the illegal carriages tended to make them safer, there was no question of prosecuting the offending companies. Instead, a clause was introduced into a Bill then before Parliament, removing the limit on the weight of carriages.[2]

Another comparable example was the illegal borrowing common among early railway companies. Their Acts usually provided that loan capital should not exceed one-third of the share capital. It was a widespread practice for companies to evade this restriction by the issue of documents—the term security cannot be used, since security was precisely what they lacked—known as Loan Notes. In 1844, the Board of Trade asked the law officers for their opinion as to the legality of these notes; they replied:

> We are of the opinion that it is not legal for a railway company to borrow money upon loan notes . . . such transactions being illegal are void and create no debt—the invalidity of the security would we apprehend, if generally known, sufficiently operate as a check on such proceedings and the Directors might we think be restrained by injunction on the application of any of the shareholders from paying any interest on such loans. We think the holders of such notes possess no security whatever—the notes are in our opinion wholly invalid and void.[3]

They did not, however, advise prosecution. What was in fact done was that the notes in existence were legalised, and companies were empowered to renew them for five years.[4] Illegal borrowing long remained a feature of railway finance.

Attempts were, of course, made to enforce private Acts. Not more than a score of the cases reported up to the end of 1840 involved any question of public interest. Where so much was new and unsettled, there seems to have been no prejudice in the courts against railways as such; if there was any judicial bias, it seems rather to have operated in their favour. It is true that in *Barrett* v. *The Stockton & Darlington Railway Company* (1840), a precedent established in dock and canal cases was extended to railways, namely that 'where the language of an Act of Parliament obtained by a company, imposing a rate

---

[1] Add. MS. 41989, 2 Jul. 1844.   [2] 5 & 6 Vict., c. 55, s. 16.
[3] MT 6/2 230/1844.   [4] 7 & 8 Vict., c. 85, s. 19.

or toll upon the public, is ambiguous, that construction is to be adopted, which is more favourable to the interests of the public, and against that of the company'.[1] But more typical, in that it went in favour of the company, was *ex parte Robbins*,[2] in which a writ of *mandamus* was sought to compel a company to carry goods. It was refused, since there was 'no clause in their Act requiring them to carry all goods offered for conveyance, although they had agreed with certain persons to carry their goods to the exclusion of all others. A *mandamus* will not be granted to enforce the general law of the land, if an action will lie.'

In *Rex* v. *Pease*, which arose out of locomotives frightening the horses of persons using the highway, it was held 'that this interference with rights of the public must be taken to have been contemplated and sanctioned by the legislature.'[3] The law on this point was amended some years later by the Railways Clauses Consolidation Act, 1845, which empowered the Board of Trade, on the application of the highway authorities, to order a company to erect screens where necessary to prevent horses being frightened.[4]

In what appear to be the two earliest cases in which parties sought compensation after having been involved in an accident —*Bridge* v. *Grand Junction Railway Company* and *Armitage* v. *Grand Junction Railway Company*—the pleas of the plaintiffs were rejected on technical grounds, and so the company escaped.[5]

Perhaps the most interesting of these early cases was *Regina* v. *Eastern Counties Railway* (1839–40). In this, the finding of the court was at first against the company, but was then reversed in a surprising way. The company was empowered to build a line from London, via Colchester to Norwich and Yarmouth. It became apparent, however, that the management had no intention of proceeding beyond Colchester, and, therefore, the court was asked to grant a writ of *mandamus* to compel the company to carry out its obligations. Lord Chief Justice Denman, in giving judgment, stated:

> the questions involved [in this case] are of much . . . importance; because, as, on the one hand, much mischief may ensue if this

---

[1] Nicholl, op. cit., ii, 443.   [2] Ibid., i, 52.   [3] Ibid., i, 58–9.
[4] 8 & 9 Vict., c. 20, s. 63.   [5] Nicholl, op. cit., i, 60.

court should improvidently enjoin the performance of things impracticable or improper, so, on the other, is there no higher duty cast upon this court than to exercise a vigilant control over persons entrusted with large and extensive powers for public purposes, and to enforce within reasonable bounds, the execution of such purposes.[1]

Two precedents from cases involving a canal and a road respectively were invoked, and the writ granted, on the ground that the company was not complying with its intention as set out in the preamble of its Act.

Impressive as Lord Denman's statement was, there were loopholes. He envisaged the possibility of the court enjoining certain things 'improvidently'; he admitted that the execution of Acts must be enforced only within 'reasonable bounds'. The company's defence throughout rested on the submission that it would be improvident to invest its entire capital, which had proved inadequate, in land, leaving none for the construction of the line. When Lord Denman heard the answer to the writ in the following year, he allowed himself to be swayed by these considerations, and gave judgment for the company.[2] This case illustrates not only the sympathetic attitude of the courts to railway companies, but also the inadequacy of the whole apparatus of judicial control to deal with the problems created by the development of the railway system.

If an individual is involved in an action, and the court finds against him, he has virtually no hope of putting things right by securing legislation to alter the law in his favour. Railway companies, created as they were by Acts of Parliament, could get out of difficulties in the courts by going back to Parliament for fresh powers. This happened, for example, in *Attorney-General* v. *Manchester & Leeds Railway Company* (1838–9).[3] The plaintiff appeared on behalf of the highway authorities, who complained that a viaduct which the company was constructing at Wakefield was not in accordance with its Act. The court refused an injunction, pending other proceedings, on receiving the company's undertaking to abide by the order of the court at a later stage. In other words, it would go on building, on the understanding that it might have to pull the whole thing down in the end. Meanwhile, the company introduced into Parliament

---

[1] Nicholl, op. cit., i, 518. [2] Ibid., ii, 260 ff. [3] Ibid., i, 436.

an amending Bill to legalise the offending viaduct. It did not inform either the highway authorities or the court. When the former discovered what was afoot, and invoked the intervention of the latter, the company abandoned the objectionable clause in the House of Commons. Had it not done so voluntarily, it could not have been forced to do so by judicial processes, for the court found itself unable to proceed further, once the company had applied to Parliament.[1]

Judicial control, then, was an unimportant factor in the public regulation of railways prior to 1840. Of public statute law there was practically none. Private Bill legislation had already reached a considerable bulk, but was little enforced, and sometimes unenforceable. Lastly, although there had been too few cases for the attitude of the courts to become clearly defined, those which had been decided had gone predominantly in favour of the companies.

Railway companies, deriving their powers from private Acts, were creatures of Parliament. Yet it was a Parliamentary committee which, as shown above, called for a department of executive government to control its creatures; and Parliament which, in 1840, delegated to the Board of Trade the powers which were the foundation of its jurisdiction over railways. How did this come about?

Before 1830, railways were scarcely mentioned at all in Parliamentary debates. Since 1758, however, they had formed an increasingly important part of the private Bill business. Sometimes the division between public and private business became blurred. The G.W.R. Bill, for example, was the subject of debate more than once in 1833 and 1834; but as O'Connell shrewdly observed, 'The chief objections to the measure seemed to be not to its principles, but its details, which he . . . considered was more a subject for the Committee than the House'.[2]

Under private Bill procedure, the most important stage, then as now, was the committee stage. But then the committees were very different from what they have since become. Indeed, in one respect they were formed on a principle diametrically opposed to that now in force. At the present time, the com-

---

[1] Nicholl, op. cit, i, 436.   [2] Hansard, xxi, 1358.

mittee is a judicial body, and impartiality is the prime virtue in its members. Then, however, the committee on a private Bill was composed of all locally interested members, and knowledge of local circumstances was the hall-mark of a good committee man. Naturally, committees formed in this way were large, and, since attendance was not compulsory, members often attended only to vote, without having heard the evidence. The votes of those who had not heard the evidence might outweigh the votes of those who had. Since members sat as representatives of the localities which would be affected by the Bill, the way was open for canvassing by interested parties. Each Bill, more-over, was considered in isolation from others of a similar nature. As a result, there was no reason to expect uniformity in the powers given to different railway companies, except in so far as Standing Orders and the common form of Parliamentary agents should secure it. Nor were the various railways author-ised considered as parts of a general system.

There was a growing awareness of the defects of the system, but it was not until 1844 that radical changes were made. These were of critical importance in the development of private Bill procedure as a whole, for

> it was the expansion of railways [that] for the first time brought more clearly than ever before into the consciousness of Parliament the conception that in private legislation there was an aspect of public, as well as one of private interest, to which no government could be indifferent; and that the function of Parliament was, not merely to act justly as between parties, but also to consider and promote the interests of the public as a whole.[1]

The main features of the new procedure, introduced experi-mentally in 1844 and made permanent in the following year, were:

(a) large, locally interested committees were replaced by small, less partial bodies.
(b) Bills were grouped so that comparable schemes were referred to the same committee.
(c) attendance was made compulsory.[2]

---

[1] O. C. Williams, *Historical Development of Private Bill Procedure and Standing Orders in the House of Commons*, London, (1948–9), i, 67.
[2] O. C. Williams, op. cit., i, 85–7.

It should not be supposed that Members were complacent about the private Bill system. On the contrary, there was a lively awareness of its failings, and the debates throw much light on the ineffectiveness of Parliamentary control of railway development. Members were subject to heavy and well-organised pressure. Some railway directors were already in Parliament—for example, Joseph Pease; some Members became railway directors—for example, Charles Russell. Other members spoke quite frankly as representatives of the companies. The Earl of Kerry, for instance, seconded the second reading of the G.W.R. Bill 'as requested by the G.W.R.'[1] The opposing landowners were also well-organised, canvassing the support of Members with the following circular:

> Opposition to the [Great] Western Railway.
> The Duke of Buckingham, Countess Berkeley; Earls Jersey, Harrington, & Cardigan; Lords Boston, Montague & Stowell; Lady Carr; Mr. Sloane Stanley, Col. Gore Langton, Mr. R. Palmer, the Provost, Fellows & Masters of Eton College, and the other opponents of this measure,—earnestly entreat the favour of your attendance in the House of Commons, on Monday, the 10th instant, at 12 o'clock, on the motion for the Second Reading.
> 34 Parliament Street,
> Mar. 8, 1834.
> With Sir W. H. . . .'s compliments.[2]

Many members, moreover, had direct financial interests in the companies on whose Bills they had to decide. When a Member's vote was disallowed on the grounds that he was a subscriber to the company whose Bill was under discussion, one speaker took the line that it was wrong to victimise one, when so many had offended in the same manner. Another pointed out that Members' names were often excluded from the published lists of subscribers, as his own had been.[3]

Sir Robert Peel supported the particular motion, but opposed the principle on which it was based; on another occasion he explained his attitude in more detail:

> The man least liable to suspicion . . . is he whose interest is most notorious. . . . But this interest is not always so apparent, though perhaps really as great, in the case of the man whose estate is

[1] Hansard, xxi, 1352.   [2] Ibid., xxi, 1362.
[3] Hansard, xxxi, 1254.

cut through by the railroad, and who has an opportunity . . . of making his own terms with the company—or in the case of the man who would be greatly though privately benefited by its execution.[1]

Most important of all, the private Bill Committee thought of itself as an umpire in a contest between private parties, not as the guardian of the public interest. This meant that it was quite exceptional for an unopposed Bill to be examined in detail at all. This aspect of the system shocked one of the new Members brought in by the Reform Bill, Richard Potter. His remarks apply to railway Bills, though occasioned by the Birkenhead Improvement Bill, 1833, on the committee for which he had served. It was an unopposed measure, and the committee had been advised to pass it formally. Potter had, however, gone through it in detail, and inserted many amendments in the public interest. He went on to entreat 'with great deference, but most earnestly . . . hon. Members to whom private Bills were referred, to look through them whether they were opposed or not'.[2] His amendments were passed, but no one spoke as to the point of principle he had raised.

Minor reforms in private Bill procedure were made in 1836, but Members were becoming aware that something more was needed. The two most important proposals were made by the Duke of Wellington in the Lords, and by James Morrison in the Commons. Both asserted 'a subsequent as well as a previous right of control over railroad affairs'. on the part of the state.[3]

The Duke intervened on the third reading of the Birmingham, Bristol & Thames Junction Bill, 1836. He wished success to the railways, but perceived a danger of monopoly; it was therefore 'desirable to insert in all these Bills some clause to enable the Government or the Parliament to revise the enactments contained in them at some future period'.[4] He did not propose retrospective action. Later, he read a clause to be inserted in all future Bills, which would have rendered the companies liable to general railway Acts passed during the same session, or within one year, whichever period should be the longer.[5] When the third reading of the Birmingham Bill

[1] Ibid., 1118–21. [2] Hansard, xvii, 1035–6.
[3] See below, p. 24. [4] Hansard, xxxiv, 1.
[5] Ibid., 498.

was resumed, he removed this clause as an amendment. Lord Clanricarde spoke against it. Any such clause, if desirable at all, should apply to all railways. Parliament would be pledged to legislation of an unknown nature. In other countries, railways had been undertaken by the state 'and the government has a right to place what restraints they pleased on the mode of conducting those works; but in this country the case is quite different, joint-stock companies managed all such undertakings'.[1] He did not, however, go on to draw the conclusion that was implied—that, therefore the government had no right to impose any regulations. Lord Londonderry pointed out that if the Regulation Act contemplated by Wellington's clause were not made retrospective, one part of a line might be under it, another not.[2] The Duke's amendment was carried, but had no effect, since no general Act did in fact follow within the period stipulated.

James Morrison's speech, introducing his motion on railway regulation in 1836, was the most able contribution to the discussion in Parliament in the 'thirties. It was also the longest, running to eleven columns.[3] He asserted that companies were given by their Acts 'what was really equivalent to a monopoly'. Competition was almost impossible for several reasons; the existing company probably was already in possession of the best line; even if it were not, it could cut its rates temporarily at any threat of competition, and raise them again as soon as it was past; and if in spite of everything a rival line were established, the two companies would be sure to make an agreement which would close the competition between them. To the question, 'even though competition might be depended upon ... would [it] be right to trust exclusively to its protection?' he replied 'No', for the Legislature is bound to prevent, as far as it can, the unnecessary waste of the public capital. It was to be expected that railway costs would fall, as a result partly of general economic growth, partly of technical advances. The maximum tolls laid down in the original Acts would become more and more ineffective as a control on rail charges. Parliament should therefore reserve the right to revise railway rates. Among various examples he gives to strengthen his argument, some were drawn from the United States.

[1] Hansard, xxxiv, 541–2.   [2] Ibid., 556.   [3] Ibid., xxxiii, 977–88.

After so prescient a speech, the remedy proposed seems rather inadequate; his motion reads:

> That in all Bills for Railways, or other public works of that description, it is made a condition, with a view to the protection of the public interests, which might otherwise be seriously compromised, that the dividends be limited to a certain rate, or that power be reserved to Parliament of revising and fixing at the end of every twenty years, the tolls chargeable on passengers and goods conveyed.

Morrison himself had already admitted the ineffectiveness of limitation of dividends, saying that it would tend to discourage efficiency, and pointing to the ease with which distribution of profits could be concealed.

In a brief but effective speech, Lord Stanley took up this point. The dividends of the Liverpool & Manchester Railway were subject to legal limitation, but it was always evaded.[1] He was opposed to this form of control, but supported the proposal to revise tolls, for 'railroads, from their very nature, must always be a virtual monopoly. It is necessary, therefore, to give the public a protection against them.'[2] Poulett Thomson also spoke in support, and no one came out in complete opposition. Morrison sought, and got, leave to withdraw his motion and bring in a Bill. Petitions were received against it, Peel declared himself opposed to it. Labouchere would not commit the government either way, and Morrison himself decided to withdraw his measure for that session. He maintained that it was still important, but that the success of the Duke of Wellington's clause made it less urgent.[3] This might have been so, had the government (or, conceivably, other private Members) taken advantage of the breathing-space secured by the Duke. But no one did, nor was Morrison's Bill ever reintroduced.

Interesting as Morrison's endeavours were, the proposed remedy probably would not have been effective. Members of both Houses were beginning to see that the problem of railway regulation was for the executive, not for the legislative, branch of government to deal with. Sir Harry Verney had already called for a tribunal which would have differed from private

[1] Cf. Pollins, loc. cit., 94.
[2] Hansard, xxxiii, 989–92. For this Bill, see P.P. 1836, iv, 723.
[3] Ibid., xxxv, 91–3, and 134.

Bill committees in being more permanent, more expert, and in having a more comprehensive oversight of railway development:

> at present it seemed to him that most of these schemes had been undertaken for the promotion of local, and not of national, interests; and in some cases, he had no doubt that public benefit had been sacrificed to private profit. He thought that somebody, in the shape of a Royal Commission, should be constituted, with supreme power to examine and decide upon the merit of conflicting plans, and to recommend that to the Legislature which seemed most worthy of adoption. The members of this Commission he would select principally from officers of the Engineers in His Majesty's service, associated with other known and competent individuals.[1]

Lord Sandon pointed to the need for a constant supervision of railways—a task which the private Bill system could not fulfil, no matter to what degree of perfection it might be brought; he 'wished that committees should exercise a subsequent as well as a previous right of investigation and control over railroad affairs by the examination of engineers and others concerned therein'.[2] Other similar proposals were made, and were to be made again.[3]

If then Parliamentary opinion on railway regulation was so strong, why was so little done? It was not because those who advocated control were defeated in debate by a party of free enterprise. Nothing is more striking in these debates than the infrequency with which the voice of economic orthodoxy is heard. It is true that one peer believed that competition from new lines would check the threat of monopoly; but when he went on to assert that that was what had actually happened with the canals, one wonders at the source of his information.[4] Joseph Pease based his arguments against a proposal for control not on principles of *laissez-faire*, but on the proposition that railways enhanced the value of property, rather than depreciating it; and that in any case, the private Bill system was control enough.[5] Speaking in the same debate, Joseph Hume laid down the principle that 'the very best check against the danger to

---

[1] Hansard, xxxi, 1113–14.   [2] Ibid., 1121.

[3] Cf. ibid., 672; xxxiv, 984; xxxv, 686; xxxvi, 1161; xliii, 590–1 and 804–5.

[4] Ibid., xxxiv, 545–8.   [5] Ibid., xxxi, 361–2.

be apprehended from these speculations is each individual's own interest.[1] On another occasion, Poulett Thomson, from the government benches, spoke in harmony with this sentiment: 'it is by the government not meddling with capital that this country has been able to obtain a superiority over every other country'.[2] That this principle was not absolute in his mind is shown by the fact that he had already told the House that 'he was not unfriendly to the great works to which these Bills related, but at the same time, he felt bound from the situation which he held in the Government, to take care that the capital of the country was not improvidently or unwisely applied'.[3] The views of the silent majority in both Houses may well have favoured non-interference; but among the articulate minority, the champions of regulation were more numerous, more forceful, and more able than their opponents.

The reason that the railway problem was not tackled earlier is that the government would neither take the initiative itself, nor follow the lead given by others, such as Morrison. The Whigs had no railway policy. During the railway crisis of 1836, a Member asked whether the government would 'suggest some course for the consideration of railway petitions and bills, by which the House would be enabled to have all such cases, especially those of rival lines, fully and completely investigated, before it came to adjudicate and decide in favour of any particular Bill'. Poulett Thomson replied that the government would not make 'any proposal . . . for preferring one line of railway to another, or even for pointing out any rule for the adoption of the house on the subject'. This negative attitude provoked the comment that it left the 'House . . . quite at sea without compass or chart'.[4]

The government's attitude to passenger duty on railways reveals a similar lack of policy. When this duty was first proposed in 1832, two important issues were raised in debate. It was urged that the new modes of transport by steam-power should be encouraged, whereas the proposed duty would have the opposite effect; and that steam road-carriages, being already penalised in various ways, would find the proposed duty the last straw. Ministers made no serious attempt to deal with

[1] Ibid., 365.
[2] Ibid., xxxvi, 1161–2.
[3] Ibid., xxxi, 684–5.
[4] Ibid., 676–82.

either of those points, treating the issue as a purely fiscal one.
As Spring Rice put it:

> The question was not whether the tax was a tax that must be
> approved of or not, but whether the revenue could afford that a
> duty, which had hitherto been collected on the stage coaches
> running, for instance, between Manchester and Liverpool,
> should be at once extinguished, without anything being substi-
> tuted for it. The revenue collected from the stage coaches could
> not be spared.[1]

In 1838, a proposal that there should be an enquiry to determine the best rail route to Scotland revealed confusion in
ministerial circles. The motion was seconded by the Attorney-
General but opposed by Poulett Thomson;[2] 'such an attempt
would be productive . . . of no practical good . . . [it was]
decidedly best to leave railways . . . in the hands of those who
were willing to embark their capital in such speculations,
subject always to the scrutiny and control of Parliament'. Later
in the year Labouchere, who was then Vice-President under
Poulett Thomson at the Board of Trade, spoke in a very different vein:

> the whole question of railways would be forced on . . . the House
> at no very distant period. They had bound the country in chains
> of iron, we were in such a state as was submitted to in no other
> country. America had taken measures to secure the interests of
> the public on railways. France had taken similar measures . . .
> that this sort of monopoly should not be established against the
> public.[3]

Baring, the Chancellor of the Exchequer, and Peel, for the
Opposition, spoke in a similar spirit.[4]

Throughout the 1830's, the government was neither anxious
to regulate railways, nor convinced of the advantage of *laissez-
faire* in railway matters. The statements of ministers reveal little
knowledge of the subject, or interest in it, and nothing that
could be called a railway policy. Occasionally, they spoke as if
railway problems were urgent; but at the end of the decade,
they were still undecided what to do. At the beginning of the
session of 1839, Poulett Thomson was asked about the work of
the Select Committee of the previous session, and whether he

---

[1] Hansard, xiv, 825.
[2] Ibid., xliii, 591–3.
[3] Ibid., xliv, 473.
[4] Ibid. 478–9.

THE NEED FOR GOVERNMENT ACTION

proposed to bring in a Bill. His reply, which should be read in
the light of the discussion summarised above, was that he

> could not positively say what the intentions of ministers were as
> to this subject but he was willing to say it was worthy of the con-
> sideration of the House . . . regulations . . . had formerly been
> neglected—not through any fault of his, but through the current
> of public feeling being then against such regulations . . . it would
> be impossible in the committees on private Bills, to introduce the
> necessary additional regulations; for these committees were in
> general occupied by private interests, and the public interests
> were too much neglected.[1]

This does not appear to be an adequate defence of government policy during the 1830's. There was a widespread recognition that railways were monopolies, not subject to the restraint
of competition. Thus the normal arguments against public
regulation did not apply. Some such regulation was desirable,
and the private Bill system could not supply it. Either a
government measure, or government support for a private Member's Bill, was necessary. Such a lead was not forthcoming
from the Whig government, who must therefore bear the main
responsibility.

[1] Ibid., xlv, 696.

2

THE EARLY YEARS OF THE
RAILWAY DEPARTMENT
1840–1844

THE years of indecision came to an end in 1840, with the introduction of the Railway Regulation Bill. In its original form[1] it was a fair reflection of the views of the Select Committee.[2] It was not a government Bill, but was introduced by Lord Seymour and James Loch, on behalf of the Select Committee. Hence the resulting measure is often referred to as Lord Seymour's Act. Loch, its other sponsor, sought Melbourne's support for it.[3] It received ministerial backing and was generally welcomed. The *Railway Times* devoted a leader to it, asserting that

> We have always declared . . . that from the moment when railways became the general, and in some sense compulsory, mode of conveyance, the public would not rest satisfied without a government superintendence of the exercise of powers granted to the companies by their respective Acts, and that it was for the interest of the proprietors themselves that such superintendence should exist.[4]

Peel, for the opposition, said that, although

> no one was more adverse to any general interference with the employment of capital than he was . . . it was impossible to deny that the railways were a practical monopoly, and that they had been established by the legislature. . . . It was their duty, therefore, to see that . . . the public rights were not interfered with.[5]

[1] P.P. 1840, iii, 427. [2] See above, pp. 8 ff.
[3] Melbourne Papers. Loch-Melbourne, 4 Jul. 1840.
[4] *Railway Times*, 13 Jun. 1840. [5] Hansard, lv, 909.

The debates on the measure were not of great interest. Perhaps the most important point which emerged was the view of the government as to the purpose of inspection. It was urged that the most able and conscientious inspector could not certify from a single visit that a line was soundly constructed. For that, constant supervision during building would be necessary. Labouchere agreed, but added that the object of inspection was not to certify the soundness of construction, but merely that the provisions of the Act had been complied with.[1] Years later, at the time of the Tay Bridge disaster, the Board of Trade was criticised because they had so lately authorised its opening. It is of some interest to find this criticism anticipated at the outset of the system of railway inspection.

Certain amendments were made during the passage of the Bill through Parliament. Section 3 of the original Bill came under very heavy criticism in the Commons.[2] In its original form, the section would have required companies to 'furnish such copies or extracts of [their] books, and make such returns in such form and manner as the [Board of Trade] shall require'. As a result of the criticism that this power was too wide, the section was amended so as to restrict this power. In its final form, it reads as follows: the Board of Trade may call for

> Returns . . . of the aggregate traffic in passengers, according to the several classes, and of the aggregate traffic in cattle and goods respectively, . . . as well as of all accidents which shall have occurred . . . attended with personal injury . . . provided always, that such returns shall be required in like manner and at the same time from all the said companies, unless [the Board of Trade] shall specially exempt any of the said companies, and shall enter the grounds of such exemption in the minutes of their proceedings.[3]

We shall see that the Board sought, and obtained, an amendment to this section as early as 1842. Had the power been conferred in its original form, it could have been used to widen and improve the range of railway statistics—for example, in matters of finance—the defectiveness of which, in early days, is widely acknowledged.

A rider was added to the section which gave power to appoint inspectors, to the effect that 'no person shall be eligible . . . who

[1] Ibid., 915.   [2] Ibid., 1179 ff.   [3] 3 & 4 Vict., c. 97, s. 3.

shall within one year of his appointment have been a director or have held any office of trust or profit under any railway company.[1] This was the result of a suggestion made in the Commons.[2] It has a modestly reasonable air, but its consequences were of some moment. Labouchere caught the point at once; he agreed that a present connection between an individual and a company should disqualify, but he was not sure 'whether the past connection of any individual was to qualify or to disqualify'.[3] In Great Britain in the year 1840 there were very few people with experience of railway engineering. Of that small number, the great majority were rendered ineligible by this clause for the office of railway inspector. The first such officers were, therefore, men who knew virtually nothing about railways. There is a humorous aspect to the situation, as we observe Pasley reading text-books on railways on the eve of taking up the post of Inspector-General.[4] But there was a serious side also. Those who were critical of the inspectors and all they stood for, could say, often with truth, that the inspectors were not by training railway men. Herapath dubbed the first Inspector-General 'Sir Signal Smith',[5] in contemptuous allusion to one of his recommendations, and his columns throughout Smith's term of office are full of accusations of ignorance. The attitude persisted long after there was any justification for it; as late as 1873, Sir Edward Watkin felt justified in drawing a contrast between the inspectors and 'practical men'—'I think the interference—the insolent interference—of these individuals is becoming almost too much for practical men to bear'.[6]

The powers conferred on the Board of Trade by the Act[7] were neither numerous nor extensive. Companies might not open lines until after one month's notice to the Board, which could appoint persons with authority to inspect railways. Both existing and future bye-laws must be submitted to the Board, which could disallow them. The Board might call for returns, within the limits specified above, and prosecute companies, through the Law Officers, in order to enforce railway Acts. Jurisdiction over junctions between private sidings and public

[1] 3 & 4 Vict., s. 5. [2] Hansard, lv, 1157–8. [3] Ibid., 1158.
[4] Add. MS. 41989, 21 Dec. and 27 Dec. 1841.
[5] *Railway Magazine*, 29 May, 1841.
[6] Cohn, ii, 604 and n. [7] 3 & 4 Vict., c. 97.

railways was transferred from Justices of the Peace, as provided for in certain private Acts, to the Board.

No reference is made in the Act to a specific Railway Department of the Board of Trade. But we have seen[1] that the Select Committee had contemplated such a department, and Lord Seymour had stated that one of the 'chief points of his Bill [was] the establishing of a board of superintendence in connexion with the Board of Trade'.[2] The Board set out its plans for the Railway Department in a letter to the Treasury.[3] It proposed to run the Department experimentally at first and 'to increase the establishment . . . as little as possible'. Since 'a considerable part of the working of the Act is naturally connected with the Statistical Branch . . . the new Railway Department should be annexed to that Branch and placed under the general supervision of Mr. Porter, the head of the Statistical Department'. The main business would, however, be in the hands of a Law Clerk, who would handle, in addition to the legal business, 'the general business and correspondence of the Department under the supervision of Mr. Porter'. A junior clerk would be needed also. No solicitor would be required, since prosecutions would be instituted through the Treasury Solicitor. As for inspection, 'it may be necessary eventually to appoint a permanent Inspector General': but for the time being, it would be better to employ an officer of the Royal Engineers or 'other competent person' as required at two guineas a day and expenses. Porter should have £200 a year in addition to his present salary, and the Law Clerk, £500 a year. The whole scheme was approved without amendment by the Treasury.[4]

Thus, the setting up of the Railway Department created little patronage, since Porter was already on the staff and inspectors were to be drawn from other branches of government service. Apart from one junior clerkship, the only post to be filled was that of Law Clerk. It went to Samuel Laing, a barrister who had been Labouchere's private secretary.[5] Later a special report on bye-laws was needed, for which Laing evidently could not find time. It was entrusted to an outsider, Arthur Symonds, a Benthamite law-reformer, who had been associated

---

[1] See above, p. 9.
[3] BT 3/29, 11 Aug. 1840.
[5] D.N.B. Article on Laing.

[2] Hansard, liv, 894.
[4] BT 1/365, 20 Aug. 1840.

with several of the great reforms of the 'thirties, and who had been employed by the Board to draft model railway Bills two years earlier.[1]

So far, the emphasis had been on the statistical and legal work of the Department. Experience soon showed, however, that its responsibility for public safety was greater than had been supposed. In the first three months 'upwards of twenty-five fatal accidents had been reported to the Board, six of which had been of such magnitude and importance as to render it indispensable to institute a protracted and searching enquiry . . . the reports . . . bring to light facts which place in the strongest point of view the necessity for the existence of a very efficient controlling power over railways.' Moreover, it was 'indispensable . . . that they should be conducted in a uniform system and not by a series of unconnected inspections and reports which, however able in themselves, would necessarily present the result of different views and contain conflicting opinions and recommendations'. A Royal Engineer officer would be preferable to a civil engineer, because cheaper; moreover, very many of the latter would be ineligible because of their connections with railway companies. Nor need a permanent officer be much more expensive. Payments to part-time inspectors in the first four months amounted to £230, whereas the salary of the officer proposed for the post of Inspector-General (Lt.-Col. Sir Frederic Smith, R.E.) would be only £900 a year, less his service pay, i.e. £570.[2] Smith was appointed, thus setting an important precedent, which has always since been followed, that railway inspection is the responsibility of officers of the Royal Engineers, serving or retired.

There was no further increase in staff until the end of 1841, when there is a reference to the Inspector-General's clerk.[3] This was almost certainly Finlay Mackenzie, who was recommended as a clerk and draughtsman on the establishment as from April, 1842.[4]

Towards the end of 1841, Smith was appointed Director of

---

[1] BT 3/39, 19 Dec. 1840. Sir Cecil Carr, 'Mechanics of Law-Making', in *Current Legal Problems*, iv, (1951). O. C. Williams, op. cit., i, 103–4.

[2] BT 3/29, 2 Dec. 1840; 5/48, 2 and 19 Dec. 1840. The part-time inspectors were Lt.-Col. R. Thomson and Capt. S. C. Melhuish.

[3] BT 5/49, 23 Dec. 1841.   [4] BT 5/50, 5 Jan. 1842.

the Royal Engineers Establishment, Chatham, of which the previous holder was Major-General C. W. Pasley. Pasley was not offered a new military appointment, and resolved to try for the post left vacant by Smith. He applied by letter to Lord Ripon. After an interview and some haggling over salary, he was appointed Inspector-General.

From our point of view, one of the most important things about Pasley is that he kept a diary, which is now in the British Museum. Frequent and regular entries during the period of almost five years during which he held the position give a vivid picture of his work. It is a document of considerable value beyond the limits of this study, for the history both of public administration and of railways.[1]

Even with so small a staff as five, it is clear that there were two distinct grades, with Porter, Pasley, and Laing in the higher and the two clerks in the lower. Among the three members of the higher grade, on the other hand, there was no established hierarchy. Although Porter was styled 'Superintendent', he was expected to give most of his time to his original work in the Statistical Department, and he did not in fact supervise the work of Pasley and Laing. These two last had direct and frequent access to the political heads of the Department, from whom they took orders, and to whom they reported. Consider, for example, the following entries in Pasley's diary:

18 Mar. 1842. Have an interview and explanation with Lord Ripon—afterwards see Mr. Gladstone . . .
19 March. 1842. See Lord Ripon this afternoon . . . takes my paper to look over.
20 Mar. 1842. When I go to the office, Mr. Laing informs me that Lord Ripon has seen and approved of my papers and his notes.

This was typical of the way in which business was handled without Porter, and so it is not surprising to find Pasley going on, 'I object to Mr. Porter being the Superintendent. Mr. Laing confirms what Sir F. Smith told me, that Porter is a sinecure [sic]—the arrangement of the Railway Department must be altered.'

[1] The volumes of Pasley's diary covering the period 1841–6 are Add. MSS. 41989–41992; this passage is based on Add. MS. 41989, 30 Nov., 3, 9, 14, 18 Dec. 1841.

Pasley was on good social terms with officers of railway companies. To take a few examples at random, he attended a party given by the Secretary of the London & Birmingham Railway, was the guest of an engineer whose line he was about to inspect, and drank champagne with the Secretary of the G.W.R.[1] Was his judgment biassed in consequence? A similar question had been raised in the early days of factory inspection.[2] There is no evidence that Pasley's judgment was biassed by good fellowship, and there is something to be said on the other side. The powers of the Board of Trade over railways were few and weak. Much of its achievement was the result of persuasion rather than legal power. For example, in Pasley's day, and for long after, there was no statutory basis for accident enquiries; yet the companies co-operated. Perhaps Pasley's social gifts contributed to the establishment of those good relations with the companies which were a valuable asset to his Department.

In the 1840's the tradition of anonymity in the civil service had not yet become established. Pasley did not feel precluded by his position from giving public expression to his political views, although he said he had 'always made a point of not interfering in the internal politics of the country, which as a military man not possessed of landed property, I consider unbecoming and unnecessary'. In Irish affairs, however, this rule did not apply. He wrote to *The Times* of the 'unaccountable supineness of the present ministers of this country, whose measures are a disgrace to them as individuals and collectively'. The letter, even though not intended for publication, was an extraordinary effusion by modern standards of civil service rectitude. He spoke on Ireland at the Institution of Civil Engineers, 'reprobating O'Connell and the inactivity of the government'. So far was he from wishing his words unspoken that, on looking into the press, he regretted finding no report of the dinner, 'as I would have wished my sentiments to appear'. He discussed politics with M.P.'s and—most remarkable of all—spoke on Irish affairs in public while on official business in Dublin.[3]

[1] Add. MS. 41990, 11 Jul. 1843, 30 Jan. and 6 Jul. 1844.
[2] M. W. Thomas, *Early Factory Legislation*, Thames Bank, (1948), 76 and 96.
[3] Add. MS. 41990, 10, 11, 15, and 17 Jul., 16 and 21 Aug., 13 and 14 Nov., and 8 Dec. 1843.

Such then was the Railway Department in its earliest years; Porter (part-time Superintendent); Laing (Law and Corresponding Clerk); Smith, and later Pasley (Inspector-General); assisted by two clerks, one of whom was also a draughtsman. The small size of the staff is important, both in relation to the bulk of work done and to the many problems not dealt with. It also affected the way in which work was done. The Department was part of a small office—the entire staff of the Board of Trade in 1840 numbered only thirty.[1] In this respect, it resembled other important public offices. The establishment of the Foreign Office in 1841 was thirty-nine,[2] excluding messengers, office-keeper, and house-keeper; that of the Colonial Office in 1862 was forty-eight.[3]

In small offices such as those, informal methods were possible and natural. The Department's officers could do business by discussion in one another's rooms, rather than by writing minutes on files. They had easy and frequent access to the President and Vice-President. It is not possible to generalise, therefore, about the way in which decisions were taken. Since the Department was new, there were no classes of routine business which were habitually left to the officers to dispose of. On the other hand, no questions were reserved for the exclusive consideration of the political heads of the Board, as was sometimes done in the Colonial Office.[4] The officers worked with the President and Vice-President so closely that we cannot normally isolate the contributions they respectively made. The former had considerable influence on policy; but the 'ministerial responsibility' of the latter was still a real responsibility, rather than the useful political fiction it was later to become.[5]

Before turning to individual cases, it is important to show the spirit in which the Department worked. Its main business, according to the original conception, was to be the enforcement of the law; but during the first four years of its existence, no

[1] Sir H. L. Smith, *Board of Trade*, Putnam (1928), 52.
[2] Sir J. Tilley and S. Gaselee, *Foreign Office*, Putnam (1933), 61.
[3] H. L. Hall, *Colonial Office*, Longmans (1937), 21.
[4] Ibid., 51.
[5] For the development of 'ministerial responsibility' in the nineteenth century, see S. E. Finer, 'Individual Responsibility of Ministers', in *Public Administration*, xxxiv (1956), 377–96.

prosecution was in fact instituted. In only one case was prosecution seriously contemplated, and then nothing came of it, because the aggrieved parties themselves brought an action.[1] There were other cases where the Department might have prosecuted, but its 'powers [were] . . . intended only for extreme cases, or when the parties have not the means of defending their rights against the aggressions of a powerful company'.[2] Similarly, the Department's jurisdiction over bye-laws proved to be only a minor responsibility,[3] while the main object of inspecting new lines soon became to ensure that they might be used with safety, rather than that they were constructed in accordance with the relevant private Acts.

By way of contrast, the Department took a much wider view of its other responsibilities than was at first envisaged. One of its most important functions—that of enquiring into accidents— grew up without any foundation in law, and remained so until 1871. Its legal powers were sometimes strained to the limit and beyond; for example, its power to require information from companies was quite specific,[4] and made no provision for enquiring into the times of trains. Yet, when correspondents complained to Gladstone that the M. & L.R. had kept them waiting more than an hour for their train, the Department asked for, and got, a return of late trains. There would be nothing odd in this had it served to exonerate the company; but in fact it showed that, of more than 500 trains, roughly one in five had run late, and that the late trains had been, on an average, twenty minutes behind time.[5] Still more remote from any delegated power was a letter addressed to the Llanelly Railway: 'a statement has been submitted . . . to the effect that [your] company has contracted for 60 sets of cast iron wheels and axles . . . at £6 . 10 . 0 per set . . . and that this price is so far below that which is generally paid . . . as to afford an impression that [they] cannot be used without danger to the public'. The company was asked for some explanation.[6] The spirit in which the

[1] MT 11/1, 5 and 17 Mar. 1841. The resulting case—*Pickford* v. *G. J. R.*— was an important one; for some consequences of it, see below, p. 128.
[2] MT 11/3, 30 Mar. 1843.
[3] See below, pp. 37–8.
[4] 3 & 4 Vict., c. 97, s. 3.
[5] BT 6/280 716, 722, and 728/1842.
[6] MT 11/1, 9 Jan. 1841.

Department worked was most clearly expressed by Laing when he spoke of a

> trust, which although not created by express legal enactment, is imposed upon [the Board] by the general understanding of Parliament and the public, of watching the proceedings of railway companies and endeavouring by amicable representations to prevent any exercise of the extraordinary powers which circumstances have vested in the directors of those bodies, adverse to the spirit by which the legislature was influenced in conferring those privileges.[1]

The most important of the Department's original powers was that of inspecting new lines. But if the line was found to be unsafe, there was no power to prevent, by administrative order, its being opened. Cases soon arose which revealed the need for such a power. In the autumn of 1841, the L.S.W. wished to open its Gosport branch, but at first postponed doing so in deference to the wishes of the Department. Later the branch was opened although the inspector had reported that it was still unsafe. Within a few days, a serious slip compelled the company to close the line. It was now winter, and because of the weather, only temporary repairs were possible. When they were complete, the line was again inspected, and the Department suggested a speed limit of 20 miles per hour until the summer. The company hedged, but eventually agreed. After a few weeks, Pasley reported that the restriction might be lifted as the works on the line were making good progress.[2] It was in consequence of cases such as this that the Board obtained power in 1842 to postpone the opening of a new line, where necessary in the interests of safety.

The Department set little store by its powers relating to bye-laws. Of 77 companies dealt with in 1840, no less than 43 either had none, or made no return. Those submitted related only to points of detail, and were, as a rule, proper in themselves. Many were defective in form, but they had not been disallowed 'where no more substantial objection appeared than the want of uniformity and correctness'. No complaints of improper administration of bye-laws had been received. In 1841 the Department

---

[1] MT 11/3, 1 Feb. 1843.
[2] BT 6/280 207/1842. MT 6/1 1026/1841; 158 and 292/1842. MT 11/2, 5 Feb. 1842.

began to move towards greater uniformity. Model bye-laws were drafted, dealing with such things as the nascent ticket system, and as opportunity offered, the Department urged companies to adopt them. Within three months, four companies had done so.[1] In 1842, they were completely adopted in four cases, and substantially, in nine more.[2] In the following year, the Department approved sixteen codes, and reported that 'on the whole they are identical with, or closely resemble, the model code'.[3] Without making any very energetic use of its powers in relation to bye-laws, the Board was successful, in a narrow field, in what it aimed to do.

One bye-law case led to an attempt by the Department to mediate in a dispute between companies. In 1842, the Manchester & Birmingham Railway was about to open. Between Crewe and Birmingham, its trains were to run over the G.J.R. The latter's terms proved unacceptable, however, and the opening was held up.[4] The G.J. now submitted, for the Board's approval, a new regulation which required, as a general rule, an interval of thirty minutes between trains.[5]

The Department had already promised the Manchester & Birmingham 'a copy of any bye-laws or regulation which may be forwarded for confirmation . . . and a full opportunity . . . of stating any objections which they may wish to offer'. This promise was now kept.[6] In reply, the company stated that the regulation would be prejudicial to it, and destructive to its independence. It wished to send a deputation, and hoped the regulation would not be confirmed.[7] The Board agreed to receive such a deputation, and the G.J. was also invited to send one.[8]

The ensuing conference may be described in Pasley's words:

> I am present at a conference between Lord Ripon and a deputation of the Manchester & Birmingham and of the G.J.R. The latter want to put an interval of 30 minutes between successive trains. This would ruin the traffic of the former, who say five minutes is enough. I had previously made up my mind that it

[1] P.P. 1842, xli, 32.
[2] P.P. 1843, xlvii, 20.
[3] P.P. 1844, xli, 14.
[4] BT 6/280 297/1842.
[5] P.P. 1843, xlvii, 17.
[6] MT 11/2, 19 and 25 Apr. 1842.
[7] BT 6/280 323/1842.
[8] MT 11/2, 29 Apr. 1842.

was so. Lord Ripon, who knows nothing of the matter, shows a good deal of sagacity in questioning both. Mr Laing also present proposes that the two parties shall go to arbitration first; for that, three directors of each might consult a competent engineer. Lord Ripon says he will refer the matter to me, as both parties had already come to the Board of Trade for reference. The Grand Junction say they do not object to perfect reciprocity, let those who come but wait the thirty minutes. They also say that public safety is their object.[1]

Pasley went north to make his enquiry, and discussed time intervals with the secretary of the M. & L.R. He noted, 'Capt. Laws informs me that at Normanton, where perhaps ninety trains pass daily, their rule is nine minutes.'[2] Later, Pasley saw 'Lord Ripon in presence of Mr. Laing. The latter is a strong advocate of the Grand Junction Railway Company. As our opinions are diametrically opposed, Lord Ripon takes the correspondence home with him.'[3] Pasley had recommended the five-minute interval. By this time, the companies were drawing together.

Mr Whithead, a member of the Manchester & Birmingham Railway Company, came confidentially to Lord Ripon and gave him advice, namely that Board of Trade should require Birmingham & Manchester [sic] Company to agree to the terms of Grand Junction for a year off-breakable [?] at six months. I advise his Lordship not to act upon this suggestion. That no *confidential* suggestion of any one individual should be received by Board of Trade. That if he acceded [?] . . . it would be taking the part of the Grand Junction, whose principles and practice were not *approved* by the public.[4]

The Department now told both companies that they would not sanction the G.J. regulation; a five-minute interval was enough in general, and eight minutes in some cases at Stafford.[5] The drafts of both were endorsed significantly, 'approved by the Earl of Ripon'.[6] The Department had waited till the last possible moment permitted by law before disallowing the regulation—presumably in hope of a settlement. Lord Ripon next did very much what Whithead had advised him to do. He

[1] Add. MS. 41989, 5 May, 1842.   [2] Ibid., 9 May, 1842.
[3] Ibid., 23 May, 1842.   [4] Add. MS. 41989, 22 Jun. 1842.
[5] MT 11/2, 25 Jun. 1842.   [6] BT 6/280.

recommended the Manchester & Birmingham to accede to an agreement for a limited period, and the company agreed.[1] By it, the traffic between Crewe and Birmingham was to be worked by the G.J.R. The Company thanked the Department most warmly, and went on to say that, but for its influence, the consequences of the dispute might have been most injurious.[2] It appears, therefore, that the victory of the G.J. was less complete than it appeared, and that the Department's intervention had enabled the Manchester & Birmingham to get better terms than it would have otherwise obtained.

The whole case shows that the Department was not content merely to discharge the very limited functions required by law, but was prepared to go much further when benefits to the public seemed likely to result. Not less significant is the fact that, confronted with a choice between the potential benefits of reduced fares through competition, and of greater safety at the expense of competition, the Department chose the latter. When told that the companies had replaced the first temporary agreement by a permanent one, the Department expressed its satisfaction 'as regards the general principle, with a view to the public safety, of avoiding the competition of rival trains over the 54 miles of railway between Birmingham and Crewe'.[3]

In another case the Department took up the complaint of a Mr. Langford against the passenger fares of the Northern & Eastern Railway. Langford lived at Ponders End, and travelled 'to and fro, the six days of the week'—an early commuter, in fact. He pointed out that whereas the fare from London to Tottenham was 1s., and that from Tottenham to Ponders End, 8d., the fare from London to Ponders End was 2s. He suggested the motive for this: 'the Directors of railways can by skilfully operating on any *one* village or town most effectually destroy *all* private competition by the post road from such locality; and having succeeded in destroying such competition in *one* place, the whole of the towns or villages on the line become in succession victims to such operations'.[4]

The complaint was conveyed to the company, which replied that 'fares for . . . the long distance on this railway are fixed so as not to exceed the rate of charge by the ordinary coach

[1] Add. MS. 41989, 29 and 30 Jun. 1842.   [2] BT 6/280 549/1842.
[3] MT 11/3, 20 Oct. 1843.   [4] BT 6/280 7/1842.

traffic . . . scale of fares rather more in favour of the public is adopted as to intermediate stations, in order to facilitate and increase the traffic . . . but not with the remotest view to a monopoly'. However, since people travelling to Ponders End on tickets to Tottenham were seeking to pay the excess fare on arrival, the company had 'determined, previously to the receipt of your letter, to remove all cause for dissatisfaction . . . by assimilating the fares'.[1]

The danger of monopoly was seen also in agreements between railway companies and coach proprietors, by which the former seemed to be extending their control over the roads themselves. The earliest of several cases in which this principle was involved concerned the G.W.R. at Steventon, which was in 1842 the station for Oxford. G. R. Phillipps, M.P., complained to Gladstone that the company had made an agreement with a coach proprietor, named Waddell, of Oxford, which in effect gave him a monopoly of the business between that place and Steventon. 'The consequence', Phillipps wrote, 'is that no coach between Birmingham and Steventon goes further than Oxford and passengers and their luggage are . . . turned into another vehicle at Oxford, where it not infrequently happens that there is no room for them. . . . We have now only one coach where there used to be four or five'. Innkeepers alleged that if they put rival coaches on the road, they would not be allowed to enter Steventon station. 'It is true', Phillipps went on, 'that they can drive up to the gates of the station about a hundred yards distant from the house for passengers: but they and their luggage must be put down frequently in the mud and rain, and subjected to the annoyance of the porters . . . not choosing to assist in carrying it to the booking office.' This letter is endorsed: 'Refer to Railway Department. Acknowledge and ask for any information as to the reasons alleged by the Company in justification. W. E. G.'[2]

To this complaint, the company replied at length. Waddell was required to meet every train at Steventon, summer and winter; this made it possible for the company to book passengers from Paddington through to Oxford by all trains. The coach waited beside the platform, thus avoiding those 'disgraceful

---

[1] MT 11/2, 5 Jan. 1842. BT 6/280 46/1842.
[2] BT 6/280 156/1842.

scenes of scrambling and importunity [such] as occurred when the line was first opened . . . and which became a source of continual complaint from the public'. The company's rule in such cases was as follows: 'after ascertaining the names of all parties engaged either in coaching or posting upon any line of road previously to the opening of the railway, they strive to secure to such parties, in as fair proportions as they can adjust, the benefit of any connection with their line'. At the same time, newcomers were not excluded. Before the opening of the line. Waddell had been the sole proprietor of coaches between London and Oxford. He had asked the company 'to exclude all other conveyances from the station, but this was distinctly refused. . . . He pleaded that it was unfair to bind him to run coaches from early and late trains with comparatively few passengers, while others could select the best trains only, and the fine weather or particular seasons of term time and those by which they might obtain great advantage over him' The company, however, had remained adamant, and rested its defence with urbanity: 'it will be a gratification to the Directors, which they think will be but due to them, to hear from you that [the Board of Trade] coincide in the propriety of their course'.[1]

It is not clear what was the outcome of this case. From it, and others like it, however, the Department learnt not only that companies had a right to make agreements with coach proprietors, but that such agreements were at least in part advantageous to the public, since they enabled companies to accept through bookings to places not served by the rail.[2] Such agreements, coupled with the regulations made for the use of station yards, necessarily favoured some coaching interests at the expense of others. Even if it could be shown that, by these means, the monopoly of the railway was being extended over the road, the Board had no power to act. A passage in the report of the Select Committee on Railways of 1844 refers to to the problem,[3] as does section 33 of the Bill[4] of that year. It was, however, struck out in committee. Subsequently, the Department dealt with such complaints by stating that no action was possible, or at most, by sending a copy to the company concerned.

[1] BT 6/280 180/1842.   [2] MT 11/2, 22 Apr. 1842.
[3] P.P. 1844, xi, 32.   [4] Ibid., iv, 415.

Accident enquiries were among the Department's most important activities, although it had no statutory power to conduct them. Why did companies afford facilities for such enquiries? To this question, which is one of the most puzzling arising from this study, the evidence affords only a partial answer. In the case of a fatal accident, an inquest was of course held, and the verdict of the coroner's jury might prove embarrassing to the company, because technically uninformed. An enquiry conducted by an inspector with knowledge of railway working, whose report would carry official sanction, might be welcome in such circumstances. As an example, we may consider an accident which occurred on the London & Brighton line in 1841. An engine-driver, giving evidence at the inquest, attributed the accident to the design of the engine, and this view was endorsed by the jury. Public alarm, already aroused by the accident itself, now became more acute, and as a result, the company withdrew the engines in question. This must have created great difficulties in working, since they constituted almost a quarter of its total complement. The company did not consider the engines a source of danger, and the Board's inspector confirmed this view. The cause of the accident, he reported, was excessive speed after heavy rain.[1] His report, by shifting the blame on to the driver, went a good way towards exonerating the company. A similar attitude was displayed by the G.W.R. when Dr. Buckland, the Oxford geologist, created a scare by alleging that the Box Tunnel was dangerous. Pasley inspected it, and Russell, the company's chairman, asked for a copy of his report. 'After the absurd but alarming rumours which have been circulated on this subject,' he said, 'it is very important to reassure the public mind.' He also wished to comfort the shareholders, and proposed to do so by putting Pasley's report before the half-yearly meeting.[2]

Recommendations made as a result of accident enquiries normally aimed at the wider adoption of devices and practices already observed on other lines. In some cases, they were 'inspectable'; that is, it was easy to discover whether companies which said they had complied, had in fact done so. For example, Pasley noted gradient posts beside the line, apparently

[1] BTHR LBR 4/6 and 5/2.
[2] BT 6/280 579/1842.

for the first time, in 1842. Years later, after an accident which was attributed to a train going too fast downhill, the Eastern Counties and Norfolk Railways complied with the Department's recommendation that they should put up gradient posts along their lines.[1] Pasley could rarely find time to make special trips to see whether recommendations had been carried out. But his work constantly took him over all the lines of the country, and he could note as he passed whether or not gradient posts, for example, had been put up. Moreover, once they were up, companies tended to keep them in use. Railway working was in its infancy, however, and there were few tangible safety devices which the Department could urge on companies.

Most of its recommendations had, therefore, to be 'non-inspectable'. When it recommended the adoption of a particular practice, it was much easier for unscrupulous companies to hood-wink the Department. The action taken following the Meudon disaster, on the Paris-Versailles line, in 1842 provides a good example.[2] It is important also as the first case in which the Department tried to ensure that railways in Great Britain would learn from experience abroad. More casualties were caused in this crash than in any accident in Britain up till that time, and one of the main reasons was that both doors of each compartment were locked, so that when the train caught fire, the passengers could not get out. At Pasley's suggestion,[3] the Department took up the question, and issued a special report.[4] But, although they reported that their recommendation not to lock both doors had been 'universally attended to',[5] the practice in fact persisted and was mentioned as a factor in accidents long after this date.[6] The Department's difficulty was not only that it had no power to enforce recommendations, but also that it could not ensure, by inspection, that where companies had voluntarily agreed to leave one door unlocked, they would in

[1] Add. MS. 41989 [29 Dec. 1842]. P.P. 1846, xxxix, 25.
[2] For this accident, see P. Dauzet, *Le Siècle des chemins de fer en France, 1821–1938*, Fontenay aux Roses (n.d.), 48.
[3] Add. MS. 41989, 14 May, 1842.
[4] P.P. 1842, xli, 1 ff.   [5] P.P. 1843, xlvii, 12.
[6] E.g. Hansard, clxxix, 1337 and 1345. 'Locking-in' was the subject of celebrated letters from Sydney Smith to the *Morning Chronicle*, lately reprinted in: W. H. Auden ed., *Selected Writings of Sydney Smith*, Faber (1957), 311–16.

fact continue to do so once the scare had passed. Of the Department's early recommendations, the majority resembled in this respect its rule on door-locking, rather than its advocacy of gradient-posts, and the value of accident enquiries was limited in consequence.

Other accident enquiries were important in that they led the Department to enquire into aspects of railway working—carriage construction and labour relations—which at first sight seem remote from public safety. On Christmas Eve, 1841, a G.W. train consisting of two third-class passenger carriages, a station truck, and seventeen goods wagons ran into a slip of earth in Sonning Cutting. Smith was soon on the spot, and wrote his report on Christmas Day. All the passengers had been thrown out of the carriages; eight had been killed, and seventeen injured. The consequences might have been less serious had the carriages and wagons been provided with buffers, as Smith had recommended in a previous accident report, and in evidence before the Select Committee of 1841. The sides should be raised from 2 feet to 4 feet 6 inches to reduce the danger of passengers being thrown out, and passengers should not be carried on luggage trains.[1]

The proposed modifications to the construction of the carriages resembled the gradient posts discussed above; they could be checked by inspection, and if carried out, would last a considerable time. The proposal that passengers should not be carried on luggage trains, on the other hand, resembled the proposal that both doors should not be locked; it was almost impossible to check by inspection what was the practice of companies, or whether they might have reverted to an earlier practice after separating goods from passengers for a time.

The company accepted the recommendations as to improved carriages. It had in fact before the accident ordered some similar to those suggested. The existing stock was modified and brought back into use within four days, and a further supply ordered shortly after.[2] The recommendation that passenger and goods traffic should be separated was not accepted, however, and mixed trains continued to run on the G.W.R. until 1844 and after.[3]

[1] P.P. 1842, xli, 113–15.
[2] Ibid., 115–16. BTHR GW 1/117, 4 Jan. 1842.
[3] BTHR GW 1/117, 4 Jan. 1842. MacDermot, i, 640–1.

The Department now undertook an enquiry into third-class travel. The objects, set out in a memorandum by Laing, were to find out what was the construction of carriages used by companies, and whether companies were in the habit of running mixed trains of passengers and goods. Laing's words on the construction of carriages are worth quoting:

> The improper construction of third class carriages as pointed out by Sir F. Smith's report, the sides and ends being only two feet high so that a moderate shock is enough to throw the passengers out of the carriage. The object of this no doubt is partly to save expense, but mainly to deter second class passengers from travelling by the third class by a fear of the exposure for eight or ten hours, without any shelter, to the cold.[1]

A general circular went out to companies, enquiring the number of trains carrying third-class passengers, the size and construction of carriages, and particularly the height of the sides, and whether they had springs and buffers; and the position of luggage wagons, if taken by passenger trains.[2] Some dozens of companies replied. A second circular went to those companies whose carriages seemed to be constructed so as to endanger the lives of passengers.[3]

In general, the replies were favourable. For example, the Midland Counties sent a copy of a minute:

> 20 Jan. 1842 . . . a letter from the Board of Trade dated the 17 Jan. 1842 having been read,
> It was Resolved,
>   That this committee approved the recommendation contained therein, and will forthwith direct alteration to be made in all the third class carriages.[4]

The L.S.W. stated that it would carry no more third-class passengers by goods trains, but take them on the normal passenger trains; the letter is endorsed: 'acquaint them that My Lords are of opinion that this is a very judicious arrangement'.[5]

Some companies dissented, however. The G.J. was advised by its engineer, Joseph Locke, against the change; 'while I possess', he wrote:

---

[1] BT 6/280.   [2] MT 11/2, 3 Jan. 1842.   [3] Ibid., 17 Jan. 1842.
[4] BT 6/280 104/1842.   [5] Ibid., 124/1842.

The greatest possible desire to adopt every suggestion which emanates from the Board of Trade, I cannot help expressing my fears that the suggestion in question is not likely to have any beneficial effects. . . . I can see nothing in the height of the sides which could guard a passenger against such an accident.[1]

The Manchester & Bolton Company, while undertaking to consider the suggestions, suggested that 'measures calculated to increase the expense of third class passenger traffic will, in many instances, cause it to be suppressed altogether'.[2]

The Sonning accident awakened the interest of the Department in the whole question of the facilities provided by the railways for the poor. The assistance of the Poor Law Commissioners was invoked, and Edwin Chadwick promised to send what information he could collect on 'the facilities for travelling by stages, waggons, vans or otherwise, enjoyed by the poorer classes prior to the introduction of the railway system, the extent to which these have been superseded by the establishment of railways, and the effect of such change in restricting or extending the means of communication at the disposal of the poorer classes'.[3] The promised information was published as an appendix to the report of Gladstone's Select Committee of 1844.[4]

The first accident in which the Department found low wages and long hours contributory factors occurred at Barnsley, on the North Midland Railway, in January, 1843. At the end of 1842, the company had cut the wages of drivers and firemen, with the result that they had all resigned in a body. Pasley went to Derby to investigate, but was told that new men had been taken on who had 'all produced good characters, and were perfectly competent for their situations'.[5] But the Barnsley enquiry—in conducting which, Pasley was guided not only by his official instructions, but also by a personal letter from Lord Ripon[6]—revealed a very different state of affairs. Of 18 men who had replaced those who had resigned, the company had discharged 10 'after a few days trial, on account of incompetence or misconduct, after having in several cases occasioned accidents. So far from having produced unexceptionable characters, at least six of the new men were discharged servants

---

[1] Ibid., 125/1842.   [2] Ibid., 101/1842.   [3] Ibid., 20/1842.
[4] P.P. 1844, xi, 640–59.   [5] P.P. 1843, xlvii, 12.   [6] Add. MS. 41964.

from other companies'.[1] The driver of the Barnsley train had been dismissed by both the L.S.W. and the G.W. between August and December, 1841.

Pasley advised George Hudson, the company's chairman, to undertake that there would be no further cuts in wages. Hudson denied any such intention, but would give no such undertaking, as it might appear a victory for the workmen.[2] The Department told the company it should not require the men to drive 146 miles a day, seven days a week, with the exception of alternate Sundays. In reply, the company sent details of the names, duties, and hours of its drivers, adding that

> the change of engine-drivers, to which you attribute this melancholy event, was forced upon the directors by the men themselves, who refused to submit to a reasonable and proper reduction, and left them no alternative but to take the course adopted, or to make the engine-drivers masters of the line, thus compromising the safety of the public by the absence of discipline and subordination. . . . The engine-men make no complaint of overexertion, and express themselves perfectly satisfied with the present arrangements.[3]

Implicit in the Department's view of this case was an argument for state intervention between employers and workers which was radically different from, say, the philanthropy of Lord Shaftesbury. It was the argument that, if wages fell below a reasonable minimum, or if hours of work exceeded a reasonable maximum, evils would ensue whose cost would be borne, not by the employers, but by society itself.

The Act of 1842 conferred on the Board powers to authorise companies to replace level crossings by bridges;[4] and to enter lands temporarily, or acquire land compulsorily, for the purpose of repairing or altering cuttings, embankments, and other works, where necessary in the interests of safety.[5]

The London & Croydon Company was the first to make use of the new procedure. It sought authority to widen cuttings at New Cross and Forest Hill. Pasley reported in its favour, but found Lord Ripon 'cautious and averse to taking people's land'. Gladstone held an enquiry, and heard the objectors.

[1] P.P. 1843, xlvii, 13. [2] Add. MS. 41989, 19 Jan. 1843.
[3] P.P. 1843, xlvii, 15 n. [4] 5 & 6 Vict., c. 55, s.13.
[5] Ibid., ss.14–15.

Following concessions by the company, and the withdrawal of the chief objector, the necessary certificate was granted. The Act was interpreted to extend to land required for a spoil-bank.[1]

A little later the company sought permission to replace the level crossing near the Dartmouth Arms (now Forest Hill) station by a bridge. In this case, the Department had to consider the objections of a public body—namely the parish in its capacity of highway authority. The parish disliked, not the proposal itself, but the line proposed for the new road under the bridge, and pressed for a straighter road. Pasley reported, however, 'that it is impracticable to carry the road over or under the railway in a direct line', and the company was authorised to go ahead with its plan.[2]

The spirit which animated the Department during its earliest years led its officers to investigate many questions beyond the minimum required by law. In many of the cases reviewed above, they failed to achieve their aims, because their powers were inadequate. The remedy, they believed, was to ask Parliament for wider powers. Pasley used this argument on Hudson and his colleagues when enquiring into the Barnsley accident: 'they object at first to grant information. I insist upon it, telling them that whatever is refused, being reasonable, will induce Parliament to arm the [Railway] Department . . . with greater power'.[3] Laing spoke in a similar tone when trying to persuade the L.S.W. to open the station yard at Woking to coaches; 'If the directors do not think proper to attend to this recommendation, it will only remain for their Lordships to take the first fitting opportunity of applying to Parliament for the necessary power to enforce what they believe to have been the spirit of the Acts relating to railways, and the intention of the legislature'.[4] We must now consider what was the influence of the Department on legislation, and how far it was successful in its attempts to get wider powers.

The accepted accounts of railway legislation[5] focus attention on the proceedings in Parliament. They analyse the evidence

[1] Add. MS. 41989, 21 Sept. and 5 Oct. 1842. MT 11/2, 6 Oct. 1842. P.P. 1843, xlvii, 24.
[2] P.P. 1843, xlvii, 25. MT 11/3, 2 Jan. 1843.
[3] Add. MS. 41989, 19 Jan. 1843.   [4] MT 11/3, 15 Feb. 1843.
[5] Cohn and Cleveland-Stevens, *passim*.

and reports of Select Committees, attribute measures to individual statesmen, summarise the arguments produced in debate, and show how the original proposals were, in many cases, modified during their passage through the houses. It is proposed to supplement these accounts by treating the subject from a different point of view, and to show the influence of the Department on legislation, and the relationship between that legislation and the Department's experience.

Within a year of the Department's foundation, the Railway Regulation Bill, 1841, sought to add materially to its powers. It was based on a report from the Department which pointed out various weaknesses in the Act of 1840, and called for greater powers:

(a) to require companies to report all accidents of a public nature, even if not attended with personal injury.
(b) to postpone the opening of a line when, on inspection, it was found to be unsafe.
(c) to set up a scheme for the examination, licensing, and registration of engine-drivers.
(d) to issue 'regulations for enforcing upon railways in general, or upon any railway in particular, such arrangements and precautions as from experience appear necessary for the public safety'.[1]

In its original form, the Bill follows the report closely.[2]

It is not surprising to find that the railway interest in general disliked the measure; more noteworthy were the means adopted to fight it. Opposition throughout centred on the proposed power to enforce safety regulations on companies, and representatives of companies, meeting at Birmingham, produced a code of signals for general adoption throughout the country.[3] The idea seems to have been to show that the proposed power was unnecessary, since the companies were voluntarily putting their own house in order. The Birmingham conference also set up a standing committee to conduct the opposition to the Bill; moderate in policy, it decided not to oppose the second reading.[4] It then put forward an amended clause which would have conferred powers on the Board narrower than originally proposed, but still far wider than any actually obtained during our

---

[1] Paraphrase of P.P. 1841, xxv, 203–8. [2] Ibid., iii, 161.
[3] *Herapath's Railway Magazine*, iii (1841), 99. [4] Ibid., 154.

period. Had it passed into law, the Board would have been able 'for the purpose of preventing accidents . . . to issue . . . such regulations respecting the lights and flags to be used as signals . . . or for the government of engine-men, guards . . . policemen or switch-men, as they shall deem necessary'.[1] This clause Labouchere would not accept, but in committee the Bill was amended in a very similar way; that is to say, the power to issue regulations was not struck out, but was restricted by being made more precise. Otherwise, the Bill emerged substantially unchanged.[2]

The government's control of legislation in the House of Commons was, of course, much less complete a century ago than it has since become. Even so, a Bill, once past the committee stage, was normally safe until it reached the House of Lords, which was usually more favourable to measures of railway regulation than the Commons.[3] But in 1841, conditions were not normal. The Whigs, nearing the end of their long spell of office, were in an extremely weak position. The opponents of the Bill were, therefore, able to secure the appointment of a Select Committee to consider 'whether it is desirable for the public safety to vest a discretionary power of issuing regulations for the prevention of accidents upon railways, in the Board of Trade, and if so, under what conditions and limitations'.[4] The Select Committee agreed with Smith, who appeared as a witness for the Board, that if any such power were delegated, the Board should have unrestricted discretion in exercising it. It went on to conclude that no such power should be delegated, and that 'the supervision of [the Railway] Department should be exercised in the way of suggestion rather than in that of positive regulation'.[5]

It was now the end of May, and, under normal conditions, there would have been time to pass the remainder of the Bill, including the scheme for a register of engine-drivers.[6] But by that time, the government was on the point of defeat. Smith,

---

[1] Ibid., 222.   [2] P.P. 1841, iii, 169 ff.   [3] Cf. Cohn, i, 86.
[4] P.P. 1841, viii, 2.   [5] P.P. 1841, viii, 4–5.
[6] For the comparable and ultimately successful campaign for the examination of Merchant navy officers, see R. Prouty, *Transformation of the Board of Trade*, Heinemann, (1957), 64–7, and J. H. Wilde, 'Creation of the Marine Department of the Board of Trade', in *Journal of Transport History*, ii (1955–6), 193–206.

writing to Saunders of the G.W.R. on the 2nd of June, pointed out the doubtful prospect for the Bill: 'if the ministry should be defeated upon Peel's motion, the dissolution would be too immediate to give us a chance of carrying our . . . Bill; otherwise we *may* get it through this session'.[1] As it turned out, the ministry was defeated two days later, and the Bill was lost.

Its defeat was not the result solely of the opposition of the railway interest, for that interest was not all hostile. George Stephenson, for example, wrote to Labouchere in support of the Bill, and suggested some of the points on which Board of Trade regulations were desirable, such as uniformity of signals, and a government stamp for wheels, frames, and axles.[2] But those members of the railway world who were opposed to the Bill were able to take advantage of the weakness of the Whig government. It was that weakness which caused the measure to founder, rather than the strength of the opposition to it.

In 1842, the Department again called for wider powers, though with some differences. There had been fewer accidents, and, in particular, the decline in the number of collisions could 'fairly be attributed in a considerable degree to the more general adoption of the precautions suggested by the Inspector General'. Fewer accidents, too, were attributed to the misconduct of drivers. The power to enforce regulations on companies, and the scheme for a register of drivers, were, therefore, now less urgent, and might be shelved.

Power to postpone the opening of new lines, and to require fuller returns of accidents, were still needed, on the other hand. In addition, the Department made the following new recommendations:

(a) the Board should have power to settle disputes between companies and such bodies as road trustees, owners of rights on lines, etc.

(b) level crossing gates should normally be kept shut across the road, not across the railway, save where the Board decided otherwise.

[1] BTHR HL 1/7.

[2] MT 6/1 568/1841. This letter has recently been printed by Mr. Rolt as an appendix to his book, *Red for Danger* (1955) but he does not bring out its significance.

(c) private gates opening on railways should normally be kept locked, and companies should be required to maintain the fences along their lines.

(d) the Board should have the power to authorise companies to acquire land compulsorily when needed to repair slips.[1]

Gladstone introduced a Bill based on these suggestions.[2] Like Labouchere's Bill in the previous session, it was essentially a departmental measure. Neither was based on the investigations of a Select Committee. Neither was the work of the statesmen who took charge of them in Parliament, save in the negative sense that the provisions of the 1841 Bill which did not figure in that of 1842 may have been left out at the instance of Lord Ripon or of Gladstone. The 1842 Bill, unlike its predecessor, had an easy passage through Parliament. Only two substantial provisions were struck out. The first of these was a clause requiring owners of private gates to keep them locked; the second, a clause which would have empowered the Board to call on railways and other interested parties to substitute bridges for dangerous level crossings, and if unable to agree, to submit to compulsory arbitration. On the other hand, the Board was empowered to authorise a company to substitute a bridge for a crossing if it wished to do so.[3]

As noted above, the railway interest anticipated the methods of modern pressure groups by conferring outside Parliament to decide its policy towards the 1841 Bill. Activity outside Parliament also took place in 1842. On the second reading, Gladstone was asked to allow time for communication, if necessary, with interested parties. He replied that they had already been in touch with the Board, and there would be opportunity for further consultation if they wished.[4] That was on 28 February, and Gladstone discussed the Bill with representatives of the companies on at least two subsequent occasions.[5] These consultations appear to have had no immediate consequences of importance; but are noteworthy as precedents. At least one subsequent railway Bill was amended more radically as a result of consultation at the Board than it was in Parliament.[6]

[1] Paraphrase of P.P. 1842, xli, 33–5. [2] P.P. 1842, iv, 27 ff.
[3] For amendments to the Bill, see P.P. 1842, iv, 37–52.
[4] Hansard, lx, 1179.
[5] Add. MS. 41989, 4 and 12 Mar. 1842. [6] See below, pp. 137–8.

In introducing the Bill, Gladstone stated that he sought greater powers 'only on specific points where experience showed that they were called for'.[1] Examples may be given of such specific points. In future, crossing gates were normally to be kept shut across the road, unless the Board permitted a company to do otherwise.[2] An enquiry in 1841 had shown that 53 companies maintained 312 crossings. Most were properly kept, but in 42 cases, gates were erected, and gate-keepers stationed, in consequence of representations from the Department.[3] It had proved possible to enforce the law by administrative means without recourse to the courts. But an anomaly had been revealed. Although the usual and wiser course was to shut the gates across the road, as required by the Highways Act, 1839, some companies (e.g. the Hull & Selby and the Newcastle & Carlisle) were required by special Acts to shut their gates across the line.[4] The section of the Act which removed this anomaly alludes to the Department's investigations: 'experience has shown that it is more conducive to safety that [crossing] gates should be kept closed across the ... road instead of across the railway.'[5]

The Act empowered the Board to authorise companies to enter lands to prevent, or repair, damage to earth-works. In case of emergency, companies might do likewise without first getting the Board's permission. The Board could also revive a company's powers of compulsory purchase, where extra land was required for such purposes.[6] The background of these provisions is to be found in the Department's records. One of Pasley's first enquiries was into a slip on the London & Croydon Railway near New Cross. He did 'not think that any engineer could have anticipated [it] ... for it is only our late experience which has developed the disadvantages of deep cuttings and high embankments in certain kinds of clay even at very moderate slopes'.[7] Soon after he investigated a similar incident on the L.S.W. Gosport branch, and the two cases led him to suggest to Lord Ripon

the expediency of obtaining for railway companies the power of occupying additional ground on each side of deep cuttings and

[1] Hansard, lx, 167.   [2] 5 & 6 Vict., c. 55, s. 9.   [3] P.P. 1842, xli, 21.
[4] Ibid.   [5] 5 & 6 Vict., c. 55, s. 9.
[6] 5 & 6 Vict., ss. 14–15.   [7] BT 6/280 64/1842.

embankments in order to increase the base of their slopes . . . for preventing slips. . . . The construction of railways being a new art, not brought gradually to perfection like other branches of engineering by the experience of ages, it can be no reflection upon the engineers who planned these works, that they did not foresee the injurious action that continued rains would produce upon such embankments and cuttings in clayey soil.[1]

The power to postpone the opening of a line,[2] and to arbitrate between companies having a portion of line in common,[3] are clearly related to cases dealt with above.[4] The power to authorise companies to replace dangerous level crossings by bridges[5] had its origin in the plain common sense of the Department rather than in its special knowledge of railways; still, cases had occurred which pointed to the desirability of such a power.[6]

The provision that carriages of laden weight exceeding four tons might be used was related to the Department's experience in a different way from any of those so far considered.[7]

No evidence has come to light to show whether the Department had any particular case in mind in suggesting the clause (later struck out) which would have required those who had private gates opening on to lines to keep them locked. But a later incident indicates the kind of danger apprehended. A man broke open two gates in order to cross a main line while hunting at Harrow, and left them open. When the London & Birmingham Company prosecuted, he pleaded guilty and was fined one shilling.[8]

The approach adopted here throws little new light on Gladstone's Act of 1844.[9] It was a personal rather than a departmental measure. The Conservative, Gladstone, had carried in 1842 a measure closely related to that which the Whig, Labouchere, had failed to carry in 1841. There is no reason to suppose that Dalhousie would have introduced the Bill of 1844 again in 1845, had Gladstone failed to carry it; still less that it would have been brought in again had a change of government

---

[1] MT 6/1 158/1842.
[2] 5 & 6 Vict., c. 55, s. 6.
[3] Ibid., s. 11.
[4] See above, pp. 37 and 38–40.
[5] 5 & 6 Vict., c. 55, s. 13.
[6] P.P. 1842, xli, 21.
[7] See above, p. 14–5.
[8] BT 6/280 831/1842.
[9] Cleveland-Stevens, Ch. V, gives a full account, summarising also Cohn's conclusions.

intervened. Gladstone's measure was based, not on a report from the Department, but on the findings of a Select Committee.[1] Although Laing was the principal witness, the most important parts of his evidence are not clearly related to the experience of the Department as reflected in its records; it consists rather of statements, which seem specially prepared for the occasion, on matters such as loan notes,[2] which were not normally within the purview of the Department. It seems likely that Laing's function was to put before the committee what Gladstone wanted it to hear. It has been suggested that Laing was the author of the Bill.[3] That he was the draftsman is very probable, but memoranda among Gladstone's papers[4] suggest that the thought was largely his. Lastly, there is the evidence afforded by the timing of the Bill, and of the influence of Gladstone's colleagues on the modifications it underwent. Gladstone did not introduce his Bill until June; but in May a memorandum of what he proposed had been circulating among his colleagues, collecting their opinions as it went.[5] Their views ranged from indifference to hostility, and it is extraordinary that he should have persevered. That he did so shows that he believed deeply in his Bill; but it is not surprising that he was forced to accept extensive amendments to it.

The main provisions of the Bill,[6] and those which suffered most by amendment,[7] dealt with revision of railway charges and purchase of railways by the state. Power to conduct these operations was transferred from the Board of Trade to the Treasury during the passage of the Bill through the Commons. These powers were never exercised and it is easy to criticise them, both on the grounds that they were too generous to the companies, and that they were not to come into effect for twenty-one years. But before reaching a final verdict on them, they should be considered in conjunction with Gladstone's policy of 'equivalents',[8] which was intended to secure reductions in charges in the immediate future.

A clause in the original Bill which stems from the experience of the Department sought to secure free access for coaches to

[1] P.P. 1844, xi, *passim.*
[2] Ibid., 73 ff., and see above, p. 15.
[3] Cohn, i, 138.
[4] Add. MS. 44734, f. 15 ff.
[5] Add. MS. 44650, f. 201 ff.
[6] P.P. 1844, iv, 415.
[7] Ibid., 435.
[8] See below, pp. 77–80.

station yards, but it was struck out in the House of Commons.[1] The only important additions to the Board's powers were those relating to cheap, or (as they soon came to be called) Parliamentary, trains.[2] Companies which derived one-third or more of their revenue from passengers, as the great majority of companies did, were to run one such train on each week-day. These trains were to stop at every station, were to run at a speed of not less than twelve miles per hour, and the fare was not to exceed one penny per mile. All these arrangements were subject to the approval of the Board of Trade, which could dispense with any of the requirements save that regarding fares. The Board was also to approve the construction of the carriages. Receipts from Parliamentary passengers were not to be subject to duty. The original proposal had been that half the duty should be remitted. The amendment, though a concession to the companies, had the effect of increasing the Department's influence over them. Since companies had to get the Department's approval before they could claim remission of duty, it is reasonable to suppose that they would have been less amenable had the financial inducement been less.

The provisions for Parliamentary trains are related in some degree to the experience of the Department.[3] We shall see below how they were implemented.[4]

The influence of the Department on private Bills also deserves consideration. We have already noted that the private Bill system did more to protect private interests than to promote the public interest.[5] To remedy this, Laing was 'to attend to all railway Bills in their progress through the House . . . and to guard against the insertion of improper clauses'.[6] Early in 1842, Hedworth Lambton, one of the Members for County Durham, drew Gladstone's attention to the Bill to incorporate George Hudson's Newcastle & Darlington Junction Company. The proposed line would incorporate portions of several existing railways, and

in all probability there will be no petitioners against the Bill . . . because the Bill will ask to pass through very little new property, and therefore the whole case would not be thoroughly sifted and

---

[1] See above, pp. 41–2.
[2] 7 & 8 Vict., c. 85, ss. 6–10.
[3] See above, pp. 45–7.
[4] See below, pp. 93–9.
[5] See above, p. 21.
[6] BT 3/29, 11 Aug. 1840.

examined before a committee of the House of Commons—feeling all this, I am anxious respectfully to call upon the Board of Trade to exercise the supervisory powers with which Parliament has invested them by desiring forthwith that a report shall be made by an able and impartial engineer on the fitness and safety to the public of the new line.[1]

A conference was held at the Board of Trade between Hudson, Robert Stephenson, and others, on behalf of the company, and Porter, Laing, and Pasley. Pasley recorded: 'Mr. Hudson is inclined to be disputatious but I cut him short. . . . We . . . declare that if they can obviate the objections on the score of safety, we will on the part of our Board make no objection to their line.'[2] Stephenson defended the proposal to incorporate sections of existing railways: 'if none of the intermediate lines had been in existence I should have selected a line nearly in the course of that now proposed'. Moreover, the whole line would be under unified management.[3] After a second meeting with Stephenson[4] Pasley reported that since the new company was to have sole management of the line, and was to add a third track to the Stanhope & Tyne railway, the projected scheme should be satisfactory.[5]

The point of the enquiry now shifted. Lord Ripon sent Pasley to make a 'personal inspection' of the proposed line, and to report on 'its fitness as regards safety'. 'It has been represented to his Lordship', the letter continues,

> that the objection . . . to which alone your former report was confined—viz., that of passing along portions of minor lines, is not the only one, and that there are some exceedingly dangerous curves, bridges, level crossings etc. upon some of the lines which it is proposed to use, especially the Durham Junction.
> Under the circumstances, Lord Ripon wishes you to examine and report upon the whole of the proposed line and Mr. Lambton . . . is to move that the second reading . . . be postponed until you have made your report.[6]

Pasley tested one of the allegedly dangerous curves by going round it at 'maximum speed—not less than 30 miles per hour'. He admitted 'that a person of weak nerves standing upon the

[1] BT 6/280 27/1842. [2] Add. MS. 41989, 2 Feb. 1842.
[3] BT 6/280 27/1842. [4] Add. MS. 41989, 7 Feb. 1842.
[5] BT 6/280 159/1842. [6] MT 11/2, 16 Feb. 1842.

engine, as we did in going, would have fancied himself in danger, but in a first class carriage, in which we returned, he would scarcely have noticed anything unusual'. He confirmed that the route was safe,[1] but later recommended two changes. The radius of a curve immediately south of the River Wear should be increased, and a speed limit of twenty miles per hour imposed; and the Washington coal railway should be carried under the main line.[2]

The Department now submitted 'an outline of the clauses which the Board of Trade will require to be inserted in the . . . Bill'.[3] Reference to the Act shows that the Department's requirements were met.[4]

Provisions in railway Bills which confer powers on the Board are not in themselves proof of the Department's influence, however. For example, the Birmingham & Gloucester Act, 1842, empowered the Board to determine, among other things, the site of the terminus of the proposed Worcester branch, regard being had to agreements already entered into.[5] In making his report, Pasley found himself practically restricted by the agreements mentioned to choosing between two sites—those suggested respectively by the company's engineer, Robert Stephenson, and by two local bodies, the Town Council and the Chamber of Commerce. His recommendation of the former was confirmed, and accepted by the latter.[6]

This case is an example of the practice which had 'recently been growing in railway committees of solving difficulties, and making provision for contingencies in particular Bills, by attaching new responsibilities to the Board of Trade'.[7] Such a practice might get out of hand. In 1844, the Department wrote to some of the more important Parliamentary agents as follows:

Mr. Gladstone's attention having been drawn to the circumstance that clauses imposing new functions on the Board of Trade have been occasionally introduced into Railway Bills . . . without any consent on the part of the Board of Trade having been obtained, I am directed by him to inform you . . . that he will oppose the

[1] BT 6/280 201/1842.   [2] RT 6/280 273/1842.
[3] MT 11/2, 31 Mar. 1842.
[4] 5 & 6 Vict., c. 80 (Local and Personal), ss. 140-3 and 149.
[5] 6 & 7 Vict., c. 53 (Local and Personal), ss. 47-8.
[6] P.P. 1844, xli, 435; MT 11/4, 29 Apr. 1844; MT 6/2 344/1844.
[7] P.P. 1844, xi, 24.

reception of the Report, or Third Reading of any Bill . . . containing any clause involving the exercise of new functions on the part of the Board of Trade unless where his express consent has been applied for and given to such clause prior to its introduction.[1]

During the early years of the Department, the normal course was not to interfere with private Bills.[2] Cases had arisen however, in which it departed from the normal course. In doing so, it found itself capable of influencing such Bills, and gained experience of the methods by which such influence might be exerted. The attempt to extend the Department's influence to all private railway Bills will form one of the main themes of the next chapter.

[1] MT 11/4, 16 Mar. 1844.　　　　　[2] MT 11/3, 20 Mar. 1843.

3

THE RAILWAY BOARD
AND ITS AFTERMATH
1844–1846

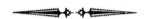

IN August, 1844, an important change took place in the form and function of the Railway Department. The staff was increased and the principal officers—known henceforth as the 'Five Kings'—were formed into a Railway Board, presided over by Dalhousie. The new Board, following the recommendation of Gladstone's Select Committee and Resolutions of the House of Commons,[1] began to prepare a most ambitious series of reports Their purpose was to guide Parliament through the whole of the railway Bills of the coming session, and to recommend for each scheme whether it should be passed, postponed, or rejected. Had the experiment succeeded, it would have had most important consequences. Every new scheme would have been subject to critical examination before reaching Parliament, and the influence of the government would have been brought to bear on the growth of the British railway system. But the experiment did not succeed. Less than a year later, both Board and reports came to an end.

The Board and its failure are therefore deserving of the closest study. Unfortunately, previous accounts of it[2] are marred by serious misconceptions. The Railway Board has been treated

---

[1] P.P. 1844, xi, 22 ff; C. J. xcix (1844), 520.
[2] Cohn, i, 176 ff. E. A. Pratt, *History of Inland Transport in England* (Kegan Paul), 1912, 269 ff. Cleveland-Stevens, 132 ff.

as a new department,[1] whereas it was merely the old Department in a new guise. It has been assumed that the purpose of forming the Railway Board was to prepare the reports. The reports are said to have had little or no effect, and at the same time, to have aroused intense opposition. The dissolution of the Board is represented as a concession by the government to outraged opinion.[2] All these assumptions will be reconsidered. The fundamental point is that there was no necessary connection between the two experiments. The reports could have been prepared equally well had the Board not been set up. On the other hand, the Board might have come into existence even if the reports had not been decided upon. Similarly, the Board might have continued after the termination of the reports, and the reports might have continued after the winding-up of the board. Distinct explanations must be sought for the setting up and abolition of the Board and for the cessation of the reports.

The Railway Board was set up as a result of Gladstone's attempts to rid himself of responsibility for railways altogether. He pointed out to Peel in June, 1844, that that responsibility had already increased and would go on increasing. Parliament's handling of railway legislation was unsatisfactory, and he doubted whether 'it can be properly conducted during the next few years without *both* a reconstruction of the present Railway Department . . . and likewise some new arrangement for the discharge of the Parliamentary duties in connection with railways which are to fall upon the Government'. To deal properly with railway questions might lead to neglect of other responsibilities of the Board of Trade. One solution would be to remove railways from the jurisdiction of the Board altogether. An 'official person' should be made responsible for railway matters in Parliament, or a Commission appointed for a term of years. Gladstone had a personal reason for wishing to hand over railway business; 'My own connection with railway interests, in part personally, but much more through my immediate relatives, is such as in point of public decency to offer a serious

---

[1] Cleveland-Stevens avoids this particular error.

[2] This view is expressed most clearly by R. Prouty, *Transformation of the Board of Trade*, Heinemann (1957), 11: 'The railway proprietors resented interference and Parliament was jealous of the Board's powers. The next year [it] was dismissed.'

impediment to my discharging the functions contemplated'[1]—
i.e. the preparation of reports on railway schemes.

Peel replied that he was willing to strengthen the Board of
Trade, but not to set up a new department for railways outside
it.[2] Gladstone now suggested 'that the Vice-President of the
Board of Trade . . . should, with the principal officers of the
Railway Department . . . constitute a Board for the discharge
of the extra-Parliamentary business'.[3] It was in this form that
the Board was set up.

There were interesting gaps in Gladstone's argument. He
suggested a new 'ministry' or 'board'[4] for railway affairs, but
apparently saw nothing to choose between them. Nor did Peel
take him up on this point. This suggestion having been turned
down, he proposed a hybrid form, neither 'ministry' nor 'board'
but he did not discuss simply transferring railway business to
Dalhousie, assisted by the Railway Department in its existing
shape. In particular, he did not attempt to show that the
proposed Board would be any more competent than the existing
Department to prepare the contemplated reports on railway
schemes. The Railway Board was not a result of the decision to
prepare such reports, but of Gladstone's desire to dissociate
himself as much as possible from them, and from railway business in general.

Gladstone had secured Dalhousie's agreement to his plan for
the Railway Board before submitting it to Peel,[5] and the responsibility for it rested on Dalhousie's shoulders from beginning
to end. Although the minute under which it was constituted
stated that 'the President or Vice-President of [the Board of
Trade] will act as the head of [the Railway Board]',[6] Gladstone
never in fact attended at all, whereas Dalhousie missed only
one meeting.[7] Dalhousie's promotion to the post of President,
on Gladstone's resignation early in 1845, made no difference in
his attendance at the Railway Board. He did not even share his

---

[1] Add. MS. 44734, f. 124–5 and f. 128–9.
[2] Add. MS. 44560, f. 208–9.
[3] Add. MS. 44734, f. 128–9.
[4] For these terms, see F. M. G. Willson, 'Ministries & Boards: some
aspects of Administrative Development since 1832', in *Public Administration,*
xxxiii (1955), 43–58.
[5] Add. MS. 44650, f. 213.   [6] Add. MS. 44734, f. 167.
[7] MT 13/3, 12 Apr. 1845.

work there with the new Vice-President, Clerk. The one meeting which Dalhousie missed was also the one meeting Clerk attended.

While Gladstone remained President, he gave Dalhousie a free hand. Indeed, any detailed supervision was out of the question during the first critical weeks of the Railway Board's existence, since Gladstone was in Scotland. Dalhousie reported to him there what he had done, and Gladstone replied:[1]

> Your accounts of the Railway Department give me great satisfaction—it has occured to me to ask whether you could conveniently send me the draft minutes of the Railway Department, by glancing over which, I might keep in some degree abreast of your proceedings. *It is in this way that I carry on ordinary relations with the Mint. But it need not be thought of if it is likely to be troublesome.*

When a difference arose between Pasley and Dalhousie, the former asked that it should be referred to Gladstone, who replied: 'I think [he] was wrong in desiring a reference to me . . . after you had told him that your mind was made up. . . . Even if my opinion were contrary to yours, . . . which it is not, I would without hesitation surrender it.'[2] On Gladstone's resignation, he left a memorandum on the state of business in the Board of Trade, from which that of the Railway Board was specifically excluded.[3] His reasons almost certainly were, firstly that he was not sufficiently abreast of the railway business to include it, and secondly that it was unnecessary to do so, since Dalhousie would remain in charge of it.

Before considering the working of the Railway Board, several lesser matters must first be dealt with. Even had there been no changed mode of working, and no increase in the Department's responsibilities, more staff would have been necessary.[4] In addition to clerks, two new senior officers were employed. These were Coddington, as Assistant Inspector, and Capt. Donatus O'Brien. The appointment of the latter is of particular interest. Gladstone had told Peel that 'a person should be attached to the Railway Department who has the special qualification

---

[1] S.R.O. Dalhousie Papers, 7/14: my italics. Gladstone was Master of the Mint as well as President of the Board of Trade.
[2] S.R.O. Dalhousie Papers, 7/14, 12 Oct. 1844.
[3] Ibid., 7/46.
[4] Add. MS. 44734, f. 156–9.

of practical experience in railway matters',[1] and the 1844 Act had removed the former ban on the employment of railway men as inspectors.[2] O'Brien did not become an inspector, however, but took the new post of General Secretary. He had been Secretary of the G.N.E. and a director of the Newcastle & Darlington Junction Railway. A not less important qualification, under the conditions of patronage, was that he had been private secretary to Sir James Graham.[3]

The appointment of the new clerks raised an important question of principle. There happened to be redundant clerks at Chelsea Hospital, and Trevelyan,[4] of the Treasury, proposed that the vacancies should be filled by transfer. This threat to the patronage of the Board of Trade aroused Gladstone's ire, but he authorised Dalhousie, if hard pressed, 'to make the best choice you can out of the list . . . always taking care, however, to save our honour as against the Treasury, for they certainly have made a violent assault upon it'. The dispute ended in a compromise. Dalhousie appealed to Goulburn, who represented Trevelyan's letter as no more than a friendly suggestion, and not in any way an attempt to tamper with the Board's rights. On learning this, Dalhousie accepted the suggestion, remarking that he was glad the Treasury claimed no right to make present or future appointments.[5]

Changes also took place affecting the existing staff. The distribution of seats on the new Board aroused what Dalhousie called a 'great controversy as to precedency'. Since the Board was to superintend the Department's work, should Porter still be styled 'Superintendent'? Dalhousie dubbed him 'Senior Member' instead. Porter was satisfied and Pasley's old resentment of him mollified. Laing became Law Secretary instead of Law Clerk, and one of the clerks, MacGregor, was given the new post of Registrar. He seems to have acted as a deputy for Laing and O'Brien and was soon signing letters for the Department.[6]

---

[1] Add. MS. 44734, f. 129. [2] 7 & 8 Vict., c. 85, s. 15.

[3] Hansard, lxxvii, 291 ff.

[4] Later Sir Charles Trevelyan, the protagonist of civil service reform.

[5] S.R.O. Dalhousie Papers, 7/14, 24 and 26 Aug. 1844, and 7/11, 29 and 30 Aug. 1844.

[6] S.R.O. Dalhousie Papers, 7/10, 12–14 Aug. 1844, and 7/16, 13 Aug. 1844, MT 11/4, 10 Jul. 1844.

The appointment of a second inspector raised the question of relations between him and Pasley. On the face of it, there should have been no problem. Pasley was Inspector-General and Coddington, Assistant Inspector; not unnaturally, Pasley treated Coddington, in fact as in name, as an assistant. Such a course was calculated to avoid the difficulty of conflicting opinions which had been envisaged in the early days both of factory and of railway inspection.[1] Dalhousie confessed, however, that he had far less faith in Pasley than in Coddington. He treated them as equals, asserting his right to order the Captain, over the head of the Major-General, to undertake a particular inspection. 'The Assistant Inspector was not appointed to become a mere copying clerk of the Inspector-General,' he wrote. 'It surely would be absurd that we should tie ourselves down to one opinion . . . when we have *two* opinions at command.' Dalhousie's favour made Coddington resent Pasley's attitude; as the latter wrote:

> An explanation with Coddington. His feelings are hurt, because I prevented him from acting independently of me, he being my Assistant. He complains that his opinions are set aside by me, I having objected to his sending in independent reports.

Observing that Pasley enjoyed direct access to Dalhousie, two permanent secretaries, and Porter notwithstanding, Coddington thought the principle should be carried one stage lower, namely, to himself; to quote Pasley once again:

> Captain Coddington and I have a difference of opinion. He wishes to be considered on a par with me, and to communicate direct with Lord Dalhousie, not only in my absence but at all times. I speak to his Lordship, who seems as usual to make difficulties.

Whatever difficulties he made on this occasion, Dalhousie settled the question by treating the two on the same footing. Such a course might have led to unnecessary trouble had they put in contradictory reports, in which case he would have been the lay judge between conflicting experts. But, although the matter was not satisfactorily settled in principle, no difficulty in practice seems to have arisen.[2]

[1] M. W. Thomas, op. cit., 245–7; and see above, p. 32.
[2] S.R.O. Dalhousie Papers, 7/14, 14 Dec. 1844. Add. MS. 41991, 16 Dec. 1844, and 16–17 Jan. 1845.

The extra staff created a problem of accommodation. Dalhousie turned down the offer of extra rooms in Great George Street, on the ground that they should all stay 'under one roof, if it can be accomplished by any amount of squeezing. I think it is possible to arrange this', he told Gladstone.

> General Pasley is willing to give Capt. Coddington a place in his room, retaining also the clerk there. Mr. Laing and Dr. D. MacGregor have each a small room. The second clerk is bestowed somewhere upstairs. By getting a new table, I can hold the Board and receive deputations in my room; and if we can only find a place for Capt. O'Brien we shall be able to make a shift for the winter.[1]

O'Brien was put in with Courtenay, Dalhousie's private secretary.[2]

The Board of Trade had shared with the Privy Council the building of which Dalhousie spoke since its completion by Soane in 1827. It stood on the corner of Whitehall and Downing Street. By the autumn of 1844, it had become too small, partly as a result of the expansion of the Railway Department. A plan dated September, 1844, shows a proposed new building to house the Department immediately behind the existing offices. The scheme was not carried out, but in 1845–6 the entire building was enlarged by Barry. Soane's design had not been one of his happiest; its principal feature was a façade of columns too heavy in appearance for the structure, which was partly of two, partly of three, storeys. Barry demolished the remains of a Tudor tennis-court, and extended the building on the north. He also added a storey so that his building was (and is) partly three storeys, and partly four, in height. He raised Soane's columns to embrace the first floor only; the effect was much enhanced by the greater height of the building. At first known as the New Treasury Offices, it housed from 1846 the Board of Trade, together with the Privy Council, the Treasury, and the Home Office.[3] The records of the Department do not show in

---

[1] S.R.O. Dalhousie Papers, 7/10, Nov. 1844.

[2] Ibid., 7/14, 8 Nov., 1844.

[3] G. S. Dugdale, *Whitehall Through the Centuries*, Phoenix House (1950). 136. Plates 54, 74, and 75 show Soane's Building; 69 and 76, Barry's. L.C.C. *Survey of London*, xiv; Plate 71 shows Soane's building; 74 reproduces the plan of Sept. 1844; ibid., xv: Plate 77 reproduces Barry's plan: 78 shows his building.

any detail what effect this upheaval had on its work. But it is worth bearing in mind that during the period of Dalhousie's responsibility for railway affairs—the period of the Railway Mania—the building in which he and his staff worked underwent a major transformation.

Problems of staff and accommodation were, however, the least of Dalhousie's many troubles. One incurable disability was that he was in the House of Lords. Such was the strength of the railway interest in the Commons that the success or failure of railway policy was determined there. He counted, of course, on Gladstone's co-operation; writing to him in November, 1844, Dalhousie remarked that 'on the introduction of the Bills into the Commons, constant communication will probably become necessary with you'.[1] Did Gladstone ever mean to give him that co-operation? After outlining to Peel the proposed Railway Board, Gladstone had added the ambiguous suggestion 'that when the next session arrives, such arrangements as circumstances recommend be made for the business in Parliament'.[2] Thoughts of resignation were in his mind as early as June, 1844, and in writing of them to Peel, he mentioned also the difficulty he felt in being responsible for railways because of his family's interest in them.[3] It is possible that that difficulty may have weighed with him as well as his avowed objection to the Maynooth grant, when he made up his mind to resign on the eve of the session of 1845.

That resignation left Dalhousie in a position of great difficulty. Had Gladstone remained, he would have handled the railway business as President of the Board of Trade with a seat in the Cabinet and more than three years' experience of railway politics. As it was, Dalhousie had to rely on the new Vice-President, Sir George Clerk, who had no previous experience of railway affairs. As for Dalhousie himself, he succeeded to the vacant post as President of the Board of Trade, but not to Gladstone's seat in the Cabinet. It is a remarkable thing that for ten critical months of the Railway Mania, Peel did not think it necessary to have a representative there from the Board of Trade.

---

[1] S.R.O. Dalhousie Papers, 7/10, Nov. 1844.
[2] Add. MS. 44734, f. 128–9.
[3] Add. MS. 40470, f. 224 ff.

I. The President's Room at the Board of Trade, 1845.

II. The Railway Mania: Correcting Plans at a Tavern as the Closing Date for Deposit Draws Near.

In this situation, Dalhousie stood in need of all the support he could get. Unfortunately, the Railway Board, far from providing support, weakened his position further. When he spoke on any other aspect of the Board of Trade's work, he spoke as a responsible minister of the Crown. When he spoke on railways, on the other hand, he could be represented as no more than the spokesman of 'a few clerks in a subordinate government office'.[1] Though such an allegation was untrue, it was eminently plausible. To the outside observer the Board seemed, in Labouchere's words, 'a cumbrous and inconvenient mode of proceeding [which] raised subordinate members of the Board of Trade to a parity with the President or Vice-President'.[2] It appeared, that is, to detract from Dalhousie's ministerial responsibility.

The doctrine of ministerial responsibility was different in form in the 1840's from what it has since become.[3] Responsibility was thought of far more as a matter of fact, much less as a useful fiction. The fact of responsibility, Palmerston had explained to the young Queen Victoria, meant that ministers were obliged to do their own work. They were 'liable any day and every day to defend themselves in Parliament; in order to do this they must be minutely acquainted with all the details of the business of their offices, and the only way of being constantly armed with such information is to conduct and direct those details themselves'.[4] Palmerston's practice, moreover, conformed with his preaching; even his Under-Secretaries 'were no more than mere clerks and did not interfere in matters of policy'.[5]

As a matter of fact, of the men who served as President or Vice-President of the Board of Trade during our period, Dalhousie came nearest to the Palmerstonian ideal in his grasp of

---

[1] *Railways & the Board of Trade*, London (3rd ed. 1845), 10 and 12.

[2] Hansard, lxxxvii, 541.

[3] For recent discussions of the subject, see S. E. Finer, 'Individual Responsibility of Ministers', in *Public Administration*, xxxiv (1956), and B. B. Schaffer 'The Idea of the Ministerial Department', in *Australian Journal of Politics & History*, iii (1957–8), 60–78.

[4] *Letters of Queen Victoria*, 1st ser, ed. A. C. Benson and Viscount Esher. London (1907), i, 136.

[5] C. K. Webster, 'Lord Palmerston at Work, 1830–1841', in *Politica*, i (1934–5), 137.

railway affairs. The Railway Board served as a screen, however, to conceal that fact from men's eyes. The form in which its reports were presented was largely responsible for this. When the summary verdict on a scheme was decided on for publication in the *London Gazette*, the formula employed was as follows: 'My Lords with the several members of the Railway Board having deliberated thereon, resolve that report be made to Parliament' etc.[1] This put the Board in its true position as an advisory body. But when the reports themselves appeared, they bore the signatures of the members,[2] from which it was reasonable to conclude that the Board was an executive body, and Dalhousie no more than *Primus inter Pares*. This decision as to signatures was part of Gladstone's unfortunate legacy.[3]

By the time Parliament received the first reports, rumours were going round of dissensions in the Board. Lord Howick asked whether Members could infer from the five signatures that the reports were unanimous. On the answer to that question, their weight would depend. Another Member referred to a speculation that Pasley had abstained from voting on a particular report. The government refused any information as to the views of individual members of the Board.[4] But an unfortunate impression remained. If votes were taken at the Board, why should members stop at abstaining? Might not a situation arise in which Dalhousie would find himself outvoted by his subordinate officers?[5]

The records provide no evidence that votes were taken at the Board, and show quite clearly that Dalhousie would not have considered himself bound, in any case, by the vote of a hostile majority. A difference between Dalhousie and Pasley led the former to lay 'down the law respecting Board proceedings in a most despotic manner', and to state the 'rule by which the Railway Board would necessarily be governed':

> if in preparing a report to be laid before Parliament, a difference should arise between the member of the Privy Council . . .

[1] E.g. MT 13/3, 4 Feb. 1845.
[2] For these reports, see P.P. 1845, xxxix.
[3] Add. MS. 44734, f. 168.
[4] For these exchanges, see Hansard, lxxvii, 530–41.
[5] For similar difficulties at the Board of Health, see R. A. Lewis, *Edwin Chadwick & the Public Health Movement, 1832–1854*, Longmans (1952), 145, 267, and 345.

presiding and the Inspector General, the Secretary, or any other member of the Board, the institution of this new form of the Railway Department would require . . . that the dissentient members should nevertheless sign the report, if called upon to do so by the presiding member. . . . If any concurrence of circumstances should make it the duty of the presiding member to insist on the signature of the dissentient member, then it would be for that gentleman to consider whether he should affix his name to the report, or whether he would prefer to resign his office.[1]

This letter seems to have been the start of the rumours referred to above. After the opening of the session, Dalhousie mentioned to the Board the embarrassment created for Peel by rumours of disagreements among its members. 'He would ask no questions', Pasley recorded.

> but hoped that no member . . . would give any hint. I observed that after being told by him that I must sign every paper . . . or resign . . . I had certainly stated to confidential friends that the rule and practice of the Board was that every member should sign; but that it could not be expected we should all be unanimous, five men never were on all questions.[2]

Pasley's concluding remark was, of course, a truism, and his diary provides ample evidence of its application to the Railway Board. But the effect of the Board procedure, coupled with his indiscretion, was that the reports carried less weight than anonymous reports from the Board of Trade, or reports signed by Dalhousie alone, would have done had no Railway Board ever been set up.

From the foregoing, it will be apparent that Dalhousie's difficulties would have been considerable even if conditions in the railway world had been normal. In fact they were highly abnormal—one of the reasons for reorganising the Department had been to enable it to weather the coming storm. The Railway Mania was beginning, and plans for 248 Bills were deposited with the Board in November, 1844. Of these, 121 passed in 1845, and some of the remainder, by a special dispensation, were carried forward to the following session. This was the greatest number of railway Bills hitherto promoted in any one

---

[1] Add. MS. 41991, 17 Oct., 13, 15, and 17 Nov. 1844. The Board's minutes (MT 13/1, 17 Oct. 1844) give no hint of the original cause of the dispute.
[2] Add. MS. 41991, 18 Feb. 1845.

session. Indeed, at the end of 1844, barely more than 3,000 miles of line had been authorised by all preceding Acts, with a capital not much more than £100 millions. The Acts of 1845 alone authorised the construction of a further 2,700 miles, with an additional capital of £59 millions.[1] No one foresaw that even these figures would be surpassed in 1846.

Dalhousie had to prepare reports for Parliament on all these schemes, to implement the Parliamentary train provisions of the 1844 Act,[2] to carry on all the Department's normal work and part of the other work of the Board of Trade—all under the difficulties discussed above. The pressure under which he (and his staff) were working should be borne in mind when the preparation of the reports is discussed. 'We have found it absolutely necessary', Dalhousie told a correspondent in December, 1844, 'to limit the reception of deputations to two days in the week, in order to give us a chance of getting through the immense amount of work before us.'[3] In April, 1845, some of the schemes had still not been looked at by either Pasley or Coddington.[4] Laing's health broke down, and he had to take several weeks' leave; he thought of resigning, but Dalhousie urged him not to do so.[5] Dalhousie's health was permanently impaired by overwork during this period. In November, 1844, he wrote to Gladstone, in reference to an item of business which he had neglected, 'I passed two such terrible months in September and October that I sometimes did not well know what I was about; and this must be my apology'.[6]

It was in this atmosphere that the Board prepared its reports.

---

[1] F. S. Williams, *Our Iron Roads*, London (1852), 57. Cleveland-Stevens, 24–5.

[2] See below, p. 93–99.

[3] S.R.O. Dalhousie Papers, 7/10, 7 Dec. 1844.

[4] Add. MS. 41991, 2 Apr. 1845.

[5] Ibid., 27 Mar. 1845. S.R.O. Dalhousie Papers, 7/10, 28 Mar. 1845.

[6] Ibid., 19 Nov. 1844. There is a double irony about this note; firstly, because the recipient had been in Scotland when he might have been in London to share the burden; and secondly, because of the contrast between the Department and the office whose business Dalhousie had neglected; his note continues: 'It is a mercy the thing occurred with the Board of Control: for considering that the President [Ripon] has not been seen or heard of for nearly four months, and that one of the Secretaries is in Egypt while the other is in Italy, they of all people have no right to complain of remissness of any kind'.

Companies readily supplied information about their plans for the coming session; the first to do so was the Manchester & Leeds, whose statement arrived in the middle of August, 1844.[1] Dalhousie described the next stage to Gladstone:

> Having determined the projects which are first to be considered, I have arranged that the engineer officers should enter upon the examination of the engineering character of the line, and the secretaries upon the analysis of its traffic case and its general features simultaneously: that they should respectively submit to me a short report of the result of their examinations, upon which I write a memorandum, to be circulated among the members of the Board previously to the project being placed on the minutes for consideration and decision.[2]

Dalhousie's personal memorandum book[3] contains many of these papers, and shows how great was his own contribution to the reports.

Meanwhile, the officers met deputations from the promoters, who were in general anxious to be heard. The first such conference was arranged as early as August, 1844.[4] When the written and oral statements of the promoters had been considered, it was the duty of the secretaries 'to apprise the head of the Board whenever points arise upon which it appears desirable that he should hear the parties, or upon which the Board should be summoned'.[5] It was necessary to consider also the views of many interested parties other than railway companies. Most were from influential bodies such as local authorities, canal companies, dock and harbour commissioners, and groups of industrialists. Some, on the other hand, presumably took up very little of the Board's time; for example, the memorial of the Court Leet and Court Baron of Ilfracombe, or a pamphlet entitled 'A Forester's Thoughts on the Gloucester & Dean Forest Railway Scheme'.[6]

At the end of the year, the first decisions were reached,[7] and announced in the *London Gazette*. At the same time, the Board

---

[1] MT 11/4, 15 Aug. 1844.
[2] S.R.O. Dalhousie Papers, 7/14, 14 Dec. 1844.
[3] Ibid., 7/28.
[4] MT 11/4, 17 Aug. 1844.
[5] MT 13/1, 14 Aug. 1844.
[6] MT 11/5, 27, 30, and 31 Dec. 1844. MT 11/6, 6, 7 and 17 Jan. 1845.
[7] MT 13/2, 24 Dec. 1844.

informed Parliamentary agents of the decisions regarding their lines. Where those decisions were favourable, the Board reserved the right 'of recommending any conditions and modifications which may appear necessary' in the Bill at a later stage.[1] When a company complained that the decisions should not have been published without reasoned statements in support, the Board replied that it was in the public interest to announce the decisions at the earliest possible moment, but that the grounds for them must be reserved for the reports to Parliament.[2] The final stage in the long process was the approval of those reports. The Board passed the first in February, 1845.[3]

Before considering the effect of the reports on Parliament, their effect on the companies will be discussed. The first point to be noticed is that they made the Board of Trade an important centre of the railway world. As we have seen in the previous chapter, prominent railwaymen had occasionally visited the Board before 1844. What had been the exception now became the rule. Having come once on deputations, railwaymen got into a habit of coming for other purposes. A significant anecdote relating to the lease by the Midland Railway of the Birmingham & Bristol in January, 1845, illustrates this. The G.W.R. had been negotiating for control of the line, but offered terms which were not acceptable. Ellis, Vice-Chairman of the Midland under George Hudson, now intervened on his own responsibility and took a lease of it. It was a dramatic coup. From our point of view, the point of the story is that although he was under no obligation to do so, 'Ellis at once went to the Board of Trade to inform them of the fact'. By an ironic chance, he met there Saunders, Secretary of the G.W.R., but did not tell him the news.[4]

A less distinguished visitor gave a vivid account of a visit to the Department at the period. William Rocke, an engineer, had tried in vain to get a hearing for his ideas about safety on railways.

> Some time ago I was in London. I then got to see Mr. Porter at the Board of Trade. I then explained to him the danger and he appeared quite satisfied and offered to interduce me to Genreal Pasley, and we whent into the Genreal's apartment, and Mr

[1] MT 11/5, 31 Dec. 1844.
[2] MT 11/6, 11 Jan. 1845.
[3] MT 13/3, 13 Feb. 1845.
[4] MacDermot, i, 214–5.

Porter interduced me to the Genreal. The General in a very sharp tone said, 'I cannot spare time'. I see Mr. Porter's face reden and he left the office, and I bid the Genreal good morning and left. The next day I received a note from Mr. Porter wishing me to call before I left London. I then stoped a day longer in London and called, but to my surprise when I called, Mr. Porter then said, 'I cannot spare time'. I do suppose he had seen the Genreal or he whole not of behaved so.[1]

In some cases, the Board's reports led promoters to change their plans without waiting for the verdict of Parliament. Dalhousie himself spoke of them 'demolishing a number of worthless schemes'[2] but without giving examples. We know, however, that the Gloucester & Dean Forest project was dropped for the time being as a result of the Board's report, and that the G.W.R. had at first intended to withdraw its support from the O.W.W. unless the Board reported in its favour.[3] In other cases, companies were brought together under the influence of the Board; the groups promoting rival lines to Harwich, for example, were 'both willing to co-operate in the formation of the line which may receive [a] favourable report'.[4] The most important instance, however, of the Board's direct influence on companies' plans was the agreement between the G.W. and the L.S.W.

Schemes proposed in the autumn of 1844 held the prospect not only of competition between these important companies, but also of increased complications between the broad and narrow gauges. The L.S.W. already had power to build a line from Bishopstoke to Salisbury; it was now supporting schemes to extend the narrow gauge from Salisbury to Falmouth. Such a route would have competed with the G.W. main line to the west. The latter agreed to back the Southampton & Dorchester Railway, which had been formed independently, provided it were built on the broad gauge. The Southampton & Dorchester had already failed to reach agreement with the L.S.W., which now faced the prospect that the westward expansion of the narrow gauge from its original terminus at Southampton might be blocked. In this situation, it was important for the companies to know what would be the Board's recommendations to

[1] S.R.O. Dalhousie Papers, 7/39. Spelling as in the original.
[2] Ibid., 7/20.
[3] MacDermot, i, 192 and 220.
[4] MT 13/3, 4 Mar. 1845.

Parliament. Dalhousie met their representatives in September, 1844, and at their request, told them the provisional decision on their schemes.[1]

At a second conference, the companies' plans remained unchanged.[2] But when the decision had been published, the L.S.W. fell in with the Board's wishes. Dalhousie told Gladstone that its chairman, 'Chaplin, has just been here to say that he thinks they will not go to Parliament and that the Great Western will transfer [the Southampton & Dorchester] to the [L.S.W.] quietly. This leaves nothing to be wished for.'[3] Chaplin's expectations were realised and on 16 January, 1845, the companies concluded an agreement, from which they bound themselves not to depart without the sanction of the Board of Trade. As a result, the L.S.W. withdrew its schemes.[4]

Difficulties soon arose as to the interpretation of the agreement. After first declining to intervene, the Board received deputations from the companies, and ruled on the points in dispute. As a result, the understanding between the companies was preserved, and the schemes authorised in 1845 were in accordance with the agreement.[5] From our point of view, the details of the dispute are not important; what is significant is the contrast between the attitude of the Board of Trade in the summer of 1845 and in the autumn of that year. In the interval, the principle of reporting to Parliament on railway schemes had been given up. The L.S.W. considered new schemes brought forward for the session of 1846 not in accordance with the agreement of January, 1845. The Board, however, declined to intervene further; and took no action when the company stated that since the Board declined to interfere, it would proceed to take that course which it thought proper.[6] That course involved the abandonment of the agreement with the G.W.R.

---

[1] MT 13/1, 16 Sep. 1844. Cf. J. Simmons, 'South Western v. Great Western: railway competition in Devon & Cornwall', *Journal of Transport History*, iv (1959–60), 13–36.

[2] Add. MS. 41991, 4 Oct. 1844.

[3] S.R.O. Dalhousie Papers, 7/10, 3 Jan. 1845.

[4] MacDermot, i, 279–80. MT 13/3, 7 Feb. 1845.

[5] MT 11/6, 22 Apr., 8 and 24 May, 4, 10, and 24 Jun. 1845. MT 13/3, 19 Apr., 8 and 24 May, 2, 10, and 26 Jun. 1845. Add. MS. 41991, 21 May, 1845.

[6] MT 11/7, 1 Nov. 1845. MT 13/4, 1 and 17 Nov. 1845.

The most important direct effect of the reports on the companies has still to be discussed. Before doing so, we must first consider the doctrine of 'equivalents'. By 1844, there was a widespread feeling that railway charges were too high, and that competition would not reduce them. To the forms of competition already recognised as ineffective,[1] competition between rival railways had now to be added. Lines might compete for a time, but then would unite. Witness the Birmingham & Derby and the Midland Counties which had vanished in the Midland amalgamation of 1844.[2] Yet the average Member of Parliament felt it would be unjust to reduce companies' charges by a general Act, since it was Parliament itself which had authorised them. But might it not be possible to persuade companies to reduce their own charges in return for corresponding advantages,[3] of which the most important was protection against competition?

This doctrine appears to have originated with Gladstone.[4] Certainly, he placed great stress on it; at one point, he came near to arguing that the Board's reports would be justified, even if Parliament ignored them, provided the companies made sufficient concessions to secure favourable verdicts on their own schemes.[5] This might have been true for one session; but in the long run, the companies would not have valued the reports unless Parliament normally acted on them. Seen as 'equivalents', the Board's reports were complementary to the policy of revision embodied in Gladstone's 1844 Act,[6] and were the answer to the criticism that that Act would do nothing to reduce fares immediately.[7] Moreover, had the policy of 'equivalents' formed the basis of relations between the government and the companies for a period of years, much experience of revision of charges would have accumulated. Hence, when the relevant sections of the 1844 Act came into effect, one of the main difficulties in implementing them—namely, the government's lack of knowledge of the subject—would not have existed.

The doctrine of 'equivalents' was potentially an instrument of great power, and if it has correctly been attributed here

[1] See above, p. 8.   [2] Cleveland-Stevens, 42–51.
[3] P.P. 1844, xi, 30 and 597–8.   [4] Add. MS. 44734, f. 43.
[5] S.R.O. Dalhousie Papers, 7/14, 3 Jan. 1844.
[6] See above, p. 56.   [7] Hansard, lxxvi, 529.

to Gladstone, was his most original contribution to railway policy. Yet its importance has not hitherto been recognised because the manner in which the Department implemented it concealed it from public view. Dalhousie described the practice of the Department to Gladstone in a letter which merits quotation at length:

> I quite agree with you . . . that we ought not to drive hard bargains with the companies. We have not hitherto attempted to do so and we do not intend doing so. In truth it is not necessary; for [they] are in every instance showing great fairness and readiness in offering reasonable and sufficient concessions to the public. . . . For the most part the companies have themselves made the first approach . . . [where they have not] I have requested Mr. Laing to see the . . . company in question . . . and [he] begs to know from them what terms they propose to give in the event of theirs being preferred.[1]

But what if a company failed to keep its promise? Since it would normally embody its offer in a clause for insertion in a Bill before Parliament, the Department would have to watch the progress of Bills with great care. We have seen that, in recommending schemes, it reserved the right to suggest amendments at a later stage,[2] and Dalhousie agreed with Gladstone that 'with regard to the London & Birmingham guarantees, we must of course watch against any clause in their Bill which would . . . [make] their promised revision a nullity'.[3] The Railway Board did in fact spend much time going through Bills while they were before each House of Parliament.[4]

Dalhousie also foresaw the possibility that a company might seek to evade provisions inserted in its own Acts. To guard against this danger, the Department must reserve its freedom of action for the future. He told Gladstone:

> With regard to the question . . . 'whether we mean to say anything about these concessions in our report', and which you observe upon as calculated to tie up the hands of government and indirectly the hands also of Parliament, I would reply that we have not proposed to make any mention . . . of the conditions on which we give the preference to the old companies in any given case. . . .

[1] S.R.O. Dalhousie Papers, 7/10, 6 Jan. 1845.
[2] See above, p. 74.
[3] S.R.O. Dalhousie Papers, 7/10, 7 Feb. 1845.
[4] E.g. MT 13/3, 7 Feb. and 26 Jun. 1845.

I do not think it would be wise for us to give . . . a sanction to any line on *condition* of their giving certain terms. The terms given by old companies ought to come as voluntary offers previously made by them, and not as conditions compulsorily imposed by us.[1]

The government would not be pledged, and if any company alleged the contrary, its 'own letter is here to refute them, and there is no other document of any kind in existence on which such an allegation could be founded'.[2] Moreover, once the session was past, companies would normally be committed by the clauses inserted in their Acts. If, therefore, new competitive schemes came forward, the companies, 'must rest—and do securely rest—on the faith of government to defend them, *so long as circumstances remain the same*'.[3] If meanwhile circumstances had changed, the government could, through the Department's reports, encourage the new schemes.[4]

A consequence of Dalhousie's determination to preserve the government's freedom of action in future negotiations was that very little was known of the companies' concessions at the time. There are one or two references to such offers in print,[5] but in general they have left no trace except in the records of the Department. Dalhousie himself gave certain examples, and from all sources, we know of eight important companies which offered terms for protection against competition. They were:

Eastern Counties	L.S.W.
G.J.R.	Manchester & Leeds
London & Birmingham	Midland
London & Brighton	S.E.R.[6]

Of a different kind was the offer made by the Liverpool & Manchester to secure approval for its proposed amalgamation with the G.J.R.[7] Several new companies also made similar offers,[8] of which the most important was the Cambridge and Lincoln.[9]

---

[1] S.R.O. Dalhousie Papers, 7/10, 6 Jan. 1845.
[2] Ibid.   [3] Ibid.   [4] Ibid.
[5] E.g. Hansard, lxxvii, 363. P.P. 1845, xxxix, 251.
[6] S.R.O. Dalhousie Papers, 7/10, 6 Jan. 1845. MT 11/6, 25 Mar. 1845, MT 13/3, 6, 13, 21 and 30 Jan., 7 and 20 Feb. 1845.
[7] MT 11/6, 31 Jul. 1845. MT 13/3, 4 Mar. and 2 Aug. 1845.
[8] MT 13/3, 28 Jan., 7 and 20 Feb. 1845.
[9] MT 13/3, 20 Feb. 1845.

Very few details of the companies' offers have survived. But for the purpose of this study, the important point is that sufficient companies of importance responded to show that the policy of 'equivalents' was workable. Had they not done so, their lack of response might have been a reason for abandoning the reports on railway schemes. As it was, there was every reason to suppose that the policy would succeed—though a longer period than one year might be necessary—provided Parliament proved receptive to the Department's recommendations.

It has been held that their effect was negligible.[1] There are grounds for thinking that this view underrates their importance; but before considering them, certain allegations which were made at the time call for notice. If true, they would go far to account for any lack of respect shown by Members for the reports.

Since the purpose of the reports was normally to recommend certain schemes at the expense of others, it was to be expected that the disappointed parties would cry out against them. Certainly Dalhousie foresaw such an outcry.[2] Charges against the Railway Board should, therefore, be examined with care. For example, the most important scheme to be condemned was that which eventually came into being as the G.N.R.; it is significant that the historian of that company was among those who have done most to perpetuate the allegations against the Board.[3] Its reports were said to be inaccurate. There was probably some truth in this, as a result of the small staff and inadequate time available. At one period, Coddington was examining plans at the rate of 100 miles a day,[4] and anyone who has studied the deposited plans of railways will realise the risk of inaccuracy he was running. But in the case of the schemes for a line from London to York, there is a special factor to take into account. It happened that Pasley's daughter died in December, 1844, and as a result, he spent a few days at home. It was there, and not at the office, that he examined the

[1] E.g. Pratt, op. cit., 276. Cleveland-Stevens, 141.
[2] S.R.O. Dalhousie Papers, 7/10, 28 Dec. 1844.
[3] G. H. Grinling, *History of the G.N.R., 1845–1902*, London (new issue, 1903), 30 ff. For the Board's report, see P.P. 1845, xxxix, 147 ff.
[4] S.R.O. Dalhousie Papers, 7/14, 14 Dec. 1844.

London-York plans.[1] Under such circumstances, it seems likely that there would be a special risk of inaccuracy, because of his state of mind, and perhaps because of lack of a plan table, works of reference, and similar facilities.

Another charge was that the Board had not had the time to prepare reliable reports, since the plans had not been deposited until 30 November, 1844.[2] It has been shown above that the Board did not wait for the deposit of the plans, but began work on the schemes more than three months earlier.[3] A further criticism was that the proceedings of the Railway Board were veiled in secrecy.[4] Dalhousie answered this by pointing out that the Board had not the power to act as a public tribunal, summoning witnesses and taking evidence on oath.[5] More might have been said. Both the Department before, and the Commissioners of Railways afterwards, in cases involving more than one company, submitted copies of statements from each to the other (or others) and invited comments, before reaching their own decision.[6] Had the Railway Board adopted such a procedure, there would have been little ground for the charge of secrecy. But there was not the time, and there was not the staff; documents had been pouring in at the rate of 9,000 a year,[7] and Parliament could not wait. In any case, the Board was not a court, nor were its decisions judicial in character; it was an agency of government, and its reports served to promote the policy of 'equivalents'.

The last allegations to be noticed here reveal incidentally the high cash value placed on the reports in some quarters. It was said that the Board's decisions in certain cases were known in some quarters before they had appeared in the *London Gazette*, and that those in the know had used this information to their own advantage on the Stock Exchange.[8] Dalhousie denied that there had been any leakage, and described the almost

---

[1] Add. MS. 41991, 26 and 31 Dec. 1844, 1 Jan. 1845.

[2] *Railways & the Board of Trade* (3rd ed. 1845), 12 and 20. The author also makes the charge of inaccuracy, 22.

[3] See above, p. 73.

[4] *Railways & the Board of Trade* (3rd ed. 1845), 21.

[5] Hansard, lxxvii, 355.

[6] See above, p. 38 and below, pp. 122–3.

[7] Hansard, lxxvii, 359.

[8] *Railways & the Board of Trade* (3rd ed. 1845), 24–6.

melodramatically elaborate procedure adopted to prevent it.[1] Closely related was the suggestion that the fact of O'Brien's brother being general manager to the S.E.R. had influenced the Board's report on schemes in which that company was interested. Dalhousie denied any such influence, pointing out that the company had offered valuable advantages to the public.[2] Pasley saw Laing's influence uppermost in the report,[3] not O'Brien's. Even ungrounded allegations of this kind gained credence because they conformed with the general belief that the Board's reports were worth much to promoters of schemes. One estimate put the value of a favourable report at £5,000, and it was said that a recommendation from the Board would send the shares of one company up by £20.[4] Those who thought in this way must also have expected that the reports would have great authority with Parliament.

What authority did they have in fact? Where committees of the House of Commons made reports at variance with those of the Board, they had to state their reasons for doing so. In only twenty-three cases did this happen,[5] and in each instance reasoned arguments were given. The tone of these statements suggests that the committees had taken the reports seriously and had not treated them 'as waste paper'.[6] In only two examples was there any disagreement as to facts. In some cases, circumstances had changed since the Board's report, and so a different decision was justified. For example, the Leeds, Dewsbury & Manchester had come to an agreement with the rival company preferred by the Board, and its Bill had been passed in consequence. In other cases, the disagreement was very slight; for instance, the Board had suggested that clauses be inserted in two Bills to secure the completion of the lines; the committees had not thought such clauses necessary. Although the figures do not exactly tally, the statements from the committees confirm in a general way Dalhousie's own assessment of the influence of the reports. The Board had reported on 245

---

[1] Hansard, lxxvii, 365–6.   [2] Hansard, lxxvii, 360–3.
[3] Add. MS. 41991, 12 Feb. 1845.
[4] *Railways & the Board of Trade*, (3rd ed. 1845), 23. Hansard, lxxvii, 143.
[5] P.P. 1845, xxxix, 19 ff.
[6] T. H. Farrer, Permanent Secretary to the Board of Trade, said in 1881 that the 1844 reports had been treated 'as waste paper'; cf. Pratt, op. cit., 276.

schemes, and Parliament had reversed its verdict in only six cases; in four or five more, schemes had been authorised at once, where the Board had recommended postponement.[1]

All this is not to say that the Board's reports were the cause of Parliament's decisions. The report on a particular scheme was only one of many factors, and it would be difficult enough to assess its relative importance even had each case been referred to a single man. Since each case was in fact referred to a committee, it is impossible now (and was probably impossible then) to estimate how far the report influenced its decision. What can be said is that there was a significant correlation between the recommendations of the Board and the decisions of Parliament. The twenty-three cases of disagreement may be compared either with the 245 schemes reported on or with the 121 Acts passed. In either case, the proportion of disagreements was small. But mathematical finality is impossible because of the Bills which were held over for the following session. The most important case in which Parliament disagreed with the Board—that relating to the scheme finally authorised by the G.N.R. Act, 1846—was one of them. For that very reason, it is not a good basis for generalising about the effect of the reports.[2] By the time the hearings were resumed, the reports had been discontinued, and one would not expect their influence on the proceedings in 1846 to have been anything other than negligible.

To sum up, the result of the experiment at the middle of June, 1845, was not unsatisfactory. The reports themselves were not perfect; but the Department would have been able greatly to improve them in subsequent years in the light of experience, especially if given more time and more staff to prepare them. Parliament had coincided (to put it no higher) with the Board in reaching its decisions sufficiently often to confirm the companies in their first belief that a favourable report was worth having, and worth giving some 'equivalent' for. It looked as though the foundation had been laid for a new relation of great importance between the government and the railways. Yet it was at this very moment that the reports were given up.

The reason can be stated very simply—Peel's lack of support for Dalhousie. At an early stage, it had become apparent that

[1] S.R.O. Dalhousie Papers, 7/20.   [2] Cleveland-Stevens, 140–1.

an important factor in the success of the reports was how far the government would intervene in private business. Never before had a department exercised a regular supervision over a whole class of private Bills.[1] When a correspondent raised this question in November, 1844, Dalhousie wrote to ask Gladstone 'whether it is the intention of government to support in Parliament every railway scheme in whose favour the government board may report'. On the one hand, there were matters, such as the objections of property owners, for which Parliament, not the Railway Board, was the proper tribunal.

> On the other . . ., I recollect that in the minutes of yourself, Sir Robert Peel and others the probability of assistance being necessary for you in the House of Commons . . . was much dwelt upon. From this, I infer that a greater charge than formerly is intended to be taken of railway Bills by the government in that House. I should be glad, therefore, to learn your views on that point; *as I never talked with you about it.*[2]

Gladstone was evasive, and Dalhousie could tell his correspondent no more than that 'we cannot now attempt to lay down any invariable rule, but must reserve a discretion to act according to circumstances in each case'.[3] In spite of this, Dalhousie clearly assumed in January, 1845, that, in preparing his reports, he spoke for the government as a whole.[4]

When the question was raised in the Commons at the beginning of the session, Gladstone was no longer responsible for answering it, for he had just resigned. Peel replied that he must consult Dalhousie, and after doing so, stated that the latter 'was entirely of the opinion with himself that it never was the intention of the government to fetter the House by any opinions or reports presented by [the Board of Trade; there was not] . . . the most distant intention of compromising the neutrality of the government upon such questions'.[5] When Dalhousie himself later spoke in similar vein,[6] his words must be taken as a statement of government policy rather than of his personal belief,

[1] O. C. Williams, op. cit., i, 67.
[2] S.R.O. Dalhousie Papers, 7/10, 19 Nov. 1844. My italics.
[3] Ibid., 21 Nov. 1844.
[4] Ibid., 6 Jan. 1845, quoted at length above, pp. 78-9.
[5] Hansard, lxxvii, 174-5.
[6] Ibid., 351 ff.

III. The Railway Office at the Board of Trade, 1844-1845.

IV. The Railway Board Receives a Deputation, 1845.

which as we have seen had been very different only a few weeks earlier.

Peel's lukewarm attitude must have diminished the authority of the reports in Members' eyes. But no decisive harm was done until the report stage of the O.W.W. Bill. The Board had favoured a rival line on the narrow as opposed to the broad gauge, and sponsored by the London & Birmingham instead of the G.W.R., on the ground that the break of gauge should occur at Oxford rather than farther north.[1] The principle underlying this decision was similar to that embodied in the agreement between the G.W. and L.S.W. discussed above,[2]—namely, that the gauges should be confined to distinct districts. A further consideration was the offer of revised charges by the London & Birmingham.[3] The Commons' committee, however, set aside this report, though not without attempting to meet the Board's criticism. To meet the first objection, they provided for the mixed gauge, and to meet the second, required similar terms from the G.W.R. and inserted clauses to that effect in the Bill.[4]

It was not so much the decision of the committee which damaged the Board's prestige, as the manner of its reception in the House, for the majority in its favour there included several members of the government, including Peel himself. Dalhousie was naturally incensed. He wrote to Peel at once to voice his

mortification . . . in learning the course pursued . . . by yourself and other members of the government. When I last year received in addition to my other duties the charge of superintending the new Railway Department, I foresaw that the task would be one of great difficulty, great anxiety, and that it would bring upon those engaged in it much personal ill will and annoyance. [But he had counted on] full encouragement and countenance from members of the government. . . . [Instead] I have the mortification of finding that you have departed, as you stated, from the ordinary practice which leads the ministers of the Crown to stand neutral and to abstain from interfering in private business at all; that, without any necessity whatever for your being present in the House, without any duty whatever requiring you to give an opinion; you had gone out of your way to oppose your own Board —had virtually recommended the House to reject its report; and had enforced that recommendation by a vote.[5]

[1] P.P. 1845, xxxix, 250.   [2] See above, pp. 75-6.
[3] P.P. 1845, xxxix, 251.   [4] Ibid., 27-8.
[5] S.R.O. Dalhousie Papers, 7/15, 21 Jun. 1845.

Four more members of the Cabinet, and seven other ministers, had done likewise; 'whatever might have been your intentions, the practical effect of the step you have taken is to overturn the authority . . . of the Railway Department and to throw discredit on the officer who conducts it'.[1]

Peel defended himself by posing the question, if the Select Committee and the Railway Department reached different conclusions, should the latter prevail? 'If it ought, let us relinquish committees, compulsory attendance and the whole of the machinery we have erected, and at once admit that the Report of the Board of Trade is to be decisive in every case without exception.' Parliament must prevail, especially since reforms in private Bill procedure had been introduced at the same time, and with the same aim, as the Board's Reports. The choice had been less simple than Dalhousie had supposed.

> I saw before me the results of active canvass by powerful companies. . . . I felt it to be my duty, a duty which I discharged in opposition to the wishes and interests of my constituents and my own, to prevent so far as my vote could prevent it, the unanimous decision of a Committee which had most zealously discharged its duty, being overruled by members, few of whom had read a word of the evidence, many of whom were brought together by dint of private canvass, and were prepared to vote on other considerations than those of the merits of the questions.

He regretted the pain he had given, but would do the same again.[2]

Dalhousie now suggested that the Board should give up reporting on Bills, unless asked to do so, and Peel agreed.[3] Of the members of the Railway Board, Laing resigned from the public service; Porter and Pasley reverted to their previous positions—the latter noting his pleasure in doing so;[4] and O'Brien remained, as the chief non-technical officer of the Department. The Railway Board was at an end.[5] It had indeed been dismissed,[6] but at Dalhousie's own desire.

---

[1] S.R.O. Dalhousie Papers, 7/15, 21 Jun. 1845.
[2] Ibid., Peel to Dalhousie, 22 Jun. 1845.
[3] Ibid., 22 and 23 Jun. 1845.
[4] Add. MS. 41991, 23 Jul. 1845.
[5] It met for the last time on 23 Jul. 1845; MT 13/3.
[6] See above, p. 62.

Although Peel had agreed with equanimity to the abandonment of the Department's reports, there is reason to suppose that the further progress of the Railway Mania led to a change in his views. Within four months he was writing to Clerk that 'the whole subject of railway legislation, the measures to be adopted immediately on the meeting of Parliament . . . deserves the fullest consideration'. Clerk replied:

> it may perhaps be necessary to appoint a preliminary committee invested with nearly the same functions as those of the Railway Department last year—to *select* and recommend among competing lines, that which will be most advantageous for the public. This committee would have equal facilities with the Board of Trade to form a correct judgment, and the House of Commons would be more disposed to defer to their recommendations.

In his next letter, Peel spoke of discussion in the press as to:

> the course to be taken in Parliament with regard to railway Bills. . . . It appears to me absolutely necessary that timely consideration should be given to it and that the government should be enabled to announce their views . . . at the opening of Parliament . . . the Board of Trade is the department which must take the matter in hand.[1]

This exchange shows that Peel and Clerk recognised the existence of a problem but not that they had any idea what the solution to it might be. But when Dalhousie reported on 1 December, 1845, that promoters had deposited plans for 788 railway schemes—more than three times the record number deposited a year before[2]—Peel at last took action. He set up a committee of ministers[3]

> to consider . . . railway legislation in the next session. We shall be discredited if we are not prepared . . . at the very opening of the session to give our advice to Parliament—to lay down at once some definite course. It will not do to appoint a Select Committee and leave them to consider a definite course.

The government might appoint 'a commission of impartial and intelligent men, if such can be found', to select those

---

[1] Add. MSS. 40578, f. 218–9, and 221; 40579, f. 147.
[2] S.R.O. Dalhousie Papers, 7/15, 1 Dec. 1845.
[3] Add. MS. 40580, f. 212–5, on which the remainder of this paragraph is based.

schemes 'which appear most conducive to the public interests'. Their report 'might be laid before a Select Committee—and then there might be *Parliamentary authority* (if the Committee agreed with the Commission) for the guidance of the House of Commons'.

The committee got off to a bad start. It was the beginning of the Corn Law crisis, and Peel tendered his resignation only three days after setting up the committee. However, it did meet, and reported to Peel in January, 1846.[1] Its report was in Dalhousie's keeping in July, 1846,[2] but has since disappeared. It seems clear, however, that it had little influence on the course of events. In the light of the Department's experience, Peel's scheme was impracticable simply because there was not time enough to sift all the schemes and recommend the best to Parliament in the way he had envisaged. When Parliament met, Peel stated that the government 'had . . . felt it their duty . . . rather to appeal to the authority of a committee of the House of Commons than to submit any plan of our own for solving the railway difficulty which must ensue during the session'[3]— the very course he had ruled out only a few weeks before.

The immediate consequence of Peel's lack of support for Dalhousie was to remove a curb to speculation that might have prevented the Railway Mania from growing to such serious proportions; and the long-term one, the abandonment of the attempt to regulate companies' charges and the extension of the railway network. The memory of Dalhousie's work lived on. In 1846, the Duke of Richmond attributed the failure of the reports to Peel's 'throwing [Dalhousie] entirely overboard'. In 1852, Lord Harrowby asserted that 'it would have been much better if Parliament had carried out properly the scheme of Lord Dalhousie . . . to assign somewhat of a monopoly to each railway company over their respective districts, under proper regulations for the protection of the public'. In evidence before Cardwell's committee of 1853, Saunders testified to the influence of the reports on companies, while Laing, who had meanwhile become chairman of the L.B.S.C. and entered Parliament, revived the doctrine of 'equivalents'. A year later, a Member connected with the railway interest told the House

---

[1] S.R.O. Dalhousie Papers, 7/39, 25 Jul. 1846.
[2] Ibid. [3] Hansard, lxxxiii, 188.

that Dalhousie had in 1845 'proposed a scheme by which the country was partitioned out among the great companies, and that the House, acting under the advice of the late Sir Robert Peel, deliberately rejected that plan'. In 1866, the Earl of Carnarvon related how 'in 1843 or 1844, when these railway schemes first came before Parliament in considerable numbers, Lord Dalhousie . . . drew up, as I have always heard, a scheme in which he laid down certain broad lines of railway communication through the country. It is much to be regretted that scheme was not carried out.' Finally, one of Dalhousie's biographers summed up his policy in these words:

> Had his advice been followed, some two-thirds of the enormous outlay since squandered on our railway system would have been saved, and the disastrous panic which followed the Railway Mania of 1845–6 would in all likelihood have been averted. But Peel lacked the courage, if not the will, to press upon Parliament a measure for which the country at large seemed far from ripe.[1]

It would be unprofitable to divide the truth from the error in these statements, several of which belong to the world of legend rather than of historical judgment. But legends grow up around great men and noble deeds. The legend of Dalhousie's railway policy is evidence of its importance and of the grave consequences of its overthrow. However, his main contribution to railway development was to be made in India, not Britain.

It has been shown that the Railway Board was merely an advisory body. Dalhousie remained personally responsible for all decisions. After it had come to an end, he kept the railway business in his own hands, and drew up new rules for the Department which placed the officers in a distinctly subordinate rôle.[2] In practice his code proved too rigorous. For example, it was laid down that 'no official reply can be given verbally by any of the officers . . . all business . . . must be submitted in writing to the Lords of the Committee [i.e. Dalhousie or Clerk] by whom alone an official reply can be given, which reply will

---

[1] Hansard, lxxxv, 1059; cxxiii, 237; cxxxii, 1234; clxxxi, 1279. P.P. 1852–3, xxxviii, 26 ff. and 189. L. J. Trotter, *Life of the Marquis of Dalhousie*, London (1889), 20. For other similar expressions of opinion, see Hansard, lxxxix, 1205; cxxxii, 603–4; and cxliv, 1270.
[2] MT 13/3, 5 Aug. 1845.

be transmitted in writing'.[1] In spite of this, at least one letter was 'acknowledged verbally' by MacGregor.[2] Another rule stated that 'if any application be made, or any letter be addressed to any officer of the Department . . . no reply should be made, nor any step taken . . . until the letter has been submitted to the Lords of the Committee and . . . instructions regarding it have been received'.[3] This implied that such letters should be submitted to Dalhousie as soon as possible. Nevertheless, Coddington kept some papers more than two months before even registering them.[4]

Some important implications of the power to inspect new lines began to reveal themselves during this period. When Pasley inspected a portion of the line between Sheffield and Manchester, he reported that though the line was not complete, the company might open it 'on their own responsibility'. Dalhousie objected to this since

> the willingness of the railway company . . . to assume the responsibility . . . does not remove [it] from us. . . . In all your future proceedings, therefore, I would request you not to authorise the opening of any line whatever, which is not certified to be in a complete state, fit for the use of the public, either by yourself or the Assistant Inspector.[5]

Although he went on to say that 'nothing can be more distinct and explicit than the requirements of the Act of Parliament', it is clear that neither he nor Pasley did in fact understand it at the time. The Board could postpone the opening of a line, on the inspector's recommendation; but it had no power to authorise the opening, nor was any such authorisation required. Unless the inspector recommended postponement, the company could go ahead and open the line as soon as the period of notice expired.[6] Pasley only discovered this after more than four years as Inspector-General.[7] Therefore, although he had behaved tactlessly in seeming to usurp Dalhousie's prerogative, he had acted in accordance with the law. Since he had not recommended such a step, Dalhousie could not have postponed the opening in any case.

[1] MT 13/3, 5 Aug. 1845.   [2] MT 13/4, 17 Dec. 1845.
[3] MT 13/3, 5 Aug. 1845.   [4] MT 13/4, 13 Oct. 1845.
[5] S.R.O. Dalhousie Papers, 7/10, 15 Aug. 1844.
[6] 5 & 6 Vict., c. 55, ss. 4 and 6.   [7] Add. MS. 41991, 28 Apr. 1846.

Where an opening was postponed, the company had no right of appeal to the courts—an example of delegated power which the nineteenth century accepted much more calmly than the twentieth century. But there was a mode of appeal in an informal sense. Parties of sufficient influence and standing could appeal to the President to repudiate his inspector's report and revoke the order. This was what happened in the case of the Whitehaven Junction. Dalhousie told Pasley that

> Lord Lonsdale and Mr. George Stephenson were insolent to him, and said, 'What could R.E.'s possibly know about railways?' And therefore though he would not otherwise object to compromising or meeting them half-way, he does not like being bullied into concession.[1]

Nevertheless, he ordered a further inspection, and approved the opening.[2]

A further development was that the notion of a new line proved more comprehensive than at first realised. One of the grounds for postponing an opening was 'incompleteness of the . . . permanent way'. The Board would therefore have been justified in postponing the opening of a line where two tracks had been authorised but only one was complete. What of the case, however, where one track was already open, and the company wished to open a second? Would it be a new line, within the meaning of the Act? The problem seems to have arisen for the first time on the Maidstone branch of the S.E.R. The Department was in doubt and took counsel's opinion, which was favourable, before acting.[3] But, given the power, was it expedient to use it? Pasley thought not: he wrote

> Lord Dalhousie has prevented the second line of rails of the Maidstone branch of the S.E. from being used. Thus the Department for public safety opposes it by causing one line to be used instead of two. If a collision occurs, blame will attach to him.[4]

[1] Add. MS. 41991, 24 Dec. 1845.
[2] Ibid., 30 Dec. 1845. In spite of what has just been said, it would be pedantic to deny that the Board did, in a non-legal sense, approve, or authorise, openings unless it postponed them; these words will, therefore, be used where appropriate in the remainder of this study.
[3] MT 11/8, 24 Apr. 1846. MT 6/3, 419/1846.
[4] Add. MS. 41992, 28 Apr. 1846.

This case was a precedent, and from then on, the Department regularly inspected additional tracks of existing lines as if they were new lines.[1]

The most striking thing to notice in the Department's attitude to accidents is the number of serious cases passed over without enquiry. For example, when a rear collision in fog occurred on the Manchester & Birmingham, the company made no mention of having used detonator signals, as the Department had recommended. In spite of that, the Department's minute reads: 'There does not appear to be any necessity for further investigation'.[2] Similarly, when half a dozen people were injured in a collision at Croydon, the Department considered the 'accident very slight' and did not order an enquiry.[3]

When an enquiry was ordered, the inspector reported to the President of the Board, and the reports were normally presented to Parliament once a year. At a later date, the Department held that publicity for the reports was valuable, since it would rouse public opinion, and so make companies more amenable to inspectors' recommendations.[4] But at this period, publicity was shunned, and the Department refused to supply copies of reports to the press.[5] In the case of a fatal accident, however, a difficulty might arise if the inspector was asked to give evidence at the inquest. For example, Pasley attributed an accident on the Midland Railway in November, 1844, to the 'extreme zeal mixed with the extreme stupidity' of Lightfoot, the station-master at Nottingham.[6] He could not attend the inquest, so sent the coroner a summary of his findings. Dalhousie was incensed, as was Gladstone, to whom he reported the incident. Both considered Pasley guilty of a breach of confidence, and Gladstone decided that one of them must reprimand Pasley; it was 'a very difficult and painful question on account of the fact that we are both so much [his] juniors'.[7] Dalhousie agreed to do so, but put it off since he did not wish to 'darken the old man's Christmas',[8]—the prospects for which were already dark, since he had just lost his daughter.

[1] E.g. MT 13/5, 9 Jul. 1846.   [2] MT 13/4, 17 Nov. 1845.
[3] MT 13/5, 18 Apr. 1846.   [4] See below, p. 145.
[5] MT 13/4, 13 Oct. 1845.   [6] Add. MS. 41991, 23 Nov. 1844.
[7] S.R.O. Dalhousie Papers, 7/14, 18 Dec. 1844.
[8] Ibid., 7/10, 26 Dec. 1844.

Another similar case arose just over a year later. As a result of an accident at Thetford, the coroner asked the Department if Pasley might attend the inquest, and he was ordered to do so. Pasley's evidence contradicted that of another witness, G. P. Bidder, the railway engineer, and criticised the design of the engine involved in the accident, which was by Robert Stephenson. These views were reported inaccurately in *The Times*, and attacked in the railway press. Dalhousie advised Pasley to ignore what the papers were saying, but the latter wrote to *The Times*, which inserted a corrected version of his evidence. Dalhousie reprimanded him in writing, and ordered him not to publish letters relating to his official duties without permission.[1]

Pasley had behaved indiscreetly, but his position was difficult. In the Nottingham case, he would not have been blamed had he attended the inquest, and there attributed the accident to Lightfoot.[2] Was it any more a breach of confidence to do so by letter? In the Thetford case, Dalhousie did not criticise Pasley for expressing controversial views. Once they were in print, was it any more a breach of confidence to have them corrected? There was an important question of principle involved, which reprimands did nothing to settle. If the findings of accident enquiries were confidential, it was unreasonable to ask inspectors to attend inquests. If, on the other hand, inspectors must attend inquests, some publicity was inevitable, and the practice of refusing copies of reports to the press, merely arbitrary.[3]

In addition to its existing duties, the Department had important new powers to exercise, namely those relating to Parliamentary trains under the 1844 Act. The enforcement of these provisions required so much work that it seems likely they would largely have remained a dead letter but for the Board's powers. Its energetic action is all the more remarkable since

[1] MT 11/8, 6 Jan. 1846. MT 13/5, 8 Jan. 1846. S.R.O. Dalhousie Papers, 7/16, 26 Jan., 7 and 9 Feb. 1846. Add. MS. 41992, 12 Jan.–1 Feb. 1846 *passim*.

[2] For an example of an inspector attributing an accident to an individual, where the coroner's jury had blamed the company, see above, p. 43.

[3] For similar disputes as to what the factory inspectors should include in their printed reports to Parliament, and what they should report to the Home Office by letter, see M. W. Thomas, op. cit., 254–8 and 261–3.

the introduction of the scheme coincided with the preparation of the reports on new projects.

Even had the Department given each company's proposals the minimum of attention before approving them, a large amount of work would have been necessary. Since the trains were to stop at every station, and the fares to be not more than one penny a mile, it was necessary to check the fare between each pair of stations against the mileage. Thus while the Department refused to approve the arrangements proposed by the Manchester & Leeds because the fares in general were too high, in the case of the G.J. and the Manchester & Birmingham, only fares between particular places were found to be excessive.[1] The two companies last-named agreed to reduce them.[2] Times had to be checked in a similar way, to ensure that the minimum speed of twelve miles an hour was maintained. The Department disapproved one of the G.J.'s trains because it was too slow.[3]

In fact, the Department gave companies' plans more than the minimum of attention. For example, Rugby was at this period an important junction for passengers on the Midland and London & Birmingham railways. The Department held up approval of the times proposed by the former until the latter's scheme arrived, in order to see what connections there were between the trains of the companies. It appears that they were reasonably good, for the times of both companies were approved.[4] Similarly, the London & Brighton was asked to explain why it proposed to run its Parliamentary trains between 6 and 10 p.m. Its explanation was presumably satisfactory, for the arrangement was sanctioned.[5]

The Department's main concern, however, was the construction of the carriages for the Parliamentary traffic. The Act provided only that 'the carriages . . . shall be provided with seats and . . . protected from the weather;' but this was to be done 'in a manner satisfactory to the [Board of Trade]'.[6] Clearly, the Department could have considered the carriages of each company on their merits, approving any that conformed with the very meagre specification laid down. In fact, it went

[1] MT 11/4, 30 Aug. 1844. MT 13/1, 24 Sept. 1844, and 30 Sept. 1844.
[2] MT 13/3, 5 and 10 Oct. 1844. [3] MT 11/4, 25 Sept. 1844.
[4] MT 13/1, 21 Sept. 1844. MT 11/4, 15 Nov. 1844.
[5] MT 13/1, 16 and 23 Oct. 1844. [6] 7 & 8 Vict., c. 85, s. 6.

further than this, setting up standards to which all companies should conform, and insisting on more than the letter of the law required. This verdict contradicts previous accounts,[1] according to which the Parliamentary carriage was a by-word for discomfort and inconvenience. It was, of course, inferior to those of a later age, but to suppose such comparisons valid is one of the elementary fallacies of history. The true contrast is with the accommodation provided for the poor at an earlier date.[2] By that test the Parliamentary carriage was a notable improvement.

The most obvious illustration of this is the fact that in a number of cases second-class carriages were used on Parliamentary trains.[3] As a result, the second-class passengers benefited also. This was notably the case on the G.W.R., where the second-, as well as the third-class passengers had previously travelled in open carriages. They were notorious for their discomfort, as is shown, for example, by the suggestion that Porter might have statistics 'to show how many of any 100 men would survive for one month, a journey of 50 miles in winter in a 2nd or 3rd-class carriage on the G.W.R.' Now[4] that the company had to provide roofs for its Parliamentary passengers, it was of course forced to abolish its open second class.[5]

As soon as the first applications from companies came in, a report on the requirements for carriages was called for.[6] When the Joint Locomotive Committee of the London & Croydon, London & Brighton and S.E.R. wrote that they were 'about to order a large number of 3rd Class carriages and requesting the opinion of the Department as to the kind of roofs which these carriages ought to have', the reply was postponed till Pasley had reported on the subject.[7] He went to see them, and thought them 'good but rather narrow'. The next day he saw those

---

[1] E.g. C. H. Ellis, *19th Century Railway Carriages*, Hamilton C. E. (1949), 31.
[2] For the results of a survey made in 1842, see P.P. 1842, xli, 23–6; and see above, p. 46.
[3] E.g. by the North Union; MT 13/1, 6 Nov. 1844, by the Bristol & Gloucester (temporarily); MT 13/3, 12 Apr. 1845; and on the Leeds-Bradford line; MT 11/8, 12 Sept. 1846.
[4] *Railways & the Board of Trade*, (3rd ed., 1845), 13.
[5] MacDermot, i, 641.   [6] MT 13/1, 27 Aug. 1844.
[7] Ibid., 17 Sept. 1844.

which the L.S.W. was building, and advised the designer, Joseph Beattie, to look at those ordered for the Joint Committee.[1] The Department asked other companies to send drawings of their proposed carriages; for example, the G.J., which was told at the same time that carriages 'open at the sides the same as 2nd class carriages' would not do.[2]

By November, 1844, the Department had acquired much information about the companies' plans. When those of the Manchester & Birmingham came up for consideration, the Railway Board came to a decision as to what standards it would require. Minute 410[3] reads:

> Acquaint the company that my Lords cannot certify any carriage for the cheap 3rd class train to be sufficiently protected from the weather, in the sense of the Act, unless it is capable of being entirely closed when necessity may require, with provisions for the admission of light and air.

Pasley's report indicates how the carriages proposed fell short of this ideal. He recommended that the company should board up the sides, leaving three or four openings on each side, fitted with moveable shutters or blinds. There should be some means for admitting light when the shutters were closed.[4] Copies of Minute 410 were sent to a number of companies whose proposed carriages were unsatisfactory, including the following:[5]

Y.N.M.	Edinburgh & Glasgow
London & Birmingham	Sheffield & Manchester
G.N.E.	Newcastle & Darlington Junct.
North Union	G.J.

It was in effect a regulation under the Act, although the Act gave the Board no specific power to make regulations. Moreover, it seems clearly to have gone beyond the Act in prescribing that the carriages must admit light when closed against the weather. Minute 410 was the origin of delegated legislation in the Department. Hitherto, the Department had used its powers only in relation to individual cases; now it exerted them to establish minimum standards below which no company should fall.

---

[1] Add. MS. 41991, 5 and 6 Oct. 1844. [2] MT 13/1, 6 Nov. 1844.
[3] Ibid., 12 Nov. 1844. [4] Ibid.
[5] Ibid., 12 and 28 Nov. and 4 Dec. 1844.

What was the Parliamentary carriage like? The greatest difference between it and the accommodation hitherto provided for the poor is that it had enclosed sides and a roof, with provision for light and ventilation.[1] The open carriage did not disappear at once. At least one company was allowed to use them for Parliamentary traffic until the new stock was ready.[2] Another offered to add open third-class carriages to two fast trains a day, instead of running a Parliamentary with covered carriages, but the Department would not agree.[3] The open carriage continued in use for many years on excursion trains.[4] But after 1844, it was exceptional, whereas before it had been almost universal for the poor. Seats were prescribed by the Act, and various amenities, such as glass windows, backs to the seats, and (in one case) oil-lamps, were provided by many companies.[5] Under pressure, they provided more than the minimum required by Parliament, though still less than the Department aimed for.

Some companies, particularly in Scotland and the north of England, were already providing facilities better in some respects than those provided for in the Act. The bait of remission of passenger duty induced some of them to ask the Department to class ordinary services as Parliamentary trains. The Newcastle and North Shields, which applied as early as September, 1844, will serve as an illustration. Its case was that it carried third-class passengers on all trains at less than a penny a mile. The Department eventually backed its claim, and the duty was remitted on all its third-class passengers, but only after discussion with Goulburn, the Chancellor of the Exchequer.[6] The Glasgow, Paisley & Greenock wished to carry the principle even further. This company carried second-class passengers at less than a penny a mile, and wished them to count as Parliamentary passengers as well as those in the third class. The Department entertained the claim, but Goulburn turned it down. It got remission for all its third-class traffic, however.

[1] According to Dalhousie, only one company had not met these requirements at the end of 1845: S.R.O. Dalhousie Papers, 7/29.

[2] MT 11/4, 15 Nov. 1844.   [3] MT 13/1, 17 Oct. 1844.

[4] C. H. Ellis, *19th Century Railway Carriages* (1949), 36.

[5] P.P. 1845, xxxix, 33 ff.

[6] MT 13/1, 18 Sept., 17 Oct., and 1 Nov. 1844. MT 13/3, 6 Jan. 1845. MT 11/6, 12 Jun. 1845.

The Department remarked that though its trains were not in strict compliance with the Act, apparently because of an inferior type of carriage, it deserved remission since its service was more beneficial than a single Parliamentary train would be.[1]

The threat that the remission of duty might be withdrawn proved a useful weapon in persuading companies to comply with the Department's wishes. It was used with effect on the Eastern Counties, which in May, 1845, had still not brought its carriages up to the desired standard. The company promised that they would be ready for inspection within ten days, and they were approved within a month.[2]

It will be seen how much work the enforcement of the Act created. Before the Department had passed the plans for the last of the lines open in 1844, some companies were applying to change the arrangements in force.[3] As new lines opened, details of the services proposed had to be approved. A company like the Manchester & Leeds, which had met all the requirements by 1 November, 1844, when the Act came into effect, was highly exceptional.[4] In most cases, the Department approved the times and the fares, and allowed the companies time to bring the carriages up to standard. In no case was legal action taken to enforce the Act in this period, and a case in which it was considered suggests the limitation of such action for the Department's purposes. The Department sanctioned the times proposed by the Edinburgh & Glasgow in November, 1844, but not its carriages. It again refused to pass them in April, 1845, on the grounds that there was 'no provision ... for the admission of light when the carriages are closed'. In November, 1845, Coddington reported that the company had done nothing to improve its carriages. The Department threatened prosecution unless the required alterations were made by 20 December, 1845. It is not clear whether the company complied or not; but the Lord Advocate, with whom Dalhousie had corresponded about the prosecution, had put his finger on the weakness in the case. 'On looking into the statute,' he wrote,

[1] MT 13/2, 24 and 30 Dec. 1844. MT 13/3, 6 Jan. and 26 Jun. 1845. MT 11/6, 12 Jun. 1845. S.R.O. Dalhousie Papers, 7/11.
[2] MT 13/3, 9 and 20 May, 1845. MT 11/6, 4 Jun. 1845.
[3] E.g. MT 11/6, 18 Jan. 1845. MT 13/3, 30 Jan. and 4 Mar. 1845.
[4] MT 13/1, 1 Nov. 1844.

'I do not observe anything as to "light and air". I . . . infer that you bring that matter under the words "protected from the weather in a manner satisfactory to the [Board of Trade]" '.[1] Would the courts have taken a similar view, if the Department had sought to enforce, not the Act, but Minute 410. The failure of one company to comply was the loss of an engagement; but the failure of a prosecution, which would have become a leading case, would have been the loss of the whole campaign. It is not surprising that the Department preferred the more flexible administrative methods of enforcement.

Gladstone's Act of 1844 was a turning-point in railway legislation. Between that date and 1868, public general Acts conferred few new powers on the Board of Trade. Nor were such Acts closely linked with the Department's administrative experience. Where new powers were bestowed, moreover, they often provided cheap and convenient procedure for companies to use, rather than means by which the Department could regulate their activities in the public interest.

The Clauses Acts of 1845 provide several illustrations of this type of delegated power. They were the work of James Booth,[2] then Speaker's Counsel, but who later played an important part in railway affairs as Joint Permanent Secretary to the Board of Trade. In framing them, he had the needs of railway promoters particularly in mind. The Companies Clauses Consolidation Act, the Companies Clauses Consolidation (Scotland) Act, and the Lands Clauses Consolidation Act, gave the Board of Trade power to appoint an umpire in order to prevent the breakdown of arbitration, when one party at least was a railway company, and when requested to do so by one of the parties.[3]

The Railway Clauses Consolidation Act, and the similar Act for Scotland, bestowed further powers on the Board. Where a company wished to deviate from its authorised levels, the Board might authorise it to do so, and settle any differences between the company and neighbouring landowners.[4] On the application of highway authorities, the Board might order companies

---

[1] MT 11/1, 16 Nov. 1844. MT 11/6, 22 Apr. 1845. MT 11/7, 4 Dec. 1845. MT 13/4, 20 Nov. and 31 Dec. 1845. S.R.O. Dalhousie Papers, 7/29.
[2] O. C. Williams, op. cit., i, 107.
[3] 8 & 9 Vict., cc. 16–18, ss. 131, 134, and 28 respectively.
[4] Ibid., c. 20, s. 12 and c. 33, s. 12.

to erect screens between rail and road in order to avert the danger of 'horses being frightened by the sight of the engines or carriages travelling upon the railway'.[1] The Board could authorise modifications in the construction of 'any road or bridge, or other public work of an engineering nature'.[2] Provision was made for the appointment of umpires in arbitration cases similar to those mentioned above; i.e., by the Board generally, and by the Lord Ordinary in Scotland.[3]

Companies were quick to make use of these procedures. One company applied for a certificate to make a deviation even before the Act had been passed, while the Southampton & Dorchester obtained permission to meet the wishes of Southampton Corporation by lengthening a tunnel.[4]

One other Act of 1845 reflects the experience of the Department. This was 'An Act to restrict the powers of selling or leasing railways contained in certain Acts of Parliament relating to such railways', which laid down that such transactions were not to be carried through under powers already obtained but must be the subject of fresh application to Parliament.[5]

The background of this Act was the purchase by George Hudson of the G.N.E.[6] That company had originally proposed to build a line between York and Newcastle, but had in fact constructed only the section south of Darlington. Hudson's Newcastle & Darlington had completed the scheme, and his object in getting control of the G.N.E. was to amalgamate the two companies and place the whole line under unified management. When the Department learnt of the deal, it took the opinion of the Law Officers as to its legality. They advised the Department in June, 1845, that it was illegal but would be hard to prevent by legal action. They were supported in this view by the Lord Advocate. When the company submitted a draft of the lease, the English Law Officers went through it, and confirmed their former verdict that the transaction was *ultra vires*. The company should seek a new Act. The Department passed

[1] 8 & 9 Vict., cc. 16–18, s. 63 and s. 55 respectively.
[2] Ibid., s. 66 and s. 58 respectively.   [3] Ibid., s. 129 and s. 122.
[4] MT 11/6, 28 May, 1845. MT 11/8, 27 Feb. 1846. MT 13/5, 18 Feb. 1846.
[5] 8 & 9 Vict., c. 96.
[6] Cf. W. W. Tomlinson, *North Eastern Railway*, Newcastle-upon-Tyne (1914), 459 ff.; Cleveland-Stevens, 34.

V. Outside the Board of Trade, Sunday Night, 30 November, 1845, the Closing Date for the Deposit of Railway Plans for the Session of 1846. Note the Scaffolding; see p. 67.

VI. The Steps of the Board of Trade, Sunday, 30 November, 1845, the Last Day for the Deposit of Railway Plans for the Session of 1846. Note the Scaffolding; see p. 67.

on this opinion to the company, which agreed to do so.[1] The lease was eventually sanctioned by an Act of 1846.[2]

The Department had little responsibility for the Gauge Regulation Act, 1846,[3] nor did that measure confer any new powers on the Board. It originated in the report of a Royal Commission,[4] set up at the suggestion of the House of Commons. Dalhousie passed on an application from Smith, the former Inspector-General, for membership of the Commission,[5] but otherwise had no say in its composition. The Department advised the Commission how to interpret one point in their terms of reference,[6] but made no important contribution to its work. The only witness from the Department was Pasley, who was called last and whose evidence was very brief compared with that of the companies' engineers.

When the report appeared it was referred to the Board, and Dalhousie advised Peel to legislate at once.[7] But the times were not propitious because of the Corn Law question, and it was not until June that the Board's recommendations were laid before the House of Commons, and resolutions founded on them adopted.[8] The Bill itself was not drafted till after Peel's fall, and then at the Home Office, though in consultation with the Board.[9]

The Gauge Regulation Act was a most unsatisfactory measure. It did not achieve uniformity of gauge, nor even prevent a very considerable increase in the mileage of the broad gauge. These consequences, however, were only in part the responsibility of the Board.[10]

One other statute of 1846 calls for only brief mention. This was 'An Act to facilitate the dissolution of certain railway companies'.[11] Its purpose was to provide a simple procedure whereby companies which wished to go no further with their Acts of incorporation, because of the financial crisis then prevailing,

---

[1] MT 6/2, 2119, 2592, 2721, 2785/1845. MT 11/6, 8 Jul. and 25 Oct. 1845. MT 13/3, 7 Jul. 1845. MT 13/4, 13 Oct. and 1 Nov. 1845.
[2] 9 & 10 Vict., c. 242 (Local & Personal).
[3] Ibid., c. 57.
[4] P.P. 1846, xvi.   [5] S.R.O. Dalhousie Papers, 7/15.
[6] MT 13/3, 12 Aug. 1845.   [7] Add. MS. 40576, f. 585.
[8] Hansard, lxxxvii, 595–6 and 631.   [9] MT 13/5, 15 Jul. 1846.
[10] For the gauge question in general, see Cleveland-Stevens, 57–8; and MacDermot, i, 229 ff.   [11] 9 & 10 Vict., c. 28.

could go into voluntary liquidation. Dalhousie was closely interested in the measure, but since it was devised for the unique circumstances of the time, its effect was transient. It conferred no powers on the Board. Dalhousie explained to Peel that it had been prepared in consultation with Glyn,[1] chairman of the London & Birmingham. It may, therefore, be significant that another railway magnate, George Hudson, sponsored a similar measure, which, however, never got further than the second reading in the Commons.[2]

[1] Add. MS. 40589, f. 244–53.   [2] C. J. ci (1846), 813.

4

THE COMMISSIONERS OF
RAILWAYS
1846–1851

WHEN the Whigs returned to power in 1846, they passed an Act[1] which set up a new department, independent of the Board of Trade, called the Commissioners of Railways. There were to be not more than five Commissioners, of whom the President and two others might be paid. The President and the unpaid Commissioners might sit in Parliament. Any two of the Commissioners were given power to act for all—a provision which had an important bearing on the attendance at meetings of the Commissioners. The powers of the Board of Trade in relation to railways were transferred to the Commissioners, but the Act gave them no new powers of any importance.

The Act reflects closely the ideas of a Select Committee presided over by James Morrison.[2] The trend of the evidence given before it was that jurisdiction over railways should be taken from the Board of Trade and given to a new body to be set up on the lines of the Railway Board but carrying more weight. How should such a body be constituted? One of the witnesses expressed the general feeling concisely[3] when he said that it should be 'a mixed Board, make up of people in high authority, or of high rank, with others to aid them'. The Railway Board had not been such a body, and it had lacked time.

---

[1] 9 & 10 Vict., c. 105.   [2] For Morrison, see above, pp. 21–3.
[3] P.P. 1846, xiv, 111.

No sooner had it been set up than 'there was a shoal of railway schemes poured in upon them which they could not possibly overtake, however hard and however willingly they might work'.

The only Board of Trade witness to give evidence was Porter, and he spoke solely about statistics.[1] Morrison even drafted the forms which were circularised to companies seeking information.[2] It was Morrison, too, who moved that Commissioners of Railways be set up.[3] The House of Commons adopted a resolution from his Committee 'that it is expedient that a department of the executive government, so constituted as to obtain public confidence, be established for the superintendence of railway business',[4] and the government introduced a Bill on the following day. It passed rapidly through all its stages without substantial amendment—perhaps because it was so late in the session.[5]

The government promised to introduce a Bill in the following session to extend the Commissioners' powers.[6] Other resolutions of the Committee, which were reported to, but not adopted by, the Commons,[7] make it clear that they were thinking mainly of equipping the new body with power to conduct preliminary enquiries and gather information necessary for reports to Parliament on railway Bills. But by the time the Commissioners began work in November, 1846, the situation had completely changed from what it had been in 1844. Then the Railway Mania had been just getting under way, now its force was all but spent. There was no need for a new department to curb excessive railway promotion.

In choosing the Commissioners, the government followed precisely the prescription quoted above—'a mixed Board, made up of people in high authority, or of high rank, with others to aid them'. Russell invited Dalhousie to take the office of President, free of any obligation to support his government, provided he would undertake not to act with the Opposition. Dalhousie declined, however, preferring complete independence.[8] Russell

[1] P.P. 1846, xiv, 290 ff.   [2] Ibid., 293–570.
[3] Hansard, lxxxviii, 845.   [4] C. J. 1846, 1225.
[5] Ibid., 1235, 1st Reading 19 Aug.: 1303, Royal Assent, 28 Aug.
[6] Hansard, lxxxviii, 847.   [7] C. J. 1846, 1180.
[8] PRO 30/22/5B. Dalhousie-Russell, 24 Aug. 1846.

chose instead Edward Strutt, M.P., whom Charles Wood, then Chancellor of the Exchequer, thought 'best in point of work' among several candidates.[1] Earl Granville got one of the unpaid posts and represented the new department in the Lords. The other paid Commissioners were Sir Edward Ryan, a retired Indian judge, and Captain (later Major, and finally Colonel) Brandreth, R.E. A seat at the board had first been offered to the distinguished military engineer Sir John Burgoyne. When he turned it down,[2] Russell took Brandreth at Charles Wood's suggestion from the post of Director of Works at the Admiralty. Auckland, the First Lord, was enthusiastic about the choice; Brandreth was 'an incomparable officer . . . in all our great works . . . our reliance was on him . . . it will not be easy to supply his place'.[3] There remained one unpaid Commissioner-ship, for Russell thought it 'best to constitute our Railway Board of four only at first. After a few weeks we shall know what aid they want.'[4] In the event, it was never filled.

Although the Commissioners were in form separate from the Board of Trade throughout the five years of their existence, their period of true independence was much less. At first, they had their own offices in Great George Street, Westminster,[5] but by September, 1847, they had moved to Whitehall, where they shared not only the same building as the Board of Trade but even its coal supply.[6]

Early in 1848, Strutt lost his seat on an election petition, and resigned his position as President. He was succeeded by Henry Labouchere, who was already President of the Board of Trade. About the same time, Brandreth died.[7] Colonel Alderson, R.E., one of the officers suggested by Burgoyne in 1846,[8] took his place until the end of 1848, but thereafter the Commissioners managed without an engineering member. Meanwhile, Granville had become Vice-President of the Board of Trade. Thus, as a result of being situated in the same building, and of

[1] Ibid., Wood-Russell, Aug. 1846.
[2] Ibid., 5C. Burgoyne-Russell, 4 Sept. 1846.
[3] Ibid., Auckland-Russell, 26 Sept. 1846.
[4] Ibid., 5D. Russell-Wood, 30 Oct. [1846].
[5] MT 13/6, 10 Nov. 1846.
[6] MT 13/7, 15 Sept. 1847. MT/8, 20 Dec. 1848.
[7] MT 11/12, 13 Mar. 1848.
[8] PRO 30/22/5C. Burgoyne-Russell, 4 Sept. 1846.

Labouchere's and Granville's overlapping appointments, the Commissioners of Railways had become by 1848 in fact, though not in name, a department of the Board of Trade. There was pressure from the House of Commons, on grounds of economy, for a fusion of the Commissioners with the Board.[1] When it took place in 1851 it was only a belated recognition of a state of affairs which had in fact existed for three and a half years.

Three of the six men who served as Commissioners of Railways—Strutt, Brandreth, and Alderson—had too little time to gain any thorough grasp of railway problems. Of the remainder, Labouchere attended very few of the meetings—fifteen in 1848 and the same number in 1849—and seems to have taken little part in the proceedings. Granville attended a large number of the meetings, but does not seem to have made any notable individual contribution to railway policy. His biographer devotes only two pages to his five years with the Commissioners and Board of Trade as opposed to thirty-five to his ten weeks at the Foreign Office in 1851–2.[2] Ryan served long enough and attended regularly enough to master railway affairs, and the minute books leave one with an impression of his ability and conscientiousness; but there is no suggestion that he was a man of vision, in railway policy at least.

The Commissioners met frequently, and their minutes form a record of the great majority of the decisions taken, even on routine matters. Each Commissioner was in a sufficiently independent position to disagree with the President, and during the period when they were four in number, there was a possibility of serious discord, and even deadlock, in the transaction of business. The minutes, however, reveal no sign that such a situation actually arose.

Another consequence of the independent status of the Commissioners was that they could, and did, absent themselves from meetings frequently and for long periods at a time. During the first six months, all attended with reasonable regularity. There were 100 meetings, of which Strutt attended 88, Granville 62, Ryan 96, and Brandreth 84. After Labouchere had replaced Strutt, however, the business fell mainly into the hands of the

[1] Cleveland-Stevens, 150–2.
[2] Lord E. Fitzmaurice, *Life of Lord Granville, 1815–1891*, London (1905) i, 40–2 and 43–78.

other two paid members. This was possible because of the provision that two of the Commissioners were sufficient to act. During the second half of 1848, there were 139 meetings, of which Labouchere attended 6, Granville 50, Ryan all, and Alderson 103. At only three meetings were all four Commissioners present. A decision of some importance was taken at one of these meetings—it related to a prosecution of the G.W.R. for alleged excessive charges[1]—but in general there was no connection between the numbers attending and the importance of the business done. Indeed, the first step in the G.W.R. prosecution was taken at a meeting attended only by Ryan and Alderson.[2]

The final stage was reached in 1851, when there were 238 meetings, at none of which were more than two Commissioners present. One of these was always Ryan. The other was normally Granville, but for a period of two months in the summer, his place was taken by Labouchere.[3]

We have seen that the government was influenced in setting up the Commissioners by the criticisms that had been made of the Railway Board. One of the criticisms had been that the policy of the Board was decided by mere clerks. At the outset, therefore, there seems to have been an attempt to reserve policy matters exclusively for the Commissioners themselves, after reference, if necessary, to the expert members.

Thus a question relating to Parliamentary carriages, and reports from companies explaining how accidents had occurred, were referred to Brandreth.[4] On occasion, Brandreth sat independently of his colleagues to hear engineering evidence, and reported his findings to them. Sometimes they would leave him to deal with questions at his discretion. Frequently they settled items of business by deciding to write 'in the terms of Major Brandreth's minute' or 'to the effect contained in Colonel Brandreth's minute viz. . . . there should be a clear height of 18 feet throughout the breadth of the road under the bridge, and . . . one foot of this height may be obtained by lowering the road'.[5] Later, Alderson played a similar rôle. The

---

[1] MT 13/10, 26 Oct. 1848; see below, pp. 119–20.
[2] Ibid., 16 Aug. 1848.   [3] MT 13/15 *passim*.
[4] MT 13/6, 24 Nov. 1846; MT 13/7, 26 Jan., 24 Jul. 1847.
[5] MT 13/6, 24 Nov. 1846. MT 13/7, 26 Jan., 25 Mar., and 1 Nov. 1847.

Commissioners ordered that a letter be written 'in terms of Colonel Alderson's minute', confirmed the draft of another letter he had written and confirmed his instructions to one of the inspectors to enquire into an accident.[1]

Legal questions were handled in a similar way. The Commissioners might order that sets of bye-laws were 'to be altered in accordance with the notes of Sir Edward Ryan', or—apropos a dispute between the M.S.L. and a highway authority—'write . . . in conformity with Sir Edward Ryan's minute'. A dispute between the L.B.S.C. and the Grand Surrey Canal was referred to him. In some cases—for example, that relating to an application for an extension of time from the Monmouth and Hereford Company—his minute was entered in full, with the Commissioners' confirmation of it.[2]

Though at first the Commissioners worked as a Board, their officers were not all mere mechanical executants of policy. The higher officers continued to play a responsible part in the work of the office, as they had done in the Board of Trade. They were intelligent and able men who could deal with matters on their own in the light of their knowledge of the Commissioners' policy. Recognising this, the Commissioners entrusted to them a wide degree of independent action. Engineering business, for example, was not invariably dealt with through Brandreth. When the important question of the mixed gauge on the Oxford & Rugby Railway, involving a conflict of views between the G.W.R. and the L.N.W.R., came up in his absence, the Commissioners did not postpone it but delegated it to an inspector, and adopted his report direct. After first referring another matter to Brandreth, they disposed of it not by confirming his minute but one by Simmons.[3]

The rôle of the Legal Assistant, Arthur Barron, was similar to that of the engineers. The Commissioners decided bye-law applications by minuting 'write in terms of Mr. Barron's draft letter'. An objection on a point of law to an application for a certificate under the 1842 Act was referred to him. On another occasion, he was ordered to prepare a case for the opinion of

[1] MT 13/10, 26 June and 17 Nov. 1848.
[2] MT 13/7, 7 Jan. and 4 Feb. 1847. 13/8, 30 Dec. 1847. 13/10, 30 May, 1848.
[3] MT 13/8, 10 and 26 Nov., 21 and 23 Dec. 1847.

the Law Officers. And the most important legal report in the history of the Commissioners was the work of Barron, not Ryan.[1]

The officer who bore the greatest responsibility was, of course, the Secretary. The mere fact of his signature at the bottom of a letter is not in itself evidence for this fact, since most of them dealt with matters of routine, while in others he was merely giving expression to a detailed minute of the Commissioners. But many of the questions left to him to deal with at his own discretion were difficult and important. When, for example, the Lancaster & Carlisle Company wrote, 'trusting that the Commissioners will not press the alterations in the construction of their carriages for cheap trains', the Secretary replied. It was he, likewise, who answered a spokesman for the drivers of the L.N.W.R. who sought the support of the Commissioners in a dispute with their employers. The Secretary was entrusted with the task of collecting information from certain Scottish companies required to deal with a query raised by Gladstone. More delicate, though perhaps less important, was the task of reassuring the Society for the Protection of Females in Newcastle, who petitioned for 'the interference of the Railway Commissioners with reference to the placing of lights in railway carriages at night'. In a different category was the Secretary's duty of preparing the annual estimates for the Treasury.[2]

It has been shown that as time went on the Commissioners functioned less and less as a board. By 1851, although the forms of board procedure continued, the reality approximated to the ministerial pattern. One of the political heads of the Board of Trade—Granville—transacted the business with Ryan, who had become in effect joint permanent secretary for railway affairs. The latter was to be 'seen daily plying below the bar of the House of Lords to take Granville's orders or to feed him with railway figures and other facts'.[3] Such a development was possible without loss of efficiency because the officers had shown themselves capable of doing the greater part of the detailed

[1] MT 13/7, 13 Sept. 1847; 13/8, 8 Oct. 1847; 13/10, 26 Oct. 1848; 13/11, 24 Mar. and 20 Apr. 1849; see below, p. 127.
[2] MT 13/7, 20 Feb. 1847. 13/10, 4 Aug. and 6 Nov. 1848. 13/13, 6 Jun. 1850. 13/14, 23 Nov. 1850.
[3] PRO 30/22/6. Brougham-Russell, 17 Mar. 1850.

work themselves. This was specially true on the engineering side, where there was no professionally qualified Commissioner from 1849. The gap was filled by the inspectors and the Secretary, who was by that time an engineer. Before the Commissioners came to an end, it had become normal rather than exceptional for their decisions merely to confirm reports or drafts from their officers. An analysis of the first hundred minutes of May, 1851,[1] shows that in twelve instances the case was either referred to an inspector, or decided in the light of a report from one. Eight of the decisions confirmed the Secretary's drafts, while forty-nine more related to classes of business (notably Parliamentary trains) which were primarily the Secretary's responsibility. In sixteen cases, no action was taken. Only fifteen cases reached the Commissioners in a form sufficiently open to require their personal decision, including three in which Ryan's own drafts were confirmed.

At first, a fairly elaborate division of the staff into departments seems to have been contemplated. There is reference to General, Engineering, and Statistical and Topographical Departments.[2] After the failure of Strutt's Bill in 1847[3] such elaboration became unnecessary, and the entire staff worked as a single department.

The distinction between the Commissioners and their officers in relation to policy was, as we have seen, never so clear as seems at first to have been intended, and by the end, had become very blurred indeed. Among the officers themselves, however, there were two distinct grades—the higher bearing important responsibilities, and with some share in the formation of policy, the lower composed of clerks, messengers, etc.

The higher grade included the Secretary, the Legal Assistant, and the Inspectors. The first Secretary, Bruce, served for less than a year and left little mark behind him. His successor, Harness, was a Royal Engineer, who had transferred from the Home Office to take charge of the abortive Statistical and Topographical Department. Like Alderson, he had been suggested to Russell for a Commissionership by Burgoyne in 1846.[4] When

---

[1] MT 13/15, 2–19 May, 1851.
[2] MT 13/7, 3 and 22 Feb. 1847.
[3] See below, p. 126.
[4] PRO 30/22/5C. Burgoyne-Russell, 4 Sept. 1846.

he resigned in 1850, on becoming Deputy-Master of the Mint, one of the inspectors, Simmons, took his place. The Legal Assistant, Barron, served from 1847 until the functions of the Commissioners reverted to the Board of Trade.

The inspectors were all on the same footing, and no one took Pasley's place as Inspector-General.[1] Dalhousie had treated Pasley and Coddington as equals, in spite of the fact that the latter was styled Assistant Inspector, and that the danger of conflicting opinions between independent inspectors had been foreseen.[2] When a Member asked Strutt in 1847 why the Commissioners had not appointed an Inspector-General, he merely replied that 'it was thought better, under the new board, to appoint . . . officers to be called inspectors'.[3] The Commissioners presumably looked to Brandreth to resolve any professional differences that might arise among the inspectors, and since the post of Secretary was later held by an engineer, he would also have been able to play a similar rôle.

Coddington transferred to the service of the Commissioners, but after a few months left to become Secretary of the Caledonian Railway. He had been getting £600 a year, and having been offered 'an assured income for ten years of nearly £2,000 per annum . . . [he] found it was no longer compatible with his private interest to retain his appointment'.[4] Thus, the three few inspectors appointed in 1847 (Simmons, Laffan, and Wynne) started virtually from scratch—they were like apprentices without a master. Soon after his appointment, one of the new inspectors received an offer similar to Coddington's. The Commissioners, realising that long service was essential to enable the inspectors to gain practical experience, proposed to raise their salaries and, to this, the Treasury agreed. Simmons' salary had been £600, and that of the others £400, a year. Now they were

[1] Simmons' appointment as Inspector General; (MT 13/8, 17 Dec. 1849) was purely nominal; it enabled him to discharge functions under a private Act.

[2] See above, pp. 32 & 66.

[3] Hansard, xci, 324. In spite of Strutt's positive statement there was in fact a good deal of variation in the titles by which the inspectors were known; though by 1867, the present style, Inspecting Officer of Railways, was widely used. For the sake of uniformity, the term 'inspector' is used in the remainder of this study.

[4] MT 13/7, 8 Jul. 1847. MT 13/8, 24 Dec. 1847.

put on the scale £600 × £50 × £900, plus £1 10s. a day and travelling expenses when inspecting.[1]

It was common form in the railway world to denounce the inspectors for their lack of experience, but these incidents show that in fact their experience could have considerable market value—as was natural in a new and rapidly developing field. However, allowances were cut again from 1 April, 1849.[2] By that time, few companies could afford to make tempting offers to gamekeepers to turn poacher.

Most of the clerks serving under the Commissioners during their early years had previously served in the Board of Trade, as had the Registrar, MacGregor. Vacancies might be filled by putting temporary clerks on the establishment. For example, H. M. Suft had been taken on as a temporary clerk in the Railway Department in 1844, and transferred in the same capacity to the Commissioners.[3] He became established in 1847. Other vacancies were filled by patronage. For example, W. M. Bucknall and G. J. Swanston were nominated by Labouchere, subject to a declaration of competence from the Secretary. It is scarcely surprising to find no case in which the Secretary refused to certify the nominees of his chiefs; but in these instances there is reason to think they were in fact men of ability. Swanston later served as private secretary to the Vice-President and Bucknall as Librarian of the Board of Trade.[4]

The transfer of responsibility to the Commissioners was an experiment which failed. Its main result was to break the continuity of experience gained by the Railway Department, and so render it largely useless. Such an event was always possible in the very small public offices of the mid-nineteenth century. Pasley had recognised the danger; one of his arguments in favour of the appointment of an Assistant Inspector in 1844 was that it would 'perpetuate professional knowledge in this

---

[1] MT 13/7, 22 Sept. 1847. MT 13/8, 24 Dec. 1847. MT 13/9, 5 Jan. 1848. Cf. Cobden a little later: 'The permanent servants of the public can scarcely be said to be overpaid, since they were often tempted to leave the service by the superior advantages offered by private service;' q. E. Hughes, 'Civil Service Reform', in *Public Administration*, xxxii (1954), 25.

[2] MT 13/10, 22 Nov. and 4 Dec. 1848.

[3] MT 13/6, 8 Dec. 1846.

[4] MT 13/10, 28 Sept. 1848; 13/11, 26 Jul. 1849. *P.O. London Directory 1857*, 96. *Royal Kalendar 1864*, 164.

Department . . . [otherwise] all the knowledge and experience . . . that I have acquired would be lost to my successor'.[1] When Lord Lincoln suggested that instead of appointing the Commissioners it would be better to leave things as they were, since the Department had the information and staff, the Government replied that the greater part of the staff would be transferred.[2] In similar vein, Russell wrote to Strutt:

> Now I wish you to form . . . the subordinate machinery of the office. It is of the utmost importance that it should be well constituted at first, and you will probably find valuable materials in the Railway Department of the Board of Trade.[3]

By a purely arithmetical test, this policy was carried out. But the greater part of the staff—those who were transferred—were clerks and messengers. Those in senior posts—the true 'depositaries of departmental traditions'[4]—were, except for Coddington, dispersed.

Why did this happen? Pasley applied for one of the paid Commissionerships, and resolved at first that he would take that or nothing.[5] On learning of Brandreth's appointment, he felt 'mortified at seeing a junior officer placed on the Board, to command him'.[6] Nevertheless, he told Russell at an interview that he would soldier on in his present post if paid the same as Brandreth, namely, £1,500 a year. He made this condition since, 'however unjustly, . . . the merits of individuals and the importance of appointments . . . are estimated by the salary'.[7] But the government would not have him. 'Distinguished as he is as an officer both of invention and ability to instruct others, he has not given satisfaction to the public in the Railway Department', wrote Russell, recommending him at the same time for advancement from C.B. to K.C.B. and some such post as the Governorship of Jersey.[8] Pasley lost his job, the Governorship never materialised, and he was left to console himself as

[1] S.R.O. Dalhousie Papers, 7/16.
[2] Hansard, lxxxviii, 848–9.
[3] PRO 30/22/5C. Russell-Strutt, 4 Sept. 1846.
[4] q. E. Hughes, loc. cit., 38.
[5] Add. MS. 41992, 22, 24, and 31 Aug. 1846.
[6] PRO 30/22/5E. Russell-Wellington, 9 Nov. 1846.
[7] Add. MS. 41992, 3 Nov. 1846.
[8] PRO 30/22/5E. Russell-Wellington, 9 Nov. 1846.

best he might with his K.C.B.[1] Porter, too, was a candidate for a Commissionership and was disappointed at being passed over.[2]

The Commissioners quickly found the drawbacks of working without experience. Among the earliest circulars approved was one to companies asking for a copy of their bye-laws, and 'whether [they] were allowed by the [Board of Trade] . . . and if so, the date of approval'.[3] Another circular sought details of the Parliamentary trains of sixty-seven companies.[4] Evidently the Commissioners could not readily discover these items of information from the records they had taken over. On some points, certainly, the records were silent. Before they could answer a query raised by the South Devon Railway, the Commissioners had first to find out 'what was done by General Pasley . . . which Mr. Brunel has undertaken to ascertain as there are no documents to be found in this office'.[5]

Why, then, was not continuity of senior staff preserved? Patronage no doubt influenced the distribution of posts—though Russell's offer to Dalhousie suggests that it was not the paramount consideration. Porter's rejection cannot be explained in this way, in any case, for he was a Whig protégé; a year later in successfully urging his claim to the post of Joint Secretary to the Board of Trade, he employed the argument that his promotion would be popular with freetraders.[6] There was a genuine difficulty. The aim was to re-create the Railway Board without its alleged defects. To this aim, continuity had to be sacrificed. Had men like Pasley and Porter become Commissioners the opponents of railway regulation would have had an ideal slogan near at hand—'plus ça change, plus c'est la même chose!'

Of the powers taken over from the Board of Trade, the most important were those relating to the inspection of new lines. They were used vigorously, in that the opening of a great many lines was postponed; e.g. thirty-two in the period November, 1846–December, 1848.[7] But they were not used effectively, in

---

[1] Add. MS. 41992, 11 Nov. 1846, 41964. Clarendon-Pasley, 27 Dec. 1846.
[2] Bodleian Library. Clarendon Papers, 561.
[3] MT 13/6, 12 Dec. 1846.
[4] MT 11/9, 5 Dec. 1846.   [5] MT 13/7, 3 Sept. 1847.
[6] Bodleian Library. Clarendon Papers, 561.
[7] P.P. 1847–8, xxvi, 11 and 1849; xxvii, 277.

that the requirements enforced on companies had little practical effect. Typical of them were the numerous speed limits fixed.[1] Excessive speed did cause some accidents, of course, but usually only when the permanent way was defective, or when the driver was making up lost time—a practice which a government speed limit was unlikely to prevent. A more radical requirement would have been to insist on improvements in the track, or the adoption of improved safety devices, which would have made speed less dangerous. As we shall see, the inspector's powers over new lines came later to be exercised mainly to promote safety, in contrast to the original view that the object of inspection was to ensure that lines were constructed in accordance with the Acts which authorised them. No blame attaches to the inspectors for not anticipating later developments. Firstly, they lacked experience; even Coddington had served only three years, and the others began only in 1847. In the second place, safety appliances of the kind which eventually proved most effective (such as block telegraph working and interlocking signals) had scarcely been conceived as yet. There was, however, a certain change of perspective during this period. A statement of inspectors' duties in 1847 stresses their duty to ascertain that lines were built as authorised, more than their responsibility to promote safety.[2] In the following year, the emphasis is altered. The Commissioners told a correspondent who had complained of a deviation from authorised levels that they had 'no power to refuse to sanction the opening of any railway solely on the ground that the construction . . . is not in conformity with the . . . company's Acts, or the general Acts'. They went on to say that the complainant might take legal proceedings against the offending company—which implied that they did not consider the mere fact of such a deviation would justify them in prosecuting the company.[3]

The Commissioners' attitude towards accidents and accident enquiries was similar. The first point to emphasise is that they ordered enquiries into only a small proportion of the accidents reported, and it is not clear on what grounds they decided that an enquiry was needed. At their meeting on 6 November, 1847, for example, they had before them reports of three fatal

[1] Ibid., xxvi, 11. [2] MT 13/8, 24 Dec. 1847.
[3] MT 13/10, 26 Sept. 1848.

accidents. Coroners' juries had delivered verdicts of accidental death on two of them, and these were simply minuted as 'Read'. In the third case the minute reads 'ask for verdict at inquest.'[1] When it arrived, it too was 'Accidental death', and the Commissioners' minute is once more a mere 'Read'.[2] Such decisions were typical. Of fifty-two accidents reported in January and February, 1851, no action was taken in regard to forty-eight. In three of the remaining cases, the only action taken was to ask the company for further information. In only one case was an enquiry ordered.[3]

When enquiries were ordered, the resulting recommendations were rarely specific enough to be of much use. Brandreth's main contribution to railway safety was the hypothesis that wheels and axles of poor quality were more likely to break than those of good quality. At his bidding, companies were solemnly adjured to draw the attention of manufacturers to the poor quality of components they had supplied, and he drafted a circular on the subject.[4] This brought to light the fact that wheel-tapping was already a regular practice on the Eastern Counties Railway,[5] but can hardly have done much good. This was a case where those who argued that the self-interest of the companies was a better guarantee of safety than public regulation were in the right. Companies might use components which were of poor quality because they were cheap, but they had an interest in ensuring that they got the quality they paid for, without being advised to do so by a government circular.

In general the inspectors appointed to investigate accidents rarely went beyond obvious common-sense recommendations in their reports. A notable exception was the report on the collapse of the Dee Bridge on the Chester & Holyhead line in 1847, at the moment a train was passing over it. The report criticised the design of the bridge, which was in cast-iron and by Robert Stephenson; but the most important recommendation was that a Royal Commission should be appointed to enquire into the whole question of the use of cast-iron in bridges.[6] The recommendation was accepted, and the enquiry led to an

[1] MT 13/8, 6 Nov. 1847.   [2] Ibid., 10 Nov. 1847.
[3] MT 13/15.   [4] MT 13/7, 26, 28, and 30 Jan. 1847.
[5] Ibid., 2 Feb. 1847.
[6] P.P. 1847, lxiii, 257–72, and esp. 265. MT 13/7, 29 Jun. 1847.

VII. The Premises of the Board of Trade, 1846, as Rebuilt by Sir Charles Barry. See p. 67.

VIII (a). Samuel Laing.

VIII (b). General Sir Charles Pasley.

VIII (c). Captain Sir Douglas Galton.

VIII (d). Sir John Simmons.

important advance in engineering knowledge. To bring out its significance it is necessary first to consider the Department's policy towards invention and research.

As early as October, 1840,[1] an inventor wrote to try to interest the Department in his project. His letter was the first of a very great number, including some from as far afield as Amsterdam, Vienna, Berlin, and Paris.[2] The general tone of the Department in replying to these applications was one of polite discouragement. The following letter may serve as an example:

> I am directed to point out to you that the government of this country has no power of trying experiments upon railways or of enforcing the adoption of experimental improvements and that if you wish to give your invention publicity you had better take measures yourself for that purpose.[3]

Occasionally, however, it seemed worth while to look into a particular invention more closely. One inventor was asked to communicate with Pasley 'with the view of explaining to him [an] invention for causing the immediate stoppage of railway trains'.[4] In August, 1846, Clarendon saw a model of an invention 'for lessening the force of collisions on railways', which pleased him.[5] In June, 1846, the Department took the step of presenting to Parliament a report on Powell's carriage, which was intended for use on either the broad or narrow gauge, as a contribution to the solution of the gauge problem.[6]

In sponsoring the Royal Commission on cast-iron structures, the Commissioners went beyond these precedents by initiating themselves an important project of research. Their reason for this departure was that

> the last few years have rendered necessary the construction of a number of bridges, intended for the use of heavy trains passing at great speeds, in designing which the known laws relating to the strength of materials is most probably inapplicable; while the experiments requisite to ascertain those which may be applicable, are beyond the means of individuals. . . . Neither can the solution

---

[1] MT 11/1, 20 Oct. 1840.
[2] MT 11/6, 14 May, 1845. MT 11/8, 16 Jun., 18 Aug., and 23 Sept. 1846.
[3] BT 6/280.
[4] MT 11/6, 14 Aug. 1845.   [5] MT 11/8, 2 Nov. 1846.
[6] MT 13/5, 24 Jun. 1846. P.P. 1846, xxxviii, 377.

of this problem be left to time, or to the experience which might be obtained from a number of sudden and frightful accidents; the knowledge is required at once.[1]

The enquiry showed that heavy moving loads, such as trains, set up vibrations which imposed additional strain on cast-iron bridges beyond that allowed for in the formulae hitherto used.[2] Engineers would have to allow for this, and the inspectors were provided with standards by which they could test such bridges on new lines. The Commissioners called on each inspector to report on 'bridges . . . inspected by him . . . which may appear not to be as strong as the recommendations . . . require'.[3]

Reports on new lines show that the tests were in fact used.[4] The whole enquiry set a precedent for the future. The Department's *Requirements* for new lines[5] from the second edition onwards, included tests for wrought-iron as well as cast-iron bridges. The Treasury was induced to make a grant in aid of William Fairbairn's experiments on the strength of wrought-iron bridges.[6] By 1874, steel bridges were beginning to come into use; the new edition of the *Requirements* which appeared that year has a footnote which refers to the investigations on which the tests for bridges were based and goes on, 'until similar investigations have been made in regard to steel . . . it is impossible to adopt rules' for them.

In exercising their powers over Parliamentary trains, the Commissioners followed a sensibly empirical course. The provision that such trains should stop at all stations was dispensed with in the case of the N.B.R. in consideration of the fact that Parliamentary carriages were attached to all its trains.[7] Another Scottish company was allowed to use carriages inferior to the usual standard in view of the number and cheapness of its trains.[8] When the Lancaster & Carlisle proposed something similar, however, the Commissioners sternly refused. It appears that the company planned to use carriages with slatted shutters, or something of the kind, in place of windows. Coddington

---

[1] P.P. 1847–8, xxvi, 9.
[2] P.P. 1849, xxix, 9–18.
[3] MT 13/12, 20 Dec. 1849.
[4] E.g. P.P. 1851, xxx, 52.
[5] For these *Requirements*, see below, p. 182 ff.
[6] See below, p. 170.
[7] MT 11/10, 11 Mar. 1847.
[8] Ibid., 9 Mar. 1847.

pointed out the altitude of the line and the weather prevailing along it, and urged that the company should follow the example of many others in providing 'glazed windows for their third class passengers'. Drawings were sent of the carriages in use on the G.W.R., Midland, and L.S.W. railways, and the company was told that several companies 'having of their own accord as shown by the enclosed drawings adopted carriages of a very superior description to those proposed' their example had been followed on lines near the Lancaster & Carlisle. There must be glass to admit light when the carriages were closed against the weather, 'especially in exposed parts of the country'. The Commissioners eventually agreed to the company's plan to fit four glass panels in the roof of each carriage.[1]

Thus, at some cost in uniformity, the Commissioners encouraged the development of services for Parliamentary passengers considerably beyond the minimum required by the law. This policy was crowned in 1850 by extending the remission of duty to excursion trains, at the suggestion of the L. & Y., and in agreement with the Board of Inland Revenue. Circulars went out to companies, drawing their attention to the new concession, and setting out the conditions with which they must comply.[2] The new policy caused the Commissioners, and still more their successors in the Board of Trade, a great deal of work, since the details (fares, times, etc.) had usually to be considered for each train individually.

A case in which the Commissioners suffered a notable rebuff may be used to illustrate the exercise of their power to institute legal proceedings. In *Attorney-General* v. *G.W.R.* (1849–50), an injunction was sought to restrain the company from charging at a rate alleged to be higher than that sanctioned by their Acts. The background of the case was as follows. In November, 1846, the G.W.R. had bought the Birmingham, Wolverhampton & Dudley Railway, which was not yet built, and which the larger company had no power to purchase. The necessary power was conferred by the G.W.R. (Amendment & Extentions) Act, 1847, which also reduced the company's tolls and charges by roughly 25 per cent from the date of transfer of the Birmingham

[1] MT 11/9, 18 Dec. 1846. 11/10, 22 Feb., 27 Apr., and 14 May, 1847.
[2] P.P. 1851, xxx, 153–7. MT 13/13, 10 Aug. 1850. 13/14, 4 and 13 Nov. 1850.

line. The company did not deny that it was continuing to charge at the former rates, but asserted that the reduction should date, not from the purchase, but from the actual handing over, of the line. That could not yet take place, because the line was still not constructed. The court upheld the company's view of the law. The company need not reduce its charges, as the Attorney-General (for the Commissioners) had contended, from the date when the interest in the line transferred from one company to the other, but only for the date in the future when it took possession.[1]

The new duties imposed on the Commissioners must now be considered. In 1847 the House of Commons adopted a Standing Order (No. 127) under which any company seeking powers of amalgamation, purchase, sale, or lease, had first to obtain a certificate of its paid-up capital from the Commissioners.[2] Applications were normally referred to the Secretary,[3] and although most went through as a matter of course, it was occasionally necessary to refuse.[4] In any case, detailed enquiry and checking was often necessary. Apropos an enquiry from the Coventry, Nuneaton, Birmingham & Leicester Railway, which wished to lease its line to the Midland, the Commissioners minuted somewhat indignantly 'write to the company and state that the Directors are mistaken in supposing' that certificates had been granted automatically 'in all cases . . . without further enquiry into the items of the accounts. That the Commissioners have in many instances required further information, and have occasionally refused to grant certificates.'[5]

Few new powers were given to the Commissioners by legislation, and of those few, the most important were temporary powers to deal with problems left by the Railway Mania. An Act of 1847[6] empowered them to extend the time during which companies might exercise their powers, provided they applied by 20 February 1848,[7] and complied with certain conditions. In judging whether these conditions had been complied with, the Commissioners exercised judicial functions. As an example of

[1] Law Journal (Exchequer), xix, (1849–50), 407–9. *Herapath's Railway Magazine*, xi (1849), 623–4, and xii (1850), 580.
[2] O. C. Williams, op. cit. (1948–9), ii, 183.
[3] E.g. MT 13/9, 31 Jan. 1848.
[4] MT 13/11, 5 Feb. 1849.   [5] Ibid., 21 Apr. 1849.
[6] 11 & 12 Vict., c. 3.   [7] Ibid., s. 1.

the procedure adopted, let us follow the application made by the Liverpool, Manchester & Newcastle-upon-Tyne Junction Railway on 8 January, 1848. The company was told to give notice as required by the Act, and was presumably among the ninety-nine circularised on 26 February. These were asked to inform the Commissioners, for a return to the House of Commons, when the required notice had been given, and to send:

(a) copies of the newspapers in which notices had been inserted.
(b) a copy of the notice affixed to church doors in the locality.
(c) a declaration before a magistrate as to the manner in which the Act had been complied with, giving a list of the churches where notices had been exhibited, and stating that there were no other churches in the locality.

It is worth noting in passing that the compilation of such returns was a duty that took up a great deal of the Commissioners' (and the Department's) time throughout the period.

By the end of April, the company was becoming anxious because it had heard nothing and wrote to ask the reason for the delay. The Commissioners replied that objections had been filed, a copy of which would be supplied if necessary, and that the company would have the chance to give a written answer or to see the Commissioners on the subject. They were dealing with unopposed applications first. The objections were evidently dealt with, for the company at last got a warrant for extension of time on 10 July, 1848.[1]

Some cases were more complicated than this. The S.E.R., for example, was bound to complete a particular line within three years, and in case of failure to comply, to pay no dividends unless authorised by Parliament to do so. When the company applied for more time, the Commissioners held themselves precluded from issuing a warrant, since it would be a means of evading a specific penalty, relief from which had been reserved to Parliament.[2] Thus even if there were no objections, these applications called for careful study of companies' legal powers. Objections might be met by special provisions in the warrant. In one case, for example, the extension of time during which a company might purchase the land of one named individual was

[1] MT 11/12, 15 Jan., 26 Feb., 25 and 27 Apr., 1848. MT 13/10, 15 May, 1848. MT 11/13, 10 July, 1848.
[2] MT 13/9, 26 Feb. 1848.

limited to a shorter period than that allowed for the exercise of its other powers.[1]

The exercise of these temporary powers involved the Commissioners in a great deal of work. 594 of the 2,054 letters written in 1848 relate to extension of time,[2] and the business dragged on well into 1849. In all, 106 companies made applications relating to 3,650 miles of line; 4 were refused, 2 withdrawn and 129 approved prior to 1 May, 1849, at which date 12 were still under consideration.[3]

The procedure adopted for the issue of warrants of abandonment under the Act of 1850[4] was very similar and need not be described in detail. A typical application was that made by the Dunblane, Doune & Callander Railway on 19 September, 1850. The company was required to advertise its intentions in the *Edinburgh Gazette* and in one paper in each county through which the proposed line was to have passed for three successive weeks. It was also required to fix notices to church doors in the locality for three successive Sundays. The closing date for objections was 30 October, 1850, and the Commissioners, having considered the company's case 'and all such objections thereto as have been brought before us' issued their warrant on 21 November, 1850.[5]

One of the main complaints against the Railway Board was the secrecy of their proceedings.[6] The Commissioners were influenced by a desire to avoid a similar accusation. When handling a case in which more than one company was interested it was their practice to send a copy of any communication received from one to each of the others. This is brought out clearly in their exercise of powers originally conferred on the Board of Trade by the Oxford & Rugby Act, 1845, to regulate the gauge on that line. It was promoted by the G.W.R. as a broad-gauge line, to which the Board ordered the narrow gauge to be added, calling on the company to submit a plan showing how they proposed to carry out this order. All this was in July, 1846. The Commissioners, as successors to the Board, applied

---

[1] MT 13/10, 17 Aug. 1848.   [2] MT 11/12 and 13 *passim*.
[3] P.P. 1849, xxvii, 279. For a complete list of applications, see P.P. 1847-8, lxiii, 25-48.
[4] 13 & 14 Vict., c. 83.   [5] MT 6/8.
[6] See above, p. 81.

again to the company in December, 1846, and January, 1847. Between that month and March, 1847, they received first Brunel's report, then drawings to illustrate it, and lastly a model. One of the Commissioners (presumably Brandreth) and an inspector then examined a section of line laid on the mixed gauge. The Commissioners now decided 'that it would not be consistent with their duty to sanction the plan . . . without previously referring it to parties connected with the narrow gauge interests (for whose benefit the enactment in question had been inserted in the Act)'. A copy of Brunel's report was, therefore, sent to the L.N.W.R. in April, 1847. Robert Stephenson's reply did not arrive until July. That the L.N.W.R. was aware of the Commissioners' practice is shown by the fact that a second copy followed 'for the use of the G.W.' which was duly sent on. In August the latter company told the Commissioners that it declined to make any further statement. But by then it was the 'season when it is usual for. . . the officers of public departments to take their annual vacation'. In December, their decision was still awaited and the G.W.R. not unreasonably complained of the delay—a rare case of such a complaint, but partially justified. It is clear, however, that the delay between July, 1846, and March, 1847, was the fault of the G.W.R. itself, while the delay between March and August, 1847, was due to the Commissioners' anxiety not to give their ruling without consultation with the other party principally interested in the case.[1]

A similar attitude prevailed in the Commissioners' interviews with deputations from companies—interviews which easily resolved themselves into hearings before what would today be called an administrative tribunal. For example, the Commissioners were empowered[2] to approve the plans for a bridge which the L.B.S.C.R. was to erect over Trundleys Lane, Deptford. They received deputations from the company and the road trustees. After the deputations had given a general statement of their views, 'the parties retired with Colonel Alderson', the engineering member. He heard the technical evidence, and returned alone to inform his colleagues what safeguards he thought proper. The Commissioners then called in the deputations again and gave their ruling, incorporating the safeguards

[1] For a summary of the entire case, see MT 13/8, 17 Dec. 1847.
[2] Under 8 & 9 Vict., c. 20, s. 66.

recommended.[1] When deputations were received separately, the Commissioners showed themselves determined to be fair to absent parties. For example, in a dispute involving the G.W.R. and the O.W.W., the latter offered to hand in a copy of counsel's opinion on the case. Ryan declined to receive the papers 'except as public documents which might be communicated to all parties interested'.[2]

Most of the cases discussed here have been chosen as representative of various classes of business. Some cases of an unrepresentative kind are also of sufficient interest to warrant inclusion. One such was an application from the L. & Y. for help in its financial difficulties. It sought the assistance of the Commissioners to obtain four things, namely:

(1) a government loan.
(2) power to pay interest on calls.
(3) power to renew loan notes beyond the date fixed by the Act of 1844.
(4) suspension of Standing Orders for a Bill to reshape the company's capital structure.

The Commissioners adopted Ryan's minute on this application, and turned down the company's first three requests. They suggested that the loan notes should be converted to debentures, as the company had power to do. With regard to the fourth point, the Commissioners undertook that, if the Committee on Standing Orders let the Bill through, they would not oppose it.[3]

An important feature of railway development in the period dealt with in this chapter was the growth of control by railway companies over harbours and shipping services. This led to an extension of the Commissioners' powers over bye-laws. After taking the opinion of the Law Officers, they decided that their power to disallow bye-laws applied to these made by the S.E.R. for Folkestone Harbour.[4] Another result was that the Commissioners came in touch with the Steamship Owners Association, from whom they received deputations opposing the grant of powers to operate steamships to railway companies.[5] As the powers of government departments increased interest groups—

[1] MT 13/9, 20 Mar. 1848.   [2] MT 13/12, 1 Nov. 1849.
[3] MT 13/10, 15 May, 1848. 11/12, 20 and 29 May, 1848.
[4] MT 13/8, 6 Dec. 1847. P.P. 1847–8, xxvi, 16.
[5] MT 13/9, 11 Feb. 1848. Cf. 13/7, 17 May, 1847.

including of course the railway interest itself—were quick to
see the importance of consultation with them. Unfortunately,
although the records of the Commissioners provide evidence of
such consultation taking place, they give only a bare outline of
what was said.

In another unusual case, an attempt was made to involve the
Commissioners in a labour dispute, on the grounds that public
safety was at stake. The issue raised was similar to that in the
North Midland case discussed above,[1] and looks forward to the
legislation relating to hours and conditions of work on the railway at the end of the century. In August, 1848, a Mr. J. Brown
wrote from the Railway Tavern, Hampstead Road, London, to
ask the Commissioners to receive a deputation of L.N.W.
drivers in reference to a dispute between them and their employers. They refused to see the deputation, but promised to
write to the company 'as it is stated . . . that the public safety is
endangered by the present state of things'. The company
replied that 'due measures have been taken for the public
safety', and kept the Commissioners informed about the progress of the strike. The Commissioners suspected that the strike
was a factor in at least one accident, and reported that it might
yet be necessary to set up a scheme of licensing drivers,[2] such as
had been contemplated in 1841.

The period 1846–51 was not important from the point of view
of legislation. It is true that the Bill introduced by Strutt in
1847, as promised when the Commissioners were set up, would
have given them certain new powers. But those powers were
mainly to enable them to prepare reports on railway Bills,
which was originally to have been the principal function of the
Commissioners. Such reports had been prepared without the
proposed powers, and continued to be prepared after the failure
of the Bill. Their effect on private legislation was limited, primarily because the attention paid to them by Select Committees
was limited, not because of lack of power to obtain the necessary
information. The failure of the Bill was, therefore probably less
important in its effects than a reading of the text would suggest.[3]

[1] See above, pp. 47–8.
[2] MT 11/13, 4 Aug. 1848. 13/10, 11 and 14 Aug. 1848. P.P. 1849, xxvii,
281–2.   [3] P.P. 1847, iii, 415 ff. Hansard, lxxxviii, 847.

The reasons for its failure are of some interest, nevertheless. When it was introduced, almost six years had passed since the last general election, and it was realised that the next could not be long delayed. It was, therefore, a very favourable opportunity for the railway interest to oppose the Bill. Parliamentary debates give only a very imperfect impression of the strength of this opposition. By direct consultation, the railway interest persuaded Strutt substantially to amend his Bill between the first and second readings.[1] Not satisfied with that, the chairmen of nine important companies formed a committee to oppose the measure at second reading. They drew up a statement of their case, 'in order that the main objections which they entertain . . . might be brought more clearly under the notice of those most interested in railway property'. Interested parties should let M.P.'s know their views before the second reading. At least one company sent its shareholders copies of this statement on the Bill, with a covering letter urging them to 'use *every exertion* . . . in causing its rejection'.[2]

The second reading debate took place in June—four months after the Bill was introduced. Strutt announced that pressure of business and the threat of obstructive opposition had induced the government to withdraw the Bill until next session.[3] In their Annual Report, the Commissioners stressed the first of these reasons to the exclusion of the second.[4] The Bill was never in fact brought in again, and it seems clear that the opposition of the railway interest was the main reason for its failure.

Other measures were promoted independently of the Commissioners. In many private Members' Bills relating to railways, they appear to have had no hand, and they explicitly disclaimed all responsibility for Lord Monteagle's Railway Audit Bill of 1848.[5]

In promoting two measures which extended their powers— the Railways (Extension of Time) Act, 1847, and the Railways (Abandonment) Act, 1806—the Commissioners were encouraged by a number of companies; any generalisation that private parties always opposed the extension of powers of public bodies,

[1] P.P. 1847, iii, 453 ff. Hansard, xciii, 762.   [2] BTHR EC 4/2/7.
[3] Hansard, xciii, 778–9.   [4] P.P. 1847–8, xxvi, 47.
[5] MT 11/12, 17 Jan. 1848.
[6] 11 & 12 Vict., c. 3, and 13 & 14 Vict., c. 83.

though plausible, would not be true. In October, 1847, for example, a deputation from the Liverpool, Manchester & New-castle-upon-Tyne Junction Railway were asking whether the Commissioners would introduce a general Act for extension of time to save companies the expense of separate private Bills.[1] Other companies made similar suggestions.[2] Since the powers conferred were for a limited period only, a second Bill was proposed by the Stirling & Dunfermline Railway a year later.[3] However, this proposal was not adopted. Similarly, the Direct London & Portsmouth Company urged the Commissioners to bring the Railways (Abandonment) Bill, which had failed in 1849, in again in the following session.[4] This was done, though there is, of course, no reason to suppose that the company's advocacy was decisive.

More important than the public legislation for which the Commissioners were responsible was their influence on private railway Bills. It was exerted in spite of their failure to secure the powers contemplated in the Bill of 1847. In that session reports were presented on the railway Bills generally; but they had to be prepared at very short notice,[5] and, in subsequent sessions, different methods were adopted. In some cases, committee chairmen sought the Commissioners' advice. They suggested, for example, that the Aberdeen Railway should be allowed to raise additional capital, but that the proposed guaranteed dividend of 10 per cent was too high, and that it should not take preference over previous guarantes. In a Bill promoted by the Bristol & Exeter Railway, a maximum figure for any one call, and a minimum interval between calls, should be fixed.[6] Sometimes, the Commissioners influenced directly parties interested in Bills. For example, clauses relating to tolls which it had been proposed to introduce into a Bill to give the L.N.W. and the L. & Y. a joint interest in the Preston & Wyre Company were objectionable to the Commissioners, and Ryan secured a promise that they would be withdrawn.[7]

In March, 1849, Barron presented a report to the Commissioners on the principles which should guide their supervision of

---

[1] MT 13/8, 13 Oct. 1847.   [2] Ibid., 25 Oct. and 4 Nov. 1847.
[3] MT 13/10, 25 Oct. 1848.   [4] MT 13/12, 19 Oct. 1849.
[5] MT 11/10, 3 Mar. 1847. P.P. 1847, xxxi, 207 ff. (74 reports).
[6] MT 11/12, 6 Jun. 1848.   [7] MT 13/11, 2 Apr. 1849.

private railway Bills.[1] The most important of these principles was that companies should not amend the general law of railways in their own favour. In 1842, for example, it had been held in *Pickford* v. *G.J. Railway* that, where a number of parcels were contained in one large package, companies must charge for it as a single item, and not at the rate applicable to the parcels individually. In 1846, however, the Y.N.B. took power to charge for each parcel, even if they were contained in one package,[2] in spite of a last-minute attempt by Clarendon to prevent it doing so.[3] The M.S.L. included a similar clause in a Bill in 1849, but the Commissioners recommended that it be struck out, with a reference to the appropriate paragraph of Barron's report.[4] Another general rule incorporated in his report was that wherever a company was given power to construct a level crossing, the Commissioners should be given power to order a bridge in its place, should public safety require it. The Board of Trade had tried—unsuccessfully—to secure such a power as early as 1842,[5] and clauses similar in purpose had been included in some Acts of 1847.[6] Now the Commissioners pressed for their insertion in Bills from which they had been omitted.[7] These examples are typical of the way in which they went through Bills in the light of Barron's report. How much effect did such influence have? That question is discussed more fully below.[8] We may note, however, that of the five recommendations mentioned above, four were adopted wholly, and the fifth partially, in the relevant Acts.[9] What is stressed here is the fact that, in spite of the failure of the 1847 Bill,[10] supervision of private legislation went on by more discreet means.

---

[1] MT 13/11, 24 Mar. 1849.   [2] MT 11/14, 21 Jun. 1849.
[3] Hansard, lxxxviii, 697.   [4] MT 13/11, 21 Jun. 1849.
[5] See above, p. 53.   [6] P.P. 1847–8, xxvi, 24.
[7] MT 13/11, 30 Apr. 1849.   [8] See below, p. 156 ff.
[9] 11 & 12 Vict., c. 67 (Local & Personal) s. 1. Ibid., c. 77 (Local & Personal), s. 19 or c. 82 (Local & Personal), s. 30; the recommendation may have referred to either of these Acts promoted by the Bristol & Exeter Company. 12 & 13 Vict., c. 58 (Local & Personal), s. 20. Ibid., c. 74 (Local & Personal), and c. 81 (Local & Personal) do not contain the clauses to which the Commissioners had objected.
[10] See above, p. 126.

5

THE RAILWAY DEPARTMENT
1851—1867

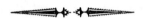

I N 1851, the government again came under pressure in
Parliament to economise by abolishing the Commissioners
of Railways.[1] As a result, responsibility for railways reverted
from the Commissioners to the Board of Trade, under an Act
which took effect from 10 October, 1851.[2] The Board took
advantage of the power conferred to employ the staff of the
Commissioners,[3] and so there was no break in continuity such
as had taken place in 1846. The officers transferred constituted
afresh the Railway Department of the Board.

Simmons served as its first head. In October, 1853, however,
he went on leave to Eastern Europe. Caught up in the events
leading up to the Crimean War, he accepted military employment, overstayed his leave, and sent in his resignation in June,
1854.[4] Galton took his place, at first as Acting Secretary, and
from 1855 onwards, as Assistant Secretary;[5] i.e., assistant to
Booth, the Joint Secretary who was responsible for the Department. On Galton's transfer to other duties in 1859, he was
succeeded, not by an engineering officer, but by MacGregor,
who had worked his way up on the clerical side of the Department. At first, he seems to have had no official title, though
eventually he was referred to as the 'Assistant to the Secretary
in the Railway Division'.[6] On the retirement of Booth, Fane,

---

[1] Hansard, cxvii, 1293-4. See also p. 106, above.
[2] 14 & 15 Vict., c. 64, s. 1.   [3] Ibid., s. 2.
[4] D.N.B.   [5] MT 13/20, 147/1854, and 18/1855.
[6] Royal Kalendar, 1864, 164.

the Legal Assistant, took charge of the Department for a time. He was responsible, not to one of the Joint Secretaries, but directly to the President.[1] Finally, at the close of the period, Herbert became head of the Department. Northcote had offered him the post some time before, on the recommendation of C. W. Fremantle, one of Disraeli's private secretaries. But Herbert declined it at first, because of his obligations as Crown Agent for Queensland.[2]

Two inspectors, Wynne and Laffan, transferred from the Commissioners to the Department. Laffan was elected to Parliament as Member for St. Ives in 1852. There were two circumstances about his resignation which throw light on the political activities of public servants a century ago. Far from requiring him to resign on being adopted as a candidate, the Board persuaded him to postpone doing so 'for the convenience of the public service' and at 'some personal inconvenience to himself'. And when he did give up his post, he did so, not on the ground that there would be anything improper in continuing, but because his duties in the House 'would interfere too much with those of an Inspector of Railways to permit me to retain that appointment either with satisfaction to myself or advantage to the public service'.[3]

Galton, who had been assistant to Simmons, replaced Laffan. In 1853, the establishment of inspectors was increased to three, and the new post was given to Tyler.[4] When Galton succeeded Simmons in 1854, he was replaced by Yolland.[5] Ross took over from Wynne in 1858, and was succeeded in his turn by Rich three years later.[6] In the last year of our period, the establishment rose to four inspectors, and Hutchinson was appointed to make up the number.

In 1867 an incident occurred which, like Laffan's election, illustrates the latitude permitted to public servants in the nineteenth century. At that period, one of the most influential of British railway magnates, Sir Edward Watkin, was chairman of the Grand Trunk Railway of Canada. Its shareholders were

[1] P.P. 1867, xxxix, 217.
[2] Disraeli Papers. Fremantle-Disraeli, 31 Dec. 1866.
[3] BT 1/498/1827. A/52.   [4] MT 13/19, 511.
[5] MT 13/20, 165/1854.
[6] *Royal Kalendar, 1859,* 164; *Royal Kalendar, 1862,* 164.

critical of its financial results and management; now they found a powerful spokesman in one of the railway inspectors, Tyler. Almost immediately he was elected to the board of directors. His double life did not seriously harm his career, for in 1870 he was made the first Chief Inspecting Officer of Railways. He became Vice-President of the railway, and it was not until 1877, after being elected President, that he finally resigned from the Board of Trade.[1]

The Commissioners' Legal Assistant, Barron, held the same position in the Department. From 1853, his responsibility was broadened, and he dealt with legal business for the Board as a whole. He served until 1855 or 1856, when he was succeeded by W. D. Fane,[2] who held the post until the last year of our period. MacGregor served as Registrar of the Department, having held similar posts in the former Department and under the Commissioners. In 1853, however, his work was handed over to a newly appointed Registrar for the Board as a whole, and he became a senior clerk.

There were eight clerks shortly after the Department was re-formed.[3] It is not clear how many there were in 1867, but since it was suggested that six would be enough,[4] it is clear that there can have been no substantial change in the actual number over the period. It is unnecessary to say much about them except that they seem to have been well above the average in ability. The general level of clerks in public offices during the period was notoriously low, and in the Board of Trade there were senior clerks who were only capable of the work of junior clerks.[5] Galton's successor, MacGregor, had started as a clerk.[6] McKenzie, who had been his sole colleague in the early days of the Department, was recommended for a personal allowance of £100 a year, because of the outstanding value of his work.[7] Other appointments held by former clerks in the Department include: Assistant in the Statistical Department, Private Secretary to the Vice-President, Deputy Accountant, and Librarian.[8]

[1] A. W. Currie, *Grand Trunk Railway of Canada*, Toronto (1957), 113, 152, and 233; and the same author's 'Sir Edward Watkin: a Canadian View', in *Journal of Transport History*, iii (1957–8), 36.

[2] *Post Office London Dir. 1857*, 95. [3] *Royal Kalendar, 1852*, 160.

[4] P.P. 1867, xxxix, 224. [5] Ibid., 228.

[6] *Royal Kalendar, 1843*, 163. [7] P.P. 1867, xxxix, 230.

[8] *Post Office London Dir. 1854*, 46; ibid. *1857*, 96; *Royal Kalendar, 1864*, 164.

Such was the staff. A report made in 1853 gives a picture of their mode of work.[1] The report itself was an important document. Prepared by Sir Charles Trevelyan, Sir Stafford Northcote, and Booth, it formed part of the wider enquiry into the work of the public offices then in progress, and led on to the celebrated Northcote-Trevelyan report on the civil service.[2] From the point of view of this study, however, its main interest lies in the description it gives of the Department, rather than in the changes proposed. It confirms the conclusion reached above, that under the Commissioners there had come into being a distinction between cases decided by the officers and cases reserved for decision by the Commissioners themselves.[3] But there were now three, rather than two, levels of decision, since one of the Joint Secretaries, Booth, interposed between the Department and the President. Thus the working of the Department was profoundly different from what it had been in the period, 1840–6. Then the political heads of the Board had been closely in touch with all the railway business. Although the officers had had great influence on questions of the highest importance, there had been no class of routine business in which the political heads normally took no part. Of the period 1844–6, in particular, it was true to say that the Department's decisions were Dalhousie's decisions. A paper which did not bear his instructions for action was so unusual as to call for explanation.[4]

The form of the surviving records, as well as their content, reflects the new mode of transacting business. At first, minutes were kept in books which appear to record decisions taken at meetings of a hypothetical railway committee of the Board of Trade. Minutes of this kind for 1852 totalled 2,123, as compared with approximately 3,400 papers received. Hence the decision in almost two-thirds of the cases dealt with, including many of a trivial and routine character, was recorded in a formal minute. Certain features of the minutes, however, make it very doubtful whether they record the proceedings of genuine meetings. There

---

[1] P.P. 1854, xxvii, 161–90.

[2] For the background of this report, see E. Hughes, 'Sir Charles Trevelyan & Civil Service Reform', in *English Historical Review*, lxiv (1949), 60–1; and the same author's 'Civil Service Reform', in *Public Administration*, xxxii (1954), 31.

[3] See above, p. 107 ff.

[4] MT 13/3, 5 Sept. 1845.

was normally no record of attendances, and the minutes were not signed by the President or Vice-President. Simmons signed the first few sets, but from early in 1852 they were not signed at all. Certain minutes in a different form strengthen the impression that it was unusual for the political heads of the Board to take part in railway business. For example, the minute appointing Galton to Simmons' post departs from the usual course by mentioning that Cardwell was present on that occasion.[1] Thus the minute books afford no evidence that the President or Vice-President took part in making the decisions recorded, though at the same time, they do not prove that they took no part.

Minute books were kept until 1856, but there was a sharp decline in the number of decisions they record, with no corresponding decline in the number of papers received. Minutes for 1856 totalled 241, as compared with approximately 3,800 documents registered. The explanation is that an alternative method of recording decisions had come into existence as from 1 July, 1853. The papers retained from the first half of that year were treated in the manner that had been usual since 1840; that is, they were folded in four, and any comments written on the blank side left exposed. Those of the second half of the year have had attached to them a minute sheet with a printed heading, 'Board of Trade Railway Department'.[2] On these sheets the officers of the Department, sometimes the Joint Secretary, and, very occasionally, the President or Vice-President, wrote their comments. At the same time, a similar change took place in the style of the minutes kept in books.[3] The minute of the Department had taken on the form now normally associated with the civil service.

It is thus possible to trace the progress of each case towards a decision. Unfortunately, only a very small proportion of the items registered each year have been preserved. For 1853, for example, only forty-nine items have been kept, whereas over four thousand items were registered that year. Nor is it clear on what basis those retained were selected; from the fact that of the forty-nine mentioned, none date from March or June, whereas eleven date from December, it seems likely that it was in part at

[1] MT 13/20, 29 Jun. 1854.   [2] MT 6/10.   [3] MT 13/20.

least a matter of chance. It is, however, reasonable to assume that those kept were, generally speaking, more important than those destroyed. Since only a small proportion of these cases were decided on by the President or Vice-President, it seems reasonable to assume, therefore, that the proportion of such cases to the whole business of the Department was no larger, and was most probably a good deal smaller.

Even before the minute books were given up, another series of the Department's records had come to an end, namely the out-letter books. Dating from the foundation of the Department in 1840, they expired in January, 1855. From that date, it is necessary to rely mainly on a single series, the correspondence and papers. When the custom of keeping copies of letters sent in a book ceased, the approved draft, or a copy, was kept with the original paper and its minute sheet instead. As time went on, the files thus formed tended to grow in size. Departmental memoranda and replies from companies were added; the minute sheet developed into a cover. The final development dates from January, 1864, from which date numbers of files on the same question were attached together, with the most recent uppermost. By the close of our period in 1867, many of the files retained are of considerable bulk. A single box suffices to hold one hundred and twenty-two retained files of 1856.[1] One of the six boxes dating from 1867, on the other hand, contains only ten files.[2]

The lowest of the three levels of decision was the Department itself. There

> the management of the details is entrusted to an Assistant Secretary, who examines the correspondence of the day, prepares the information necessary for arriving at a decision, and brings the whole of the important business in a convenient shape before the Chief Secretary, who gives him instructions upon which it becomes his duty to act. The Assistant Secretary disposes, on his own authority, of matters of smaller moment, and takes such intermediate proceedings in preparing a question for the decision of the Chief Secretary as his experience suggests.[3]

The phrase 'matter of smaller moment' seems to have been used in a strictly relative sense; they included cases relating to the opening of lines, which involved the exercise of the Board's

---

[1] MT 6/13. [2] MT 6/46. [3] P.P. 1854, xxvii, 166.

most important power. For example, it was Galton who authorised the opening of the Deeside Railway in 1853.[1] But Galton was at least an engineer; it is more surprising to find his successor, MacGregor, who was a promoted clerk, making a similar decision. Yet he appears to have ordered the Dundee, Perth & Aberdeen Railway to postpone the opening of its line in 1860. Although the file is marked for reference to Farrer and Booth, there is no indication that either of them saw it.[2]

Where reference to a higher level than that of the Department was required, a clerk would enter on the minute sheet the names of the men who were to see the file. As it circulated, each person would add his comments opposite his name, or if he had none, merely his initials. In the absence of either comment or initials it is reasonable to suppose that the individual named had not in fact seen the file. As MacGregor himself wrote on one occasion, when referring a case to an inspector, 'please write something on this to show that you have seen it'.[3]

An illustration of this process will also provide an example of a decision taken at the second level, that of the Joint Secretary. Minute 789 of 1853 reads:

789: Umpire.
Read No. 2128, 8 July, 1853.
Mr. W. G. Roy, inclosing joint application from the arbitrators in a matter in dispute between the L.N.W.R. and Shrewsbury & Birmingham Railway Companies . . . for the appointment of an umpire and suggesting that the umpire should be Mr. John Hawkshaw.
Refer to Mr. Barron; see no objection to the appointment of Mr. Hawkshaw. J. L. A. S[immons].
Mr. Barron thinks that the . . . appointment . . . rests with the Board of Trade, and recommends that an appointment should be sent to the umpire and communicated to each company.
Mr. Booth concurs in this suggestion.[4]

Appropriate letters were written on 13 July, 1853. Booth could, moreover, give a decision in cases which had been referred to the President. In October, 1864, for example, the Department had been waiting almost a month for the President's ruling on the new Batley branch of the Leeds, Bradford & Halifax Junction Railway. At last, Booth gave permission for it to open, and

[1] MT 6/10, 3136/1853.
[2] MT 6/22, 3378/1860.
[3] MT 6/38, 563/1866.
[4] MT 13/20, 789/1853.

someone wrote on the file, 'Mr. Booth directed this should go forward without Mr. Gibson's seeing it'.[1]

The highest level of decision within the Board was, of course, that of the President and Vice-President. The holders of those offices were, for the most part, men of ability, and two of them served for much longer than it is usual for British statesmen to stay in one office. These were Lord Stanley of Alderley from 1852 to 1858, first as Vice-President and then as President; and Milner Gibson, who was President from 1859 to 1866. Thus they had time to acquire a thorough knowledge of railway problems. The most distinguished President during the period covered by this chapter, Cardwell, served for only a little more than two years. His influence was reduced, moreover, by his exclusion from Aberdeen's coalition Cabinet, on the grounds that the size of the Peelite contingent should be related to their voting strength rather than to their ability. As President, too, he was responsible for the preparation of the highly important Merchant Marine Act of 1855. There is little doubt that, had he stayed longer at the Board, he would have made a more worthy contribution to railway policy than his Railway & Canal Traffic Act.[2]

What was the particular rôle of the President and Vice-President in the Department's work? For the period, 1840-6, such a question would have been meaningless. Then there had been no classes of business habitually reserved for the political heads of the Board, just as there were none in which they normally took no part. But, from 1851 onwards, the permanent officers decided the great majority of cases. It becomes important, therefore, to distinguish the kinds of business which were dealt with at the highest level.

The most obvious was the Parliamentary business, including the defence of the Department. As the Board's representatives in Parliament were no longer in close touch with the Department's routine work, they sometimes revealed a surprising ignorance of what was going on there. For example, the charge was made in the House of Commons in 1861 that as soon as 'the inspectors had acquired a certain knowledge of railways they were removed to other appointments' and that they were 'of little use

[1] MT 6/32, 2033/1864.   [2] Cleveland-Stevens, 191 ff.

because they were so constantly changed'. This was quite untrue. Although one change had just been made, the other two
inspectors had served since 1853 and 1854 respectively. Yet
Milner Gibson let the damaging accusation pass unrefuted. In
the same debate, he defended the decision not to replace Galton
by another engineer on the extraordinary ground that 'questions of science did not now often arise'.[1] As will be shown in the
next chapter, 'questions of science', such as telegraph working,
interlocking signals, and continuous brakes were by 1861 more
important in the work of the Department than ever before.

A proportion of the surviving files contain evidence that they
were referred to the political heads of the Board for decision.
How were they selected? One of the thirty-eight surviving from
the second half of 1853 may serve as an example.[2] A portion of
the Oxford, Worcester & Wolverhampton Railway had been
inspected prior to opening, and Booth recommended postponement. Cardwell added his initials, and the words 'to be signed
by Mr. Booth'—presumably to impress on the company the
solemnity of the decision. It is easy to see why this case should
have gone so high. The opening had already been postponed
several times. Both the G.W.R. and the L.N.W.R. were keenly
interested in the line, and since they possessed great Parliamentary influence, mishandling of the case might be politically
dangerous. Lord Redesdale, who lived near the line, also took a
close interest in it. As Lord Chairman of Committees in the
House of Lords, he was a figure of too much importance in
railway affairs to be ignored.[3]

One of the most important activities of the President was to
receive deputations. If full records of these meetings were made
at the time, they no longer survive. Thus, the form of the evidence may lead us to underrate the importance of the President
as decision maker. For example, between the second reading
and the committee stage of the Railway & Canal Traffic Bill,
Cardwell had amended his own measure so radically that it was
virtually a new Bill. The jurisdiction which he originally proposed to give to an administrative tribunal under the Board
of Trade was now to go to the courts. These changes had not

[1] Hansard, clxi, 1822 and 1830–1.
[2] MT 6/10, 4175/1853.
[3] For the outcome of this case, see below, p. 165.

been made in Parliament, but outside, as a result, he said, of a conference with spokesmen for the railway interest.[1] In 1861, Milner Gibson received a deputation of engine drivers, who sought a statutory limit on their hours of work in the interest (partly, at least) of public safety. The evidence for this incident is his reply to a question in the House.[2] The records of the Department are silent. The incident forms a link between the Department's earlier concern with labour questions[3] and the legislation on railwaymen's hours at the end of the century. Certain accident reports, which mention excessive hours of work as a factor harmful to safety, also testify to the Department's continuing interest in labour matters.

In the light of subsequent developments in administrative law, the function of the President as a court of appeal deserves notice. An early example has been noted already[4] but its development dates from the period after 1851. The statutes from which the Board derived its powers over railways gave no formal right of appeal against its decisions; though had a Bill of 1855 become law, there would have come into existence a power to order a company to replace any level crossing by a bridge, subject to appeal to the Judicial Committee of the Privy Council.[5]

The lack of any right of appeal was pointed out in an unusual report to the N.E.R. in 1857. The Department had held up the opening of its Bishop Auckland branch for three months, when, by way of protest, they asked the eminent engineer G. P. Bidder to give his opinion on it. The interest of the report lies, not in its engineering views which contradict, as one might expect, those of the Department's inspector at every point, but in his remarks on the Department's discretionary powers. 'The annoyance and loss', he stated, 'to which the N.E.R. Co. have been exposed . . . justifies [sic] me in making a few remarks beyond the ordinary range of a professional report.' It was unfair to deprive the public of the use of lines and the companies of revenue, but he regretted that he could suggest no remedy:

The law affords you none! There is no appeal against . . . an inspector's report except to the tribunal of which he is the officer

[1] Hansard, cxxxii, 1247.
[2] Ibid., clxii, 1063–4.
[3] See above pp. 47–8 and 125.
[4] See above, p. 91.
[5] P.P. 1854–5, i, 17.

and which may feel itself bound to uphold his report. Equity provides a remedy for every other public wrong . . . and the accumulation of cases . . . certainly ought to convince the legislature of the propriety of allowing a reference in all these matters to some really competent tribunal.[1]

There was no general rule as to the circumstances in which a company might appeal from the inspector's decision to the President of the Board. Each application seems to have been decided on its merits. When Stanley agreed to see Lord Lonsdale on the business of the Whitehaven & Furness, and the Whitehaven, Cleator & Egremont Railways, his decision to do so probably reflected the importance of Lord Lonsdale, who was a director of both companies, rather than the importance of the business he wished to discuss.[2] Discussion often turned on technical points, on which it would have been easy for the company's representatives to bemuse a layman. Hence Northcote's stipulation in a case where the inspector had required turn-tables as a condition of opening a line, that he would see representatives of the company provided Yolland could be present too. In this case, Northcote supported the inspector. His minute reads: 'Inform the parties that my Lords have carefully considered the question of the use of turntables and have come to the conclusion that they must be required in the case of any line of railway which exceeds five miles in length. Regret that they cannot depart from this decision in the present case'.[3] Another decision in a similar case only a few months later shows how arbitrary and capricious such decisions could be. The Duke of Richmond received an officer of the G.N.R., on the subject of a turn-table at Spalding, which Tyler thought necessary, but which the company was unwilling to erect. 'I am sorry', he minuted, 'the G.N.Co. will not comply . . . but in as much as we could not compel the company to use it if it was there, I see no objection to opening the line.'[4]

From time to time, the Department was in negotiation with many other public offices. In the Colonial Office during the period covered by this study, consultation with other departments caused constant difficulty and delay.[5] In this respect, the

---

[1] MT 6/14, 1348/1857.
[2] Ibid., 14/1857.
[3] MT 6/46, 1057/1867.
[4] MT 6/47, 1748/1867.
[5] H. L. Hall, *Colonial Office*, Longmans (1937), 28.

experience of the Railway Department was far happier. The probable explanation is that the initiative in consultation normally came from other branches of the public service, which needed advice or help; the Department was rarely dependent on other offices (with one important exception) in deciding its own course of action.

The exception was the Treasury. Although Treasury control of other offices was not universal in the 1840's[1] the Department was subject to it from the start. Examples of its operation have been given above.[2] Apart from salaries, the Department cost little to run; and on two occasions when representatives of the Treasury investigated its work, they recommended increases rather than reductions in the establishment.[3] It is true that the inspectors sometimes worked under considerable pressure; but this seems to have been the result of the irregularity of their duties.[4] Had there been enough to meet all calls at the busiest times, there would probably have been under-employment at slack periods. It appears, therefore, that Treasury control did not seriously hamper the Department's work.

It was normal to consult with the Admiralty about railway schemes which might endanger navigation, such as the Menai Bridge,[5] until 1864, when the responsibility was transferred from the Admiralty to the new Harbour Department of the Board of Trade itself. At the desire of the Home Office, Galton inspected the Crystal Palace after it had been re-erected on its permanent site.[6] The Department assisted the War Office to obtain the facilities accorded by law for the movement of troops

---

[1] E. Hughes, 'Sir Charles Trevelyan & Civil Service Reform, 1853–5', in *English Historical Review*, lxiv (1949), 54–5.

[2] See above, pp. 31–2.

[3] P.P. 1854, xxvii, 161 ff.; 1867, xxxix, 213 ff. These increases have already been noted in the first section of this chapter.

[4] The surviving records do not make possible the reconstruction of the inspectors' actual programme of work for specimen periods; but clearly, if committees of Parliament were waiting for reports on gradients and level crossings (see below, p. 160), if one inspector was in Ireland, investigating an accident, while another was due shortly to inspect a new line in Cornwall, the arrival of a notice from a company in the north of Scotland that a new line would be ready for inspection in ten days (see below, p. 150) might create great difficulty.

[5] MT 11/6, 23 Apr. 1845. S. Smiles, op. cit., 392.

[6] MT 13/20, 3 Jun. 1854.

by rail.[1] A statement of the law relating to the liability of railway companies to meet claims arising out of accidents was prepared, at the request of the Foreign Office, for the information
of an enquirer overseas.[2] The Department supplied the Post
Office with information and advice about the use of railways
for carrying mail. In 1854, for example, the Post Office wanted
the G.W.R. and its associated companies to accelerate the mail
to the west, and asked the Department to look into the objections raised against the proposal. Rowland Hill was told that
the attitude of the company was reasonable.[3] When the Department was contemplating legal action, it was necessary to act
through the Treasury Solicitor and the Law Officers; the latter
also gave advisory opinions on cases referred to them.[4] The
Department regularly reported on railway schemes for the
Colonial Office.[5] The remission of passenger duty on Parliamentary trains led to constant correspondence with the Board
of Inland Revenue, whose responsibility it was to collect the
duty. The Department and the Board did not see eye to eye
on all points. The Board challenged the Department's policy
of classing excursion trains as Parliamentary trains,[6] It was
natural that the Board should be zealous to protect the revenue.
On the other hand, the Department complained that the Board
sometimes remitted duty on trains which had not been approved.[7] In spite of occasional differences of this kind, it does
not appear that the Department's exercise of its powers was
materially hampered by this division of responsibility with the
Board of Inland Revenue. Indeed, the Department's work
seems to have been little affected in any way by other offices.

Although the greater part of the Department's work from
1851 onwards was of a routine nature, it took up much time,
and called for considerable care. The procedure relating to
Parliamentary trains may serve as an example. A company
which sought approval for its arrangements had to submit three
copies of its current time-table, with the relevant trains indicated by a red cross. When the Department had approved all

---

[1] MT 13/19, 12 and 23 Mar. 1853.
[2] MT 11/22, 22 Jul. 1852. [3] MT 11/27, 24 Mar. 1854.
[4] E.g. MT 11/27, 29 Mar. 1854. MT 6/12, 2636/1855.
[5] E.g. P.P. 1852-3, lv, 361. [6] MT 13/17, 8 Jun. 1852.
[7] MT 11/27, 16 Jun. 1854. And see below, p. 143.

the details, it returned one copy to the company, sent one to the Board of Inland Revenue, and kept the third for its own records.[1] Opportunity might be taken to check Parliamentary trains other than those for which approval was sought,[2] in case any should have been changed without notice.

The wide variety of grounds on which the Department refused to approve trains shows how carefully applications were scrutinised. Some examples may be tabulated:

(a) a child's excursion fare should be half the adult fare, i.e. 4½d instead of 5d.
(b) the Aberdeen Railway's train leaving Forfar at 11.45 a.m. was too early for passengers arriving there by the Scottish Midland Junction train at 11.50 a.m.
(c) details of an excursion had not been received before the date on which it was to run.
(d) an excursion fare was higher than the statutory limit.
(e) one of several trains was not shown to stop at one of the stations.
(f) G.N. through trains to Scotland, which ran over the N.B.R., could not be approved because the Department had withdrawn its approval of the N.B.R.'s own Parliamentary trains.[3]

In the period 1–20 January, 1855, taken at random, there were thirty-two applications from twenty-eight companies; the Department approved only nineteen outright.[4] When queries were raised, much delay might ensue. The West Cornwall Railway, for example, applied for retrospective remission of duty from the date of its first application. The Department pointed out that correspondence relating to its first application had extended over more than six months, and more than seven in a second case. The delay in securing remission of duty was, therefore, the company's own fault.[5] The amount of work was increased by the Department's readiness to approve more than the statutory minimum number of Parliamentary trains, and to class excursion trains as such. In 1854, for example, the Leeds Northern was running five daily in each direction.[6] In

[1] MT 11/20, 9 Nov. 1851.
[2] MT 11/25, 30 Jul. 1853.
[3] MT 11/25, 24 Aug. 1853. MT 13/17, 8 Jul. 1852. MT 11/28, 9 and 12 Aug. 1854. MT 11/30, 11 Jan. 1855. MT 13/21, 15 Feb. 1856.
[4] MT 11/30 *passim*.   [5] MT 11/23, 24 Dec. 1852.
[6] MT 11/27, 27 Apr. 1854.

the following year, almost 19,000 excursion trains were approved.[1] All these called for checking.

In enforcing the law relating to Parliamentary trains, the Department relied on the carrot of remission of duty rather than on the stick of legal action.[2] It was important, therefore, that the Board of Inland Revenue should not remit duty until the Department had approved a company's arrangements; since the requirements of the latter were the more exacting, it might be less easily satisfied than the former. For instance,

> in fixing the time of running the cheap trains, my Lords have always required that the hours selected should be those best suited for obtaining the benefits of through communications along different lines of railway for the lower class of passengers; and alterations in these often have the effect of preventing this through communication; and since the principal inducement for railway companies to adhere to the time of running the cheap trains at the hours sanctioned by this Department, is the pecuniary benefit which accrues to them from the remission of the passenger duty, my Lords are desirous that this subject should receive the consideration of the Board of Inland Revenue, in order that, if possible, arrangements may be made which shall prevent the companies from obtaining the advantages afforded by the Act. . . without complying with the requirements of that Act.[3]

The construction of the carriages gave the Department less anxiety than other aspects of the Parliamentary train. Yet even here, years after the passing of the 1844 Act, occasional shortcomings were revealed. Y.N.B. carriages, for example, were not fitted with lamps, which had been required since 1846 as 'absolutely necessary for the safety and comfort of passengers'. The Department hoped the company would supply the omission.[4] When the L.S.W. submitted drawings of the Parliamentary carriages proposed for use on its new Worting-Andover line, it was noted that they were inferior in construction to those previously approved. A hint that it might become necessary to withdraw approval from all the company's Parliamentary trains, brought a promise to modify the offending stock.[5]

---

[1] P.P. 1856, liv, 18.

[2] *Attorney-General* v. *O.W.W.R.* (1860) was a case relating to Parliamentary trains instituted by the Board of Inland Revenue, not the Board of Trade: 31 *Law Journal* (Ex), 218 and 35 *Law Journal* (Ex), 123.

[3] MT 11/27, 14 Jun. 1854.

[4] MT 11/23, 6 Nov. 1852.   [5] P.P. 1854–5, xlviii, 132.

On the other hand, a lower standard was thought adequate for excursions, and the Department sometimes sanctioned the use of open carriages for such trains.[1] The evidence throws virtually no light on the administration of the Parliamentary train provisions of the 1844 Act after 1856; but there is no reason to suppose that this branch of the Department's work became lighter or easier simply as a result of the passage of time.

Similarly with accident reports. It had been a statutory obligation for companies to report accidents since 1840, and it would be reasonable to suppose that by 1852 they would have done so as a matter of course. The evidence shows that this was not so. The Department watched the press, and on seeing news of an unreported accident, would ask the company for details.[2] Nor was it only small companies which fell short in this respect; the G.W.R., for example, was equally capable of failing to supply such information.[3]

Although the Board had no legal power to enquire into accidents, companies gave its inspectors every facility to do so. Milner-Gibson stated in 1865 that there had been no case of a company refusing to co-operate.[4] In defending himself against a complaint from the N.B.R. that his report was 'inconsistent with the real facts' Wynne described his procedure for taking evidence. The 'evidence given by servants of the company . . . was taken in the presence of two of the superior officers of the company and . . . after the examination of each witness . . . his evidence was read over to him before those officers'.[5] Laffan's report on an accident on the L.N.W.R. illustrates the lengths to which an inspector might go. The immediate cause was that the ashpan had fallen off and partially derailed the train. But he was not content to leave it at that. He suspected that the ashpan had fallen off because of bad workmanship in its fitting. Therefore, he 'proceeded to examine the company's servants in the workshops of Wolverton and Rugby, and to inspect the books in which all repairs are entered'. A new ashpan had been fitted in September, 1851, and the attachment renewed between

---

[1] MT 11/22, 18 Aug. 1852.
[2] MT 13/17, 14 Aug. 1852. MT 13/18, 12 Oct. 1852. The newspapers referred to were *The Times* and *Morning Chronicle* respectively.
[3] MT 11/30, 4 Jan. 1855.
[4] Hansard, clxxvii, 1133.   [5] MT 11/23, 27 Nov. 1852.

January and April, 1852, at Wolverton. The engine was in the shops again at Rugby in July, 1852, only a few days before the accident, when the attachment again needed attention. Laffan printed a verbatim statement by the foreman at Rugby in which he admitted bad workmanship by the man who had done the job, and the lack of supervision on his own part. In a similar statement, the Wolverton foreman not only agreed that the workmanship was bad, but went on to criticise the design itself.[1]

The accident reports for 1852 appeared in a new form.[2] Hitherto, they had been printed as appendices to the annual report of the Department, but now they came out as a separate Blue Book, with an introduction analysing the contributory factors and indicating remedies. Early in 1854, a further change took place. In response to a suggestion from Lord Monteagle,[3] reports were presented to Parliament in batches at intervals of two or three months. Where the Department felt that an accident revealed a particularly bad state of affairs, the report might be published separately. This change indicates a reversal of the Department's attitude towards publicity.[4] Previously, publicity was shunned; now reports were put out while they still had news value, in the belief that public opinion would influence companies to adopt their recommendations. They were summarised in the press, and were available to counsel in actions for damages arising out of accidents.[5]

These changes may be illustrated by the enquiry into an accident at Dudley Station on the South Staffordshire Railway in May, 1855.[6] It occurred almost on the same spot as an accident in October of the previous year. The causes of both were the same. At the point in question, there were three parallel lines, but, nevertheless, passenger traffic was worked in both directions over one of them. Nor was this merely an occasional practice. Thirty-eight trains were run daily over the single line in each direction, and six pairs of trains were timed to pass over it as nearly simultaneously as could be contrived. The wonder is, not that there were two collisions within eight months, but that they did not occur daily.

[1] P.P. 1852–3, lv, 170–4.
[2] P.P. 1854, lxii, 1 ff.
[3] Hansard, cxxx, 291–2.
[4] See above, p. 92.
[5] P.P. 1854–5, xlviii, 542.
[6] Ibid., 425 ff.

The line was leased by the company to J. R. McLean, the engineer, who was responsible for working the traffic.[1] He protested against the appearance of the report, on the grounds that 'it is surely contrary to every principle of justice, and also to the usual course, to print [such a document] in the middle of the session, and not as one of a series, but by itself.' The accident had occurred in May, and the report appeared in June. He should have had a chance to present his own defence. The Department obliged by publishing a second report, containing statements by McLean, in August, 1855.[2] This second report also contains Galton's explanation of the Department's new policy. Since the beginning of 1854, it had 'been customary to present the reports to Parliament as soon after they have been received as practicable, and . . . this course has been adopted with the view of giving as much publicity as possible to these reports'.

A complicating factor was the circumstance that the third line at Dudley had been opened without notice, and, consequently, without inspection. Of course, the Department did not want to see it closed. But Galton pointed out that the company had rendered itself liable to prosecution, and if found guilty, to a heavy fine. He hinted broadly that there would be no prosecution if a safer mode of working were adopted. McLean advised the company to avoid prosecution on grounds which have a general validity, and which probably influenced other companies in a like position. 'Even if you succeeded', he pointed out, 'in resisting legal proceedings at the suit of the Crown . . . you cannot recover any part of the expenses you might so be put to.'

The company thus found themselves under more pressures than one. In the midst of its deliberations, a Bill which authorised, among other things, new lines at Dudley, received the Royal Assent. Pending their construction, the company agreed to adopt pilot working. The Department referred to this case in their Annual Report as a bad example of the way in which a company could ignore recommendations arising out of accident enquiries, with the result that a second accident had occurred.[3] It appears that after the second accident the line was in fact

---

[1] For an account of this arrangement, see Cleveland-Stevens, 31.
[2] P.P. 1854–5, xlviii, 533 ff.   [3] P.P. 1856, liv, 311.

worked in the manner promised. At any rate, the company applied three years later for permission to do away with pilot working at Dudley. Yolland supported the company's application in view of the improvements made since 1855.[1] The whole case affords an unusually clear view of the effects of accident enquiries on companies. The Board had no statutory power to conduct such enquiries, still less to force companies to carry out any recommendations which might result. In spite of this, companies gave facilities without which such enquiries could hardly have been held, and the Board was able to exert pressure, which might prove as effective as legal power would have been, to persuade companies to adopt recommended precautions. On the other hand, the circumstances were unusual, and the case added little to the collective knowledge of the Department. As will be shown in the next chapter, the main importance of accident enquiries in this period was the way in which they yielded lessons for the future guidance of the Department in their efforts to achieve greater safety.

A case which the Department inherited from the Commissioners provides a good illustration of the use of its powers over new lines. When the Y.N.M. branch from Burton Salmon to Knottingley first opened, it crossed the River Aire by means of a temporary bridge. The first tube of a permanent tubular bridge, by Robert Stephenson, having been approved by the Commissioners, was opened in July, 1851. In November, 1851, however, the Board postponed the opening of the second tube on the ground that it was too narrow to permit trains to pass with safety, and suggested that the first tube should be widened. After further inspections and postponements had delayed the opening of the tube for six months, Stephenson submitted plans for altering it. Eventually, in October, 1852, the alterations were passed and the tube permitted to open—almost a year after it had been first inspected. The company at once carried out similar improvements on the first tube, which was inspected and permitted to reopen before the end of the year.[2]

The line which this bridge carried, though short, was of

---

[1] MT 6/17, 1990 and 3470/1858.
[2] P.P. 1851, xxx, 42. MT 13/16, 6 Nov., 4 and 30 Dec. 1851. MT 13/17, 2 Jan., 1 Apr., 1 and 29 May, 11 June, 1852. MT 13/18, 12 Oct., 10 and 20 Nov., 1852.

great importance. The Y.N.M. had built it in order to admit the G.N. traffic to York. In return, the G.N. had cut short its own line a few miles north of Doncaster. Thus, the Y.N.M. had retained a share in the London-York traffic by sacrificing its partners in the sole route hitherto available, the L.N.W. and the Midland. The deal had been a factor in the downfall of George Hudson, formerly chairman of the Y.N.M. The condemned bridge was noteworthy too; not only was it the work of one of the most eminent railway engineers, but it was of a design which he had made his own.

There was power to postpone the opening of a line in case of 'incompleteness of the works or permanent way'.[1] Yet no objections had been raised to the opening of the line, first with a temporary bridge, and then with one line only of the permanent bridge. There might be some danger in using the second tube. There was certainly danger in working the traffic of an important line through one tube only, which was, in any case, no wider than that which was kept closed. When an accident occurred, the Duke of Montrose suggested that the Department was partly to blame, since by postponing the opening of the second tube, it had made the line more dangerous.[2] The evidence does not sustain his charge, but such a reaction was natural and was anticipated when the Board first extended its powers to additional tracks of lines already open.[3]

Nevertheless, the Department's motive is not hard to understand. Postponement was the most effective means available to persuade the company to widen the bridge. Some temporary increase in danger was worth while, in order to make the line safer in the long run. The company's reasons for giving way are less easy to understand, though one factor seems to have been the desire of its ally, the G.N.R., to enjoy the full use of the line as soon as possible.[4] Whatever the motives, the case is a striking illustration of the Department's power to enforce its views by postponing the opening of a new line. But such triumphs could only be looked for occasionally. The Board could not postpone an opening for more than one month at a time, and then only on the report of an inspector. There were too few inspectors to permit monthly inspections of more than one or two lines at any

[1] 5 & 6 Vict., c. 55, s. 6.
[2] P.P. 1852-3, lv, 268.
[3] See above, p. 91.
[4] MT 11/22, 3 Aug. 1852.

given period. Moreover, the case did not become a precedent since tubular bridges remained rare. It will be shown in the next chapter that the full value of the Board's powers over new lines was realised only when each case was considered, not in isolation, but in relation to general principles derived from experience.

In a case which in some respects resembles that just discussed, a company, the O.W.W., opened a portion of line in defiance of the Board's order of postponement. The Board successfully sought an injunction to restrain the company from using the line.[1] It has been shown that the Board rarely took legal action even when there were good grounds for thinking that a company had broken the law.[2] This attitude persisted. There were certain offences of very frequent occurrence where, so far as the surviving evidence shows, proceedings at law were never seriously contemplated. Of these, failure to report an accident, and irregularities in the running of Parliamentary trains were the most important; but even the opening of a line without inspection might be similarly passed over.[3] In other instances, it was felt that action should be taken (if at all) by a private individual, rather than by a public authority. To a complaint of undue preference, the Department replied:

> it might be open to you, as the party peculiarly aggrieved, to proceed against the company under the Railway & Canal Traffic Regulation Act. But their Lordships would not consider themselves called upon to interfere under the powers given them under that Act in a case where the object immediately in view was not to obtain the removal of an obstruction or the establishment of an arrangement for the benefit of the public generally, but only to restrain the company from acting with partiality or injustice to a private individual.[4]

Even in a case where action by a private individual was inappropriate, the Department did not consider themselves necessarily bound to act. They declined to prosecute the G.N.R. for not stopping a Parliamentary train at Hatfield, stating that

---

[1] See below, p. 165. [2] See above, p. 36.
[3] MT 6/28, 2717/1863.
[4] MT 11/28, 4 Nov. 1854. The party concerned followed the Department's advice and was partially successful in the resulting action: P.P. 1857–8, li, 10. For similar advice in another case, see MT 11/24, 30 Mar. 1853.

they would 'require to be satisfied not only that the Act in question has been violated but that it will be for the public advantage that the company should be restrained from acting in violation of the Act'.[1]

Apart from the Department's general reluctance to prosecute, there were special difficulties in enforcing the provisions relating to new lines. The first arose from the requirement that a company had to give ten days' notice that a new line was ready for inspection.[2] The Department held that if the inspection did not take place within ten days of the notice, it had no power to postpone the opening. On this ground it was decided not to prosecute the Carmarthen & Cardigan Company for opening a line without authority.[3] The companies presumably took a similar view of the law, but did not invariably take advantage of the loophole. In one case, the N.B.R., while meeting the inspector's requirements, pointed out that the Board had forfeited its power to postpone the opening of the line in question by failing to inspect it within the statutory period.[4] In another case, the L.N.W. and the Midland kept a line closed for two years.[5] With so few inspectors it must often have been difficult to arrange inspections within the stipulated period. There seems to have grown up an understanding whereby the companies normally refrained from taking advantage of the Department's difficulties, while the Department abstained from legal proceedings save in extreme cases.

The Board's second difficulty was that the legal basis of an order of postponement was open to question, as, indeed, were most of its powers relating to railways after 1851. The Act of 1851 was ambiguous on its wording; it transferred to the Board the powers conferred on the Commissioners since 1846, but did not explicitly restore the powers originally conferred on the Board prior to 1846.[6] Thirdly, as time went on, an increasing proportion of the postponement orders were open to challenge on other grounds. Parliament had enacted that the opening of a

---

[1] MT 11/24, 19 and 25 Jan. 1853.   [2] 5 & 6 Vict., c. 55, s. 4.
[3] MT 6/30, 769/1864, MT 6/31.
[4] MT 6/32, 1973/1864. For further details of this case, see below, p. 191.
[5] See below, p. 193.
[6] Sir W. Hodges, *Treatise on the Law of Railways*, London (5th ed., 1869), 466 n.

line might be postponed in case 'of incompleteness of the works or permanent way'. In the example given above of the tubular bridge on the Y.N.M. Knottingley branch, would the courts have held the works to be incomplete, within the meaning of the Act, because the inspector disagreed with the company's engineer on the question of width? Was a line incomplete if not fitted with interlocking points and signals? Fane, the Legal Assistant, was inclined to think so;[1] the courts would not necessarily have upheld him. They were not competent to assess the technical issues involved. Indeed, they referred technical questions in railway cases to the Department, who acted as assessors.[2] As in the matter of Parliamentary carriages,[3] the Department was aiming at a higher standard for new lines than the minimum required by law, and so could hardly use legal means to enforce them.

The Department preferred administrative means of enforcing its standards. A case discussed elsewhere in this study,[4] *Attorney-General* v. *O.W.W.R.*, is the exception that proves the rule. The company had opened a section of track on the narrow gauge only, in defiance of the Board, although the first track of the same line was constructed on the mixed gauge. The prosecution showed that the company's Act required that the line should be capable of being worked continuously with the G.W.R., which was of course on the broad gauge. The court could, therefore, hardly fail to find that the permanent way was incomplete. The court declined to consider the validity of the Board's order, ruling that if the company wished to challenge it, its remedy would be to apply to Queen's Bench for a *mandamus* to dissolve the prohibition. The case also settled an important point of law, namely that the Board's powers over new lines extended to additional tracks of lines already open. As already shown, the Board had for years acted on such an assumption,[5] and so the finding of the court vindicated its view of the law. But if the judgment had gone the other way, and the very fact of the court's pronouncement shows that it was a dubious

---

[1] For further details of the case in which Fane gave this opinion, see below, p. 194 ff.

[2] MT 11/20, 28 Oct. 1851. MT 11/23, 17 Dec. 1852.

[3] See above, 97 and below, 200n.

[4] See p. 165.　　　　　　　　　　　　　　　[5] See above, p.91.

point, the restriction on the Board's powers would have been serious.

The public general Acts relating to railways passed during the period covered by this chapter made few additions to the powers of the Board, and the surviving records do not in all cases show how they were exercised. It seems to have been the rule, however, to keep all papers relating to cases under the Railways Companies Powers and Railways Construction Facilities Acts of 1864.[1] It has been said that the powers delegated to the Board by these Acts were never used.[2] This was not so. It is true that an objection from a single railway company could prevent the Board from granting a certificate, and the value of the measures was much reduced in consequence. Still, some certificates were granted, and an example of the procedure adopted may be given.

The first application was for power to construct an underground line in East London, to be known as the Eastern Metropolitan Railway.[3] Although unsuccessful, it illustrates the Board's practice, and has features of intrinsic interest. It took the Board quite by surprise. Booth minuted that he had expected someone to introduce a clause when the Bill was before Parliament to exclude London from its provisions altogether. The Board had not proposed such a clause itself only because the procedure might be useful for minor purposes within the metropolis, such as the enlargement of a station. 'But I never contemplated', he went on, 'the possibility of our sanctioning the making of railways under the streets of London.' There was considerable opposition to the scheme, as seventeen memorials against it showed; but they afforded no grounds for rejecting the application. Booth appears to have been relieved when the eighteenth memorial against the scheme arrived, for it was from the G.E.R. 'If this matter had not been taken out of our hands by the *notice of opposition* lodged by the G.E. company,' he wrote, 'there would have been some difficulty in deciding what to say.' Then the G.E.R. withdrew its opposition, and Booth was once more face to face with the difficulty. He now discerned what he described as a 'fatal objection' to the project. The company had not shown that it had contracted to buy land

[1] For these measures, see below, p. 155.
[2] Cleveland-Stevens, 211.
[3] MT 6/33, 305/1865.

for building stations, as the Act required. On this ground, the application was turned down.

Private Bill legislation, in contrast to the public Acts, conferred numerous new powers on the Board. There were fifty-two cases in the session of 1854, for example.[1] The evidence throws no light on the way in which many of them were used; fortunately, this is not true of one of the most important of such provisions—that by which companies were required to submit working agreements for the approval of the Board. The full development of this type of agreement belongs to the period after 1853, when Cardwell's Committee recommended it as an alternative to amalgamation, and preferable because subject to public regulation,[2] But the procedure had been worked out earlier, and it is reasonable to suppose that Cardwell's thought was influenced by the experience of the Department. An agreement between the Stockton & Darlington and Middlesbrough & Guisborough companies, for example, was under consideration while the Committee was actually sitting.[3] Cardwell's original Bill of 1854 would have conferred a general power to make such agreements on railway companies, and such a provision was included in the Clauses Act of 1863.[4]

The railway interest at first opposed the introduction of the new type of agreement.[5] But companies came to see its advantages. An early railway agreement resembled a treaty rather than a contract; if one of the parties set it aside, the other (or others) had no legal remedy. When, for example, the M.S.L. denounced a previous agreement with the L.N.W., and sought Parliamentary sanction for a new arrangement with the G.N.R., a committee of the House of Commons resolved that the original agreement had been '*ultra-vires*, and therefore *ab initio* void'.[6] Many companies decided that supervision by the Board was a price worth paying for legal recognition.

The Board learnt from its experience in this as in other matters. At first it favoured agreements for not more than ten years.[7] Later it approved longer or unlimited periods, provided

---

[1] P.P. 1854–5, xlviii, 10.
[2] The background to this recommendation is sketched in Cleveland-Stevens, 183 ff.
[3] MT 11/24, 19 Feb. 1853.
[4] See below, p. 155.
[5] Cleveland-Stevens, 196 ff.
[6] P.P. 1857–8, xv, 18.
[7] See below, p. 159.

it was empowered to make revisions in the public interest at intervals of ten years, and suggested a model clause for this purpose.[1] A further refinement was the recommendation that companies should be required to publish notices drawing the attention of the public to the Board's power of revision when the time for its exercise arrived.[2]

The changes suggested in the drafts submitted by companies were often very slight. Not untypical was the case of the Mid Wales Railway, which inserted the words 'good and sufficient' before the word 'repair' in its lease, at the suggestion of the Board.[3] It was no doubt true in most cases that the agreements 'contained nothing to be noticed by this Board', as Fane minuted on one between the L. & Y. and the G.N.[4] But it is reasonable to assume that they were more beneficial to the public interest than private agreements which had not to undergo the scrutiny of the Board.

This period saw the introduction of a considerable number of railway Bills, several of which passed into law. From the point of view of this study, however, this legislation was not of great importance. Little of it stemmed from the experience of the Department, and it made few notable additions to the Department's powers.

Of the government measures, the most important was Cardwell's Railway & Canal Traffic Act, 1854. Had the Bill passed in its original form,[5] it would have set up an elaborate administrative tribunal, under the Board of Trade, to hear traffic cases. As it was, however, the Act bestowed this jurisdiction on the Court of Common Pleas, before which the Board might appear as public prosecutor.[6] An example has already been given to show in what light the Department regarded its responsibility under this Act.[7]

Two Cheap Trains Acts[8] tidied up the law with regard to the fares which companies might charge their Parliamentary passengers for fractional portions of a mile. The immediate origin

[1] P.P. 1860, lix, 167. [2] MT 6/21, 130/1860.
[3] BTHR MW 1/9, 20 Feb. 1865. [4] MT 6/31.
[5] P.P. 1854, vi, 1.
[6] 17 & 18 Vict., c. 31, s. 3. Cf. Cleveland-Stevens, 191 ff.
[7] See above, p. 149.
[8] 21 & 22 Vict., c. 75, and 23 & 24 Vict., c. 41.

of this measure was a decision of the Irish courts, but similar difficulties had arisen with companies in Great Britain.[1] The Railway Clauses Act, 1863, incorporated a number of provisions which had become usual in railway Acts since the original measure of 1845. Several of these were the result of long sustained pressure from the Department: for example, the power to order a company to replace a level crossing by a bridge.[2] The Department had first sought a similar power as long ago as 1842,[3] and since 1848 it had usually been included in private railway Acts. Another attempt had been made in the Accidents on Railways Bill, 1855.[4] Similarly, the Act reflects the Department's attitude towards working agreements. Companies were given a general power to make such agreements with one another, subject to the approval of the Board, which was authorised to revise them, if necessary, in the public interest every ten years.[5]

The Railway Companies Powers and Railways Construction Facilities Acts, 1864,[6] should be considered together. They embody ideas first put forward by Booth as early as 1853.[7] In their original form,[8] they would have enabled companies to obtain new powers in certain cases, of which the raising of capital and construction of lines were the most important, by certificate from the Board instead of application to Parliament. During their passage through the Commons, however, two important restrictions were introduced. If a railway or canal company gave notice of opposition to any application, proceedings before the Board must cease, and the draft certificate must be laid before Parliament, which could reject it.[9]

It will be seen that Parliament greatly reduced the scope of the government's Bills. But it would be altogether too simple to imagine a government always pressing for more power, and private Members always resisting such pressure. Often it was private Members who urged the government to seek wider powers, and ministers (especially Milner-Gibson) who resisted.[10]

[1] E.g. P.P. 1856, liv, 83–7. MT 13/21, 50/1856.
[2] 26 & 27 Vict., c. 92, s. 7.　　　[3] See above, p. 53.
[4] P.P. 1854–5, i, 17.　　　[5] 26 & 27 Vict., c. 92, ss. 24–7.
[6] 27 & 28 Vict., c. 120, and c. 121.　　　[7] P.P. 1852–3, xxxviii, 264.
[8] P.P. 1864, iv, 1 and 33.
[9] 27 & 28 Vict., c. 120, ss. 7, 8, and 12–14; c. 121, ss. 9–10 and 14–15.
[10] E.g. Hansard, clvi, 220–1; clxi, 141–2; clxxvi, 1388–9.

Similarly measures promoted by private Members might confer new powers on the Board. For example, the Railway Companies Arbitration Act, 1859, empowered the Board to intervene in order to prevent the breakdown of arbitration between companies.[1]

In some cases, measures promoted by private Members were taken up by the government. The most notable example was statutory provision of means of communication between passengers, guards, and drivers. We shall see below how much importance the Department attached to this safety device.[2] The first attempt to make it compulsory was the Accidents on Railways Bill, 1855.[3] This was a government measure, introduced late in the session in the House of Lords, where it passed rapidly through all its stages.[4] In the House of Commons, the second reading was postponed on five occasions, on all but one of which it had not been reached till after midnight, and the Bill was eventually withdrawn a few days before the summer recess.[5] Eleven years later, the question was taken up by a private member. His first Bill failed, but he introduced similar measures in the two succeeding sessions.[6] On the last occasion, however, he withdrew his Bill at the committee stage, and the principle for which he had contended became law as part of the government's Regulation of Railways Act, 1868.[7] Further evidence of the Board's willingness to take up schemes promoted by others was the incorporation of the Debenture Holders' Bill, promoted by a private member, in a government Bill of 1867.[8]

The influence of the Department on private Bill legislation is harder to assess. It has been shown above that the Commissioners were in regular communication with Parliament about railway Bills.[9] The Department stepped into that relationship as the session of 1852 approached. In February of that year, it was decided to submit to the officers of both Houses observations on certain railway Bills which were thought to be 'deserving the

[1] 22 & 23 Vict., c. 59, ss. 8 and 13.   [2] See below, p. 172 ff.
[3] P.P. 1854–5, i, 17.
[4] L.J., lxxxvii (1854–5), 243 and 305.
[5] C.J., cx (1854–5), 395, 414, 420, 438, 452, and 455.
[6] P.P. 1866, v, 1; 1867, v, 463; 1867–8, iv, 367.
[7] 31 & 32 Vict., c. 119, s. 22.
[8] C.J., cxxii (1867), 231.   [9] See above, p. 127 ff.

consideration of the Select Committees to which the Bills may be referred'. Similar observations on the remaining Bills were promised, and assistance offered in scrutinising amendments.[1] Further observations followed at intervals until May, by which time the views of the Department on ninety-eight Bills had been communicated to the House of Lords. Unfortunately, the surviving records contain no copies of the observations themselves nor is it clear whether the same number of Bills was dealt with in communications to the House of Commons.[2]

Other evidence gives examples of the suggestions submitted. Henley directed that 'in addition to the observations which have been already transmitted . . . relative to the Eastern Counties Railway (Powers to use the East Anglian, etc.) Bill', the Department should point out 'that it may deserve consideration by the Committee on the Bill what bearing the purchase or the lease of the East Anglian Railway . . . may have on the construction of the lines of railway between Wisbech and Spalding, and Wisbech and Peterborough, which [have] already received the sanction of the legislature'.[3] The Department drew the attention of both Houses to all Bills by which railway companies took powers over canals.[4] Similar observations were forwarded in 1853 and 1854, but thereafter the evidence does not show whether the practice continued or not. The need for them probably vanished after the introduction of the reports on railway Bills which will be discussed below.

The Department also submitted amendments direct to promoters. For example, 'certain amendments . . . [for] the protection of the interests of the public' were sent in the hope that they would be included in a Bill introduced by the Shrewsbury & Birmingham Company.[5] That company's reply showed how anxious parties watching the progress of railway Bills were lest the Department's influence should be exercised in a manner hostile to their interests. It was necessary to send a reassurance that the amendments submitted had not been 'suggested by the L.N.W.R.Co. but . . . originated in this Department'. Similarly the Department told the North Lancashire Steam Navigation Co. that it had already drawn the

[1] MT 13/17, 12 Feb. 1852.
[2] MT 11/21 and MT 13/17 *passim.*
[3] MT 11/21, 30 Mar. 1852.
[4] Ibid., 6 Apr. 1852.
[5] MT 11/21, 28 May, 1852.

attention of Parliament to a Bill relating to railway-operated steamship services from Morecambe.[1]

From 1854 onwards, the Department prepared a report on all railway Bills for the guidance of the General Committee of the House of Commons set up in pursuance of the Report of Cardwell's Select Committee of 1853.[2] Similar reports were presented annually during the remainder of our period. They did not follow the example of Dalhousie's reports in recommending that individual Bills should be passed or rejected. They merely classified the Bills, and related them to the general principles laid down by Cardwell's committee. The reason was the Department's belief that straightforward recommendations would be rejected.[3] It may be, however, that this discreet approach had, in some cases, the opposite effect from that intended. It requires close study to see what changes the Department thought desirable in any particular Bill—closer study, in all probability, than the average Member, selected to serve on a committee on a railway Bill, was prepared to give. From the session of 1857–8 onwards, special reports on each individual Bill supplemented the general reports.[4] They made it easier for any committee so minded to adopt the Department's recommendations.

Such were the methods adopted by the Department to influence railway Bills. What effect did they have? To this question the evidence affords no conclusive answer. A great many individuals and corporations sought to influence railway Bills—landowners, industrialists, other railway companies, canal proprietors, highway trustees, local authorities of all kinds, to name only the most obvious examples—as well as the Department. To isolate the effect of one influence from among so many would be difficult if each Bill had been decided on by one individual; in fact, of course, they were referred to committees. It would be necessary to know how much each factor counted with each member, and how much weight each member carried in the committee's decision. The records do not give this information. Nevertheless, an attempt must be

[1] MT 11/21, 2 Jun. 1852. MT 13/17, 17 Apr. 1852.
[2] For an account of this Committee and the effects of its report, see Cleveland-Stevens, 179–204.
[3] P.P. 1857–8, xiv, 19 and 24. For a typical example of these reports, see P.P. 1856, lv, 491 ff.
[4] For the first set of special reports, see P.P. 1857–8, xxxi, 397–639.

made to answer so important a question. The accepted account supports the view of two of the Board's own officers, Booth and Galton, that its influence was very slight.[1] A reconsideration of the evidence suggests that it may have been somewhat under-rated.

To show that individual Bills contain provisions favoured by the Board is not, in itself, proof of the Board's influence; *post hoc* is not necessarily *propter hoc*. If, however, the Board's report on the Bills of a session is compared with its report on the resulting Acts; and if it is found that a substantial proportion of the Bills have been amended as the report had recommended, there is a strong probability that the amendments were introduced as a result of the report. The Board's report on the Bills deposited in the session of 1854–5 pointed out that only six of the Bills by which companies sought power to conclude working agree-ments limited such agreements to a period of ten years, and made them subject to the Board's approval.[2] In the event, eighteen Acts of that session conferred such powers on com-panies in Great Britain. Of that number, five had been satis-factory as Bills, six had been amended, while seven were deficient in one or both respects.[3]

Committees on railway Bills were required by Standing Orders to report, in all cases where reports from the Board of Trade had been referred to them, what action they had taken.[4] 106 such Bills survived the committee stage in the Commons in the session of 1860, on all but five of which the Board had made recommendations. Committees had adopted those recom-mendations wholly in twelve cases, and partially in fifty-three cases.[5] In the remaining instances, the committees made use of some such phrase as 'a report from the Board of Trade upon the Bill had been referred by the House to the Committee and con-sidered by them'.[6] This appears to be a polite formula for rejection. Of course, the Board's reports were not always un-favourable to the companies. By Standing Orders, the Board

---

[1] Cohn, ii, 613; F. Clifford, *History of Private Bill Legislation* (1885–7), i, 182; Cleveland-Stevens, 206–7; O. C. Williams, op. cit., i, 114. For the views of Booth and Galton, see P.P. 1857–8, xiv, 9–44.
[2] P.P. 1854–5, xlviii, 574–6.
[3] P.P. 1856, liv, 167 ff. [4] Williams, op. cit., ii, 175.
[5] Supplement to *House of Commons: Votes & Proceedings* (1860), *passim*.
[6] Ibid., 307.

was required to report, for example, on all applications from railway companies to alter the gradient of a road beyond certain limits.[1] In some cases, the recommendation adopted was that a company should be given such power.[2]

We have seen that, starting in the days of the Commissioners, it had become usual in Bills authorising level crossings to insert a clause empowering the Commissioners (later the Board) to order the company to substitute a bridge for the crossing.[3] In the session of 1852, for example, only one railway Act authorising a level crossing omitted such a provision.[4] An amendment to Standing Orders of the House of Commons, first effective in the session of 1854, required a favourable report from an officer of the Department before power could be given in any railway Act to make a level crossing.[5] A circular to Parliamentary agents sought their help in preparing these reports.[6] They had the effect of limiting the number of crossings authorised. In 1855, for example, the railway Bills which finally passed provided for 237 crossings, but only 102 were sanctioned.[7] Galton admitted that Parliament usually acted on these reports, in contrast to the majority of those prepared in his Department.[8]

A number of important Bills contain provisions which were probably inserted at the instance of the Department; but the evidence is tantalisingly inconclusive. The first example is the G.W.R., Shrewsbury & Birmingham, and Shrewsbury & Chester Railway Companies Amalgamation Bill,[9] of 1854. It required the G.W.R. to complete a double-track, narrow-gauge, route to link the Shrewsbury & Birmingham and the L.S.W. at Basingstoke within eighteen months, and precluded the company from laying down the broad gauge between Wolverhampton and Chester without permission from the Board. A passage in the Department's annual report hints that these provisions reflect its influence, but the evidence given before the Parliamentary committees throws no light on their

---

[1] O. C. Williams, op. cit., ii, 170.
[2] E.g. Supplement to *Votes & Proceedings* (1860), 215 and 219.
[3] See above, p. 128.
[4] 15 & 16 Vict., Acts (Local & Personal), *passim.*
[5] O. C. Williams, op. cit., ii, 171–2.
[6] MT 11/27, 14 Feb. 1854.
[7] P.P. 1856, liv, 7.   [8] P.P. 1857–8, xiv, 14.
[9] 17 & 18 Vict., c. 222 (Local & Personal).

origin.[1] Another amalgamation Act of 1854[2] brought the N.E.R. into existence. It empowered the Railway Department, in association with the Treasury, to introduce an amending Bill to remedy any evils that might arise[3] from the monopoly power of the new company. The evidence heard by the Lord's committee on this Bill is silent as to the origin of this clause.[4] But another unusual provision of the Act links up directly with the Department's work. The company was required to provide lights in its third-class carriages, and although this has been attributed to the efforts of a local authority,[5] the Department was pressing the company to take this very step during the passage of the Bill.

The last example to be considered here is the L. & Y. and East Lancashire Amalgamation Bill, 1858. The Board suggested the insertion of clauses requiring the company to build a new station at Wigan, and to double the Burnley branch.[6] The committee on the Bill reported that they had received and considered a report from the Board; and had received a petition from Wigan Corporation for a new station. A clause had been inserted to meet this request. It might be inferred that the clause was a result of the petition.[7] But the verbatim record of the proceedings gives a different impression. The company itself put in a clause by which it bound itself to build a new station at Wigan within two years. Counsel for the company opened this part of his case with the significant remark; 'The Chairman [of the committee] has been looking at the Board of Trade report'.[8]

As it turned out, the Bill failed to pass, and the Act by which the companies amalgamated in the following year contains no

[1] P.P. 1854–5, xlviii, 9. House of Lords Record Office: Lords' & Commons' Evidence on G.W.R., Shrewsbury & Birmingham, and Shrewsbury & Chester Railway Companies Amalgamation Bill, 1854.

[2] 17 & 18 Vict., c. 22 (Local & Personal).

[3] P.P. 1854–5, xlviii, 223.

[4] House of Lords Record Office. Lords' Evidence on the Y.N.B., Y.N.M., & Leeds Northern Railway Companies Amalgamation Bill, 1854. The Commons' evidence is missing.

[5] W. W. Tomlinson, op. cit., 525.

[6] P.P. 1857–8, xxxi, 591–3.

[7] Supplement to *Votes & Proceedings* (1857–8), 169.

[8] House of Lords Record Office. Commons' Evidence on L. & Y. & E. Lancs. Railway Co.'s Amalgamation Bill, 4 May, 1858.

provision for a new station at Wigan.[1] The reason was that the company had proceeded with the construction of the station, which opened in 1860.[2] But the Act does provide for the doubling of the Burnley branch,[3] thus carrying out the other recommendation of the Board. The company reconstructed the line within eighteen months,[4] and as will be shown below, the Board required important improvements in it before allowing it to open.[5]

These examples suggest that, while the recommendations of the Board were often turned down, their effect on railway Bills was greater than has been hitherto supposed. An important piece of evidence from the last year of our period tends to confirm this conclusion. In 1867, the Board itself, harassed by lack of staff, suggested to the appropriate officers of the two Houses of Parliament that reports on railway Bills should be given up. The idea seems to have originated with Farrer, but it was approved both by Northcote, and by his successor, the Duke of Richmond. Lord Redesdale and Dodson, speaking for the Lords and Commons respectively, opposed the idea. They were prepared to dispense with the special reports if necessary, but wished the general and level crossing reports to continue, believing them to be of value to the committees.[6] It appears that their view prevailed, for while there was a sharp fall in the number of special reports, both the other types continued.

[1] 22 & 23 Vict., c. 110 (Local & Personal).
[2] BTHR LY 1/55, 5 Jun. 1860.
[3] 22 & 23 Vict., c. 110 (Local & Personal), s. 46.
[4] BTHR LY 1/55, 3 Jul. 1860.
[5] See below, p. 181.   [6] MT 6/44, 111/1867.

6

RELATIONS WITH THE
COMPANIES

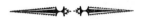

R ELATIONS between the Board and the companies could be
either normal or pathological. The normal pattern, in
spite of what railwaymen sometimes said in public,[1] was one of
good sense and moderation. The Board did not invariably seek
to enforce every provision of the law; the companies did not
invariably refuse to go one inch farther than the law required.
Through the clash of interests and difference of technical
opinion, common sense prevailed. As a result, the Board exercised considerable influence on most companies. Such influence
was negligible where the pathological pattern obtained. The
formal powers of the Board were few while the loopholes in the
law were many. Hence against a company set on defiance and
exploitation of the Board's weaknesses, little could be done.
Most of this chapter deals with the normal relationship. But
it is worth considering first a pathological case—that of the
Board's dealings with the O.W.W. Any company could have
behaved like the O.W.W., but few did. With such an extreme
case in the foreground, the perspectives of the normal relationship will assert themselves more clearly.

The outline history of the company is well known, and only
the briefest summary is necessary here.[2] It was incorporated in
1845, having been promoted under the aegis of the G.W.R. in

---

[1] For a number of examples, see H. W. Tyler, 'On Simplicity as the
Essential Element of Safety & Efficiency in the Working of Railways', in
Journal of the Royal Society of Arts, xxii (1874), 637–51.

[2] MacDermot, i, 459 ff.

opposition to a rival scheme backed by the L.N.W.R. As already shown, the passage of its Bill through the House of Commons was the immediate cause of the dissolution of the Railway Board.[1] The Commons Committee had inserted a clause requiring the Company to construct its line on the mixed gauge. As time went on, the Company's relations with the G.W.R. worsened, and it arrived at an understanding with the Company which had originally opposed it, the L.N.W.R. Hence it sought to construct its line on the narrow gauge first, and to evade its obligations to add the broad gauge. In 1860, it merged in the West Midland Amalgamation, which later was absorbed in the G.W.R.

In 1849, in common with many other companies at that time, the O.W.W. found itself almost overwhelmed by financial difficulties. But unlike other companies, there was in this case a remedy for those difficulties near at hand. Under the company's Act of incorporation, the G.W.R. was empowered, in the event of the O.W.W. proving unable to complete the line, to enter on the works, and exercise all the powers of the latter company in order to finish them. If the G.W.R. declined to exercise these powers, the Board of Trade (whose powers were, by 1849, being exercised by the Commissioners of Railways) might order it to do so. Under pressure from residents in the locality, headed by no less a man than the Duke of Marlborough, the Commissioners called on the G.W.R. to complete the line. When that company refused, they called for a report from one of their officers, who found the line unfinished and abandoned. The Commissioners thereupon ordered the G.W.R. to complete it.[2]

The G.W.R. showed no inclination to comply with the order, and a prosecution was instituted against the company.[3] It dragged on for some months but was eventually stopped, because the O.W.W. itself resumed work on the line.[4] The first section, a short branch from Abbots Wood to Worcester, opened in October, 1850.[5]

The O.W.W. was intended to be a double line, and as shown

[1] See above, p. 85 ff.
[2] This paragraph is based on P.P. 1850, xxxi, 179–221.
[3] P.P. 1851, xxx, 338–43.
[4] P.P. 1854, xxxviii, 8.
[5] MacDermot, i, 476.

above, of mixed gauge. It caused a vast amount of work to the Railway Department by seeking to open in short sections, one line at a time, and even in some cases, on the narrow gauge only at first; in almost every case, one or more postponements proved necessary. For example, the Worcester-Stoke section was postponed a fortnight; the Wolvercot Junction (where it met the G.W.R.) to Evesham section, a month; and the Tipton-Dudley section, three months.[1]

If these postponements were tiresome for the Department, they can hardly have been less so for the company. When, therefore, the second line from Evesham to Worcester, and from Brettell Lane to Dudley, was ready, it was opened without notice to the Department. After a subsequent inspection, they informed the company that these sections were dangerous and that their opening would have been postponed had the normal procedure been followed. A second report shows that after the better part of a month, and with a prosecution in the offing, only one of the Inspector's requirements had been met.[2]

Towards the end of 1853, the second line of the Evesham-Honeybourne section was inspected, and the opening postponed because the mixed gauge was not complete. An application for approval of Parliamentary trains revealed to some sharp-eyed member of the Department the curious fact that two trains were timed to pass one another on the (supposedly) single line between Evesham and Honeybourne. The company now stated that it had opened the second line; and from its records, we know that the Chairman, a solicitor by profession, held that it was not liable to any penalty for having done so. The Court of Chancery disagreed with him, however, and granted an injunction, as a result of which, the company closed the line in March, 1854. It remained closed for a year, being finally opened with the Board's sanction, in March, 1855.[3] It is worth noting that at the height of the dispute with the Board, the Company was in frequent contact with the L.N.W. and sought its approval for the course it was taking.[4] The company's engineer passed over

---

[1] P.P. 1852–3, lv, 91–4; 1854, xxxviii, 48–62, and 63–7. BTHR OWW 1/24, 21 Oct. 1853.   [2] P.P. 1854, xxxviii, 67–70.
[3] Ibid., 70–7; MT 13/20, 79/1854; BTHR OWW 1/24, 7 Dec. 1853; MacDermot, i, 503.
[4] BTHR OWW 1/24, 24 and 29 Mar., 12 Apr. 1854; 1/25 17 Apr. 1854.

the entire line from Wolvercot to Wolverhampton with a broad-gauge engine in April, 1854,[1] but the line was still far from complete; portions of the line first authorised in 1845 were still being inspected in 1858.[2]

Meanwhile, in March, 1854, the Board had instituted a prosecution against the company to recover the penalties for having opened the Evesham-Honeybourne line without sanction. The company bound itself, however, by provisions inserted in its 1854 Act, to complete the second line on the mixed gauge by 1 January, 1856, under a heavy penalty to be sued for by the Board of Trade. In the following session, it promoted two Bills by which it sought either to get rid of its broad-gauge obligations altogether and take power to remove the broad-gauge lines already laid, or at any rate to relieve itself of the obligation to lay its lines on the mixed gauge, unless ordered to do so by the Board of Trade. Both these Bills failed, and by the autumn of 1855 it was clear that it was not going to comply with its undertaking. It appealed to the President of the Board, who met deputations from the company and the G.W.R. The latter company had been pressing the Board to exact the penalties, but relented so far as to agree to the terms of a new Bill, which the O.W.W. successfully promoted in 1856. By this, it was allowed four more years to carry out its obligations, and the O.W.W. and the G.W.R. were empowered to reach agreements for the discontinuance of the broad gauge. It was also relieved from the penalties it had incurred for non-compliance with its 1854 Act.[3]

The rest of the Company's conduct was of a piece with that already discussed. An accident occurred at Hartlebury in 1856, and another at Charlbury in 1858. As a result of the second, the company paid more than £3,000 in compensation. In 1858, there occurred at Round Oak what the Department's inspector described as 'decidedly the worst railway accident that has ever occurred in this country'. A number of carriages broke away from a train as it mounted an incline, and ran backwards until they collided with a following train. What made it worse was that a very similar accident had taken place on the same part of the line five years before. The main difference was that, in the

---

[1] BTHR OWW 1/25, 19 Apr. 1854.
[2] Ibid., 1/26, 6 Aug. 1858.
[3] P.P. 1854–5, xlviii, 584–5; 1856, lv, 513–4; MacDermot, i, 513.

first case, the runaway vehicles had no brakes, while, in the second case, the brakes were adequate, but the guard abandoned the train without fully applying them. It is hard to decide which was more discreditable to the company.[1]

To turn to minor matters, the Board is found exercising its powers to order the company to build a bridge in place of a level crossing on its Chipping Norton branch prior to its opening. The company, having failed to do so, was allowed to open the branch on undertaking to build the bridge within one year. The company's Parliamentary train arrangements sometimes had to be queried, and its half-yearly returns did not always arrive on time. In short, the O.W.W. throughout its short existence showed how much a company could get away with in defiance of the powers with which the Board was endowed both under private and public Acts. Less obvious, it showed how the machinery of the Department would have ground to a standstill had every company caused it so much work. Not the least revealing fact about the company is that in the period 2 January–17 June, 1854 the Department wrote sixty-five letters to the O.W.W.—nineteen more than it wrote to the L.N.W.R.[2]

So much for a very abnormal case. In normal relations with companies, the Department's influence grew steadily, especially from 1852 onwards. This growth resulted, not from any notable increase in its powers, but from the more effective exercise of those it already possessed. The stock argument used against extending its powers was that greater regulation by the government would lessen the companies' own sense of responsibility, and so measures intended to increase public safety would in fact decrease it.[3] The companies used a similar argument in opposing the introduction of safety devices. Devices intended to make travelling safer would in fact make it more dangerous, since they would lessen the sense of responsibility of railway servants.[4]

---

[1] P.P. 1854, lxii, 231; BTHR OWW 1/26, 1, 87, and 93; Rolt, op. cit., 151–3.
[2] MT 13/20, 72 and 119/1855. BTHR OWW 1/25, 24 Jun. 1854, and 7 Mar. 1855. MT 11/27 *passim*.
[3] It would not be hard to collect dozens of references to this argument; for characteristic examples, see Cohn, i, 93; MT 6/1, 924/1841; MT 11/3, 1 May, 1843; MT 13/3, 5 Sept. 1845; MT 11/8, 10 Aug. 1846; Hansard, cxxii, 1048 (1852); clxi, 1823–4 (1861).
[4] Ibid., 126; Rolt, 65–6.

Until 1851 or thereabouts, this argument was generally accepted in the Department. The object of accident enquiries, for example, was more often than not to decide which individual had been to blame. It was, of course, true then (as indeed it is today) that the responsibility for some accidents can be fixed in this way. In one case, an accident was attributed to a pointsman 'who immediately afterwards committed suicide'.[1] In others, the Department advised companies to dismiss or prosecute drivers whom they held to be responsible for accidents.[2] So great a degree of responsibility might be fixed on the individual as to exonerate the company completely. One accident report concludes: 'I am of the opinion that this accident occurred from the recklessness of the driver, a circumstance against which it was impossible for the company to guard'.[3]

From the early 'fifties on, however, a new note began to be heard. It was said that self-interest ensured that companies and individual railway servants alike would behave in a responsible manner. Wynne came to the conclusion that this was not so. He was reporting on an accident in which an engine, appropriately named 'Mazeppa', had run away with no one on the footplate, having been left unattended but with steam up. Certain individuals were responsible; but would the accident have happened had management supervised the work of their servants more closely?

> I had much conversation on the subject of a closer supervision of the workmen with the manager . . . and his views and mine differed considerably. . . . He combatted the efficacy of a closer supervision . . . and maintained the principle of . . . making it their self interest to do their duty *strictly* without watching; that is, that steadiness of conduct would raise them to a higher grade. The principle is an excellent one, combined with an efficient control over the men and the power of ascertaining that the *supposed* steadiness *does* exist; wanting that element, I believe, it cannot be depended on, . . . and as the question is one which involves the public safety, the present system calls for at least serious consideration if not revision.[4]

[1] MT 13/17, 26 Aug. 1852.
[2] MT 11/7, 29 Nov. 1845. P.P. 1852–3, lv, 205–6.
[3] Ibid., 208.
[4] P.P. 1852–3, lv, 238–9. The accident occurred on the Shropshire Union Railway, on which the traffic was worked by the L.N.W.R.

Yolland made a similar point with greater brevity and force. The man immediately responsible for an accident at Dudley had been prosecuted and fined £5. But the fundamental cause of the accident was mismanagement, 'so that, although the assistant policeman has been prosecuted and convicted, the parties really responsible, from their supineness, for this sad accident, will altogether escape'.[1]

Was self-interest any more efficacious in making companies behave responsibly? Companies paid out large sums in compensation to the victims of accidents,[2] but this did not appear to act as a check. Enquiries into accidents had shown that

> the larger proportion had been due to causes within the control of the management; and . . . the proportion has not diminished as compared with former years. . . . And it does not appear that under the existing law in England there is any instance on record in which, although the accident may have been shown to have arisen either through the deterioration of the works or the defective arrangements and bad discipline on a railway, any superior officer of a company has been punishable. The inferior servants . . . are punishable. . . . But many cases of negligence, for which these men have been punished, have been shown . . . to be partly attributable to the defective system of working or to an insufficient establishment.[3]

Scots law differed from English in this respect, and the Department suggested that the liability of railway officers there to punishment (including imprisonment) was a partial explanation of the lower accident rate in Scotland.[4] Just as the failure of self-interest at the lower level called for closer supervision by management, so at the higher level, it called for stricter regulation by the Department.

The main factor making stricter regulation possible, without any substantial increase either of powers or of staff, was the steady growth of the Department's knowledge. How was that knowledge obtained? Inventors continued to put their projects forward; but since there was no 'power to enforce upon railway

---

[1] P.P. 1854–5, xlviii, 428 and 430.
[2] Single accidents cost the S.E.R., £25,000, and the L.N.W., £26,000: PP. 1857–8, li, 202, and BTHR LNW 1/82, 3 Jul. 1862. Accidents cost eight major companies £331,000 in the period 1849–58: Hansard, clxi, 1832.
[3] P.P. 1856, liv, 13–14.   [4] P.P. 1857–8, li, 202.

companies the adoption of inventions relating to railways' the Department 'in general thought it inexpedient to undertake to investigate and decide upon the comparative merits of such inventions and [were] in the habit of replying in that sense to the very numerous applications made to them by the proprietors of inventions'.[1] On at least one occasion, the Department itself sponsored research. A difference of opinion as to standards of strength of wrought-iron bridges between Tyler and the distinguished engineer William Fairbairn, arose in 1859. Fairbairn agreed to strengthen the bridge in question, but pointed out the desirability of more investigations of the subject. He was himself willing to undertake the necessary experiments, if the government would contribute £150 towards the cost.[2] This was done and Fairbairn's report was eventually published under the Department's auspices.[3]

Much the most important source of the Department's knowledge, however, was the practice of the railway companies themselves. Where that practice was good, it could be recommended for general adoption; where it was bad, the Department set itself to devise better methods, not merely for use on the line in question, but wherever applicable. Accident enquiries were of special importance in this way, as soon as the inspectors reduced their early obsession with personal responsibility to its proper proportion. Even where companies neglected the recommendations resulting from particular accidents, enquiries served 'to show the Inspecting Officers what additional precautions should be required from railway companies proposing to open new lines'.[4]

The growth of the Department's thought on brakes illustrates this process. In the early days of railways, brakes were worked by hand and operated on the wheels of only one carriage. If more than a single brake van were included in a train, each required a separate operator. In its first annual report, the Department had laid down a formula for the amount of brakepower per train; the last carriage, and at least every fourth carriage, of passenger trains should be fitted with brakes.[5] This formula was inherited by the Commissioners of Railways.[6]

[1] MT 11/26, 16 Nov. 1853.   [2] MT 6/19.
[3] MT 6/30; P.P. 1864, liii, 749 ff.   [4] P.P. 1857–8, li, 203.
[5] P.P. 1841, xxv, 205.   [6] P.P. 1847–8, xxvi, 8.

Inadequacy of brake power continued to feature promi-
nently among the factors to which the Department attributed
accidents. But in 1854, Tyler, reporting on an accident on the
East Lancashire line between Bury and Manchester, pointed
out that the consequences would have been worse had not three
carriages been fitted with 'Newall's brake . . . which may be
applied simultaneously, by one guard, to any number of carriages'.[1] Henceforward, the Department was concerned with
the quality as well as the quantity of brake power, emphasising
the value of the continuous variety.

> When each brake requires a separate man to work it, the number
> of brakes . . . forms an important element in the expense of the
> train, and an increased number of brake vans, beyond the number
> actually required for parcels or luggage, causes additional un-
> productive weight.
> Several plans have therefore been tried for . . . giving the engine
> driver from his tender, or the guard from his van, control over
> brakes on passenger carriages. The only one which appears to have
> been practically adopted to any extent, is by Mr. Newall, of the
> East Lancashire Railway, which is stated to be in use on the East
> Lancashire, L. & Y., M.S.L., and N.E. Railways.
> This plan enables the guard or engine-driver to apply a brake to
> every carriage in the train. . . . It is also arranged so as to afford
> a means of communication between the guard and the engine-
> driver. The principle . . . is thoroughly sound; and . . . should be
> adopted . . . at least for [fast] trains.[2]

This passage looks forward two decades to the Newark brake
trials of 1875, and more than three to the Act of 1889 which
made continuous brakes compulsory.[3] In pointing out that they
provided the guard with a means of communicating with the
driver, the Department was even more far-sighted, as will be
seen when the history of that problem is discussed. But it was
not enough to know what was needed. Little could be done to
persuade companies to adopt continuous brakes until the Board
was given the necessary power.

But legal power was not the one thing needful for successful
intervention on the part of the Department, as may be seen

[1] P.P. 1854-5, xlviii, 349. For references to brakes in later accident
reports, see, e.g., P.P. 1864, li, 658, and 1865, xlix, 128.
[2] P.P. 1856, liv, 306.
[3] For these later developments, see C. H. Ellis, *Nineteenth Century Railway
Carriages*, Hamilton C. E. (1949), 57-9, and Rolt, 158 ff.

from the history of its endeavours to secure means of communication between the different parts of a moving train. The Department's interest in this question dates from 1845, while the Commissioners issued a circular on the subject in 1847, and referred to the desirability of such a device in their report for that year. In 1851, they made enquiries in France and Belgium as to the methods in use there, and one of the first actions of the re-formed Department was to circularise recommendations arising out of those enquiries to British companies.[1] A few companies became interested in the question,[2] but little was done.

The solution proposed was simple in the extreme. Carriages should be fitted with footboards and handrails, by means of which the guard could pass along the train, either to communicate with the driver, or to investigate hand signals made by passengers to attract his attention. This suggestion was less impracticable than it may sound. On some early railways, it was the normal practice for ticket collectors to pass along the trains whilst they were in motion,[3] and three small companies relied on this means of communication for use in emergencies as late as 1857.[4] Wynne believed in it in 1853—Lord Brougham thought it practicable as late as 1864, while the Department still approved it at that date.[5]

Meanwhile, the Department addressed a copy of its 1851 circular to the Railway Clearing House Committee, and sought the help of that body in achieving the general adoption of some system of communication.[6] This development is of considerable interest in itself, since it showed that consultation was of value to the Department as well as to the companies. For this purpose, the Clearing House was not the ideal body, but it was no doubt the best available. It considered the Department's plan, but recommended an alternative method. A bell should be fitted to each engine, connected by means of a rope passing over the roof of the carriages to the guard's van, in such a manner that the guard could ring the bell in case of emergency. This system

[1] MT 13/4, 6 Dec. 1845. P.P. 1847–8, xxvi, 10; 1852–3, xcvii, 329–33.
[2] E.g. L.N.W. (MT 11/20, 20 Oct. 1851); Monmouthshire Railway & Canal Co. (BTHR HL 2/247–50).
[3] E.g. the Manchester & Leeds: MT 11/6, 7 Mar. 1845.
[4] P.P. 1857–8, li, 222–5.
[5] P.P. 1854, lxii, 228–9. Hansard, clxxvi, 1439. P.P. 1865, l, 15–16.
[6] MT 11/20, 20 Oct. 1851.

was in use in Holland and Germany.[1] Passengers should not have access to the rope—the whole discussion was marked by the companies' fear that facilities would be abused.

The Clearing House report was submitted to Cardwell's Committee of 1853,[2] which resolved in favour of the introduction of communication. The Clearing House itself recommended its constituent companies to adopt the bell and rope system from 1 January, 1854.[3] All this activity had some effect. The General Manager of the G.N. advised his board of directors to implement the plan at an estimated cost of £1,500. The public expected it, and other companies had given a lead.[4] The Bristol & Exeter introduced a system in 1854,[5] and the L.N.W. experimented with an electrical device in the same year.[6] But the returns to a further circular showed that communication was still the exception rather than the rule.[7] Hence a Bill to make it compulsory was introduced in 1855, but failed to pass.[8]

The Department first became convinced of the necessity of communication as a result of fires breaking out while trains were in motion. But an accident of a different kind will provide a better illustration here. In 1855, a train made up of G.N. and N.E. stock was travelling on the N.E.R. when the last carriage but one lost a tyre. The guard saw that something was wrong, and tried in vain to attract the driver's attention with his red flag. Then 'he attempted to cross over the carriages . . . but the carriage before him plunged so violently as to deter him from doing so, and he got into his van and put on his brake'. The result of this was not to stop the train but to break the couplings, 'and he was left helpless in his van'. The train went on for two and a quarter miles before the driver stopped it.[9]

This accident not only showed the necessity for some means of communication, but also the folly of assuming that only lack of footboards and handrails prevented guards passing along the outside of moving trains. It also showed how difficult it was for companies to introduce such devices independently of one

[1] The bell and rope system is sometimes ascribed to T. E. Harrison, the N.E.R. engineer, but the reference to its being used on the Continent casts some doubt on this.   [2] MT 11/24, 22 Mar. 1853.
[3] BTHR GN 1/275/19.   [4] Ibid.
[5] MacDermot, i, 843.   [6] MT 11/27, 22 Mar. 1854.
[7] Ibid., 11/28, 22 Jul. and 5 Aug. 1854. P.P. 1854, xlvii, 274 and 313–16.
[8] See p. 156.   [9] P.P. 1854–5, xlviii, 414–16.

another. The N.E.R. said it had introduced the bell and cord system but had discontinued it because the G.N. carriages which had to be attached to many of its trains were not fitted with the apparatus. The G.N.R. stated that all its through trains were already fitted with the same system, and that it was 'in course of being applied to every other train'. The third partner in the East Coast route, the N.B.R., went no further than to say that the three companies had agreed to a joint trial.[1] These statements may well have been excuses rather than explanations; but they show the special reasons that existed for making some communication system compulsory on all companies simultaneously.[2]

Returns to a further circular issued in 1857 show that only ten companies claimed to provide means of communication. These included the G.N.R. and N.E.R., but it is pehaps significant that the N.B.R. made no reply.[3] The question was again considered by a Select Committee in 1858, and following their recommendation, bell and cord communication between guards and drivers was widely introduced.[4] That system came in for severe criticism from Daniel Gooch, reporting in 1861 on the whole subject of communication to his board of directors. The G.W.R., in this, as in other things, had its own way of doing things. A porter travelled on the back of the tender, looking along the length of the train, and sitting in what was sometimes called an 'iron coffin', to protect him from the weather. In case of need, the guard, or passenger, could attract the porter's attention and he could warn the driver. Gooch thought the bell and cord device the only alternative worth considering. Among his reasons for thinking it inferior was the fact that it put 'the engine-man . . . in the hands of the guard only, the cord in no instance that we know of being placed so that any one else in the train can give the signal'.[5]

Hitherto the discussion had centred on the question of passengers' safety in accidents; but what of their safety from other

[1] P.P. 1854–5, xlviii, 416.

[2] For reports of other accidents in which lack of communication was mentioned, see, e.g., P.P. 1854, lxii, 51–2, 112–14; 1854–5, xlviii, 397–9, 400; 1857–8, li, 196, 219; 1863, lxii, 737.

[3] P.P. 1857–8, li, 219–25.

[4] Ellis, *Nineteenth Century Railway Carriages*, 129.

[5] BTHR HL 1/1/4.

passengers? In 1863, a maniac attacked two passengers in a train on the L.N.W.R., and in the following year a man named Muller murdered a passenger in a train on the North London Railway. These events not only aroused widespread interest in the whole question but convinced the public that communication devices were of little value unless the public had access to them.[1]

The Railway Managers' Committee of the Clearing House took up the question and, at Milner-Gibson's request, kept him informed of their deliberations. In April, 1865, they reported that the bell and cord system should be introduced on expresses and long-distance trains. It should be uniform for all companies, so as to allow of interchange of carriages, and should be so devised as to permit passengers to communicate with guards, and guards with drivers. There should be a statutory penalty for abuse. The chairman of the Clearing House vetoed a proposal to submit the report direct to Milner-Gibson because he thought they should 'avoid . . . getting in any way to have direct communication with the Board of Trade, a result which should be guarded against in every way'.[2] It is unfortunate that he did not explain his reasons more fully, because, as has already been shown, the Clearing House did to some degree fulfil the purposes of a consultative body, and Milner-Gibson had already used its forthcoming report to stave off a question in the House.[3] He also used the committee, in interviews with its chairman, as a channel for urging on the companies his view that they should themselves deal with the problem.[4] They began a series of trials and promised to let the Board know the results by the end of 1867.[5] As already described, it became compulsory in 1868 for companies to provide means of communication to which passengers should have access.[6]

Meanwhile, the Department had been urging on companies an even more important safety measure: the use of the telegraph for traffic control. Telegraph working dates from a very early period of railway history. It was used (experimentally) on the G.W.R. in 1839, throughout on the Norfolk Railway in 1844,

---

[1] Hansard, clxxii, 1285–6; clxxvi, 1388–90, 1439, 1468–9. Ellis, *Nineteenth Century Railway Carriages*, 72 and 130.
[2] BTHR GN 1/293/2. [3] Hansard, clxxvii, 116.
[4] Ibid., clxxxi, 969. [5] Ibid., cxc, 575. [6] See p. 156.

and very extensively on the S.E.R. at about the same period.[1] Other companies employed it where special difficulties occurred such as tunnels. The G.W.R. adopted it at the Box Tunnel in 1847, and the L.N.W. at Kilsby Tunnel in the following year.[2] Similarly, it was sometimes used on single lines.[3] But its general introduction was very slow, and the normal system was based on time intervals. A company's regulations would lay down that no train was to start until a specified period of time (say, five minutes) after the previous one. A case has been given above in which the Department sought to mediate in a lengthy dispute about time intervals in 1842.[4] Ten years later, it was still criticising companies for faulty working of the system in terms which implied tacit approval for the principle on which it was based. The L. & Y., for instance, was held responsible for a

> flagrant breach of the regulations framed by the company for the guidance of their servants and for the safe conduct of the traffic, trains being permitted to pass the Lostock junction at a less interval than the five minutes prescribed in the regulations as the time within which trains are not to follow each other. It appears that seven trains were allowed by the junction signalmen to pass within a quarter of an hour.[5]

By the time those words were written, however, the Department was aware of a radically different system, based on the use of telegraph instruments. The inspectors seem to have seen it in operation first on the S.E.R.[6] Galton brought out the difference between the systems clearly in a report on an accident, which showed

> how impossible it is . . . to preserve trains from collisions, when their safety depends alone upon the interval of time which elapses between the *starting* of the trains; and it adds another argument to the many which already exist in favour of adopting a system of working all trains, in which the interval . . . is one of distance . . . instead of an interval of time.[7]

The typical accident resulting from the break-down of time intervals occurred when one train ran into the rear of another

---

[1] C. E .Stretton, *Safe Railway Working*, London (1893), 48. P.P. 1846, xiv, 221–4, 580–1. [2] MacDermot, ii, 607. BTHR HL 2/19/161/16/C.
[3] MacDermot, ii, 611. [4] See above, p. 38 ff.
[5] P.P. 1852–3, lv, 148–9.
[6] MT 6/9, 292/1851. [7] P.P. 1854, lxii, 201.

on the same line. Such collisions could easily occur. The leading train might break down; or it might be a goods or excursion train not shown in the time-table and travelling more slowly than that which followed it; or the company's servants might lack watches and clocks and so not be able to preserve the proper intervals. Merely to send information about train movements along the line by telegraph provided little security against such collisions. Indeed, it might be 'not only useless, but positively mischievous', as Huish of the L.N.W. remarked on one occasion, when a telegraph message from Wolverton did not arrive at Tring until twenty minutes after the train to which it referred.[1]

The telegraph must be used, not only for information, but for control. This was done in the block system, according to which the whole line was divided into sections, and no train was allowed to enter a section until a message had been received that the preceding train had left it.[2]

Very soon after the Department had become aware of this system, it found an advocate in unexpectedly high places. In November, 1853, Cardwell received the following from Windsor Castle:

> The Prince desires me to make what appears to him a very simple suggestion with a view to prevent collisions on railroads by one train running into another in advance of it. It is, I believe, already practised on the [S.]E.R., and the precaution was adopted the other day when the Queen went to London in advance of the express train from the west.
> It is to make it imperative upon every station to have a telegraphic communication with the station next to it on either side—and no train should be allowed to leave one station till the signal was received from the next, to say that the train in advance was passed. Thus at every station the red signal by day and the red light by night would be shown the moment a train passed, and not turned off till the signal was made from the next [station] that the road was clear.

Cardwell replied:

> The suggestion you have done me the honour to communicate to me is a very valuable one.
> We have no power to enforce the adoption of it: but we have long urged it upon the companies in the way of advice.

[1] BTHR HL 2/19/161/16/D.
[2] For a recent account of the origin and development of the block system, see Rolt, esp. 32, 41–4, and 128 ff.

> I think you will like to see a report . . . made by Capt. Galton, and within this week officially communicated to the L.N.W. on this subject. It shows the importance we have attached to the precaution.

The Prince Consort's secretary closed the correspondence with the following:

> I return you Capt. Galton's report, of which I have communicated the substance to the Prince. H.R.H. desires me to thank you very much for having sent it, and to express the satisfaction with which he hears of the endeavours made by the Board of Trade to have such regulations adopted by the different railway companies as may prevent future collisions.[1]

Such a system was a marked advance on the existing arrangements for the safety of royal trains, which took the form of a sophisticated type of pilot working. In 1853, Simmons had at Cardwell's suggestion accompanied the Queen

> to and from Scotland . . . [and] travelled on the engine all the way. [There was] reason to believe that this precaution mortified the companies, and was considered a great indication of distrust. It was, however, well deserved, for the state of things at that time warranted no confidence.[2]

In 1854, rear collisions were the largest single class of accident numbering 29 of 85 reported on. 23 of the 46 collisions on double lines of railway would not have occurred, the Department asserted, had telegraphic control been in force.[3] In August 1854, therefore, a circular on the subject was issued to 225 companies.[4] It began by pointing out the frequency of rear collisions, and went on to draw attention to the weakness of the time-interval system. It then proceeded:

> With a view of effectually securing that an interval of space should under all circumstances be at all times maintained . . . the S.E.R. Co. have on portions of their railway placed electric telegraphic stations at intervals . . . and no train is allowed to pass one of these stations . . . until a notification has been received from the next station that the preceding train has passed off that portion of the line.

Certain conditions were required for the successful working of

---

[1] PRO 30/48/46.
[2] Add. MS. 43197. Cardwell-Aberdeen, 15 Aug. 1853 and 24 Jul. 1854.
[3] P.P. 1854–5, xlviii, 279.   [4] MT 11/28, 12 Aug. 1854.

the system. 'A telegraph wire should be exclusively reserved for this service; . . . the instruments used should be simple and should exhibit the signals with sufficient clearness for the signalling to be carried on by a person of ordinary intelligence.' Though the system had not been generally adopted, it had worked well on single lines and through tunnels.

The Department frequently recommended telegraph working in accident reports. The earliest example appears to have resulted from a collision near Tetbury Road Station on the G.W.R. in December, 1851. The Company adopted Galton's suggestion that the new mode of working should be used between that point and Brimscombe, where there were steep inclines, and the Sapperton Tunnel.[1] In 1855, the L.N.W. agreed to adopt it for the section between Heaton Norris and Stockport.[2] In other cases, companies were advised to make better use of the telegraph equipment they had installed. In his report on an accident at Felling, for example, Tyler pointed out that the N.E.R. had recently laid down the telegraph between Darlington and Newcastle.

> The company do not, however, prohibit two or more trains from being at the same time between any two telegraph stations, because they believe that the distance between some of these stations is too great to admit of such a prohibition being carried out, with their large traffic. They cannot, therefore, derive the great advantage, which they might otherwise obtain, from the telegraph stations that they have so judiciously established, of providing against the possibility of a collision on this crowded portion of their line. But . . . the company . . . might perhaps be induced, by a suggestion from their Lordships, to issue instructions by which all collisions between passenger trains and any other trains, might be avoided by simply directing that no train whatever should be permitted to pass a telegraph station, until the previous passenger train has passed the telegraph station next in advance, and that no passenger train should be allowed to pass a telegraph station, until the preceding train . . . whether passenger or goods . . . has passed the next telegraph station. I believe that this arrangement, at least, might be carried out with the present telegraph stations; and the only collisions that would then be possible, would be those between goods, coal and cattle trains.[3]

It does not appear what the company thought of this plan.

[1] MacDermot, ii, 610.   [2] P.P. 1854–5, xlviii, 480.
[3] Ibid., 492.

In the reports on new lines, there are many references to telegraph working. The Cornwall Railway told Yolland that it proposed to work its traffic in this way,[1] and did in fact do so from the date of its opening in 1860.[2] Sometimes the Department was able to influence the working of traffic on lines already open. For example, the Berks & Hants Railway had agreed to adopt the train staff system[3] as a condition of being allowed to open. When, therefore, it wished to go over to block working, it had to get the Department's consent. This was given, but the opportunity was taken to amend the company's telegraph regulations.[4] In at least one case, Tyler was able to suggest an important improvement in the instruments used. Some months before the Charing Cross Railway was opened, Tyler was asked to make a preliminary inspection. It was proposed to use telegraph instruments of the type then standard on the S.E.R. They gave audible signals only, and Tyler suggested that, in view of the very heavy traffic expected, visible signals were necessary as well; indeed 'he would be unable otherwise to recommend the Board of Trade to sanction the opening of the line'. The electrical superintendent of the company designed instruments to meet the Inspector's requirements and they were installed prior to the opening of the line. The S.E.R. subsequently adopted them generally throughout its system.[5]

By the middle 'sixties the Department found telegraph working a common feature of new lines. There were few cases, however, in which the opening of a line was postponed for lack of it. The first such appears to have been the second track on the L. & Y. Burnley branch. As already shown, there is a strong probability that the company only doubled this line under pressure from the Department.[6] When Tyler inspected it in June, 1860, he pointed out that there were three tunnels, and that block working should be adopted. The existing instruments

[1] MT 6/19, 1500/1859.   [2] MacDermot, ii, 278.

[3] For an explanation of this system, see Rolt, 117–18.

[4] MT 6/31, 1406/1864.

[5] MT 6/30, 45/1864. Tyler, loc. cit., 646. For other reports on new lines where telegraph working is mentioned, see MT 6/23, 2158/1861 (L.C.D.R.); MT 6/26, 3950/1862 (L.B.S.C.); MT 6/32, 1916/1864 (Vale of Neath); MT 6/44, 325/1867 (W. Cornwall).

[6] See above, pp. 161–2.

were neither adequate nor suitable.[1] Tyler must have conveyed this requirement verbally to the company, for the installation of the necessary equipment was ordered on the same day as the inspection.[2] At the next inspection, the line was passed, and opened on 1 July, 1860.[3]

The case of the Mid Wales Railway, inspected by Yolland in 1864,[4] shows that a mere promise to do as required was not always to be relied on. It was a single line of unusual length— forty-six miles. On his first inspection, Yolland recommended postponement, without making block working one of his requirements. The company's engineer called at the Department three weeks later and told MacGregor that the improvements suggested were almost complete. In his second report, Yolland made a new recommendation:

> from the very steep inclines on this railway, I do not think it can be safely worked on the train staff and ticket system, by which one train may be permitted to follow another at an interval of five minutes of time, and although the line may be opened for traffic in the first instance on this system it is to be understood that no second train is to be permitted to follow another until the first train has been ascertained by the ordinary telegraph to have passed over the portion of line to the adjacent train staff section, and that in the course of two months, the train staff and ticket system is to be abandoned and the working of the traffic is to be conducted entirely by telegraph on the block system.

Although it may have seemed unreasonable to impose this new stipulation after having already held up the opening for several weeks, the company appears to have raised no protest. It gave the required undertaking and the Department sanctioned the opening. Though the company eventually got the telegraph, it was not within the stipulated period, nor is it clear what use was made of it in working the traffic.[5]

In 1867, thirteen years after the Department had issued their first circular in favour of block working, they had still not used their powers to make it a condition for the opening of new lines

[1] MT 6/21, 1889/1860. [2] BTHR LY 1/55, 20 Jun. 1860.
[3] Ibid., 3 Jul. 1860. For a similar case involving the Midland, see MT 6/25, 2154/1862. [4] MT 6/32, 1838/1864.
[5] BTHR MW 1/1B, 12 Oct. 1865, and 1/9, 16 Jul. 1869. For a similar case, involving the G.N.R., see MT 6/32, 2033/1864; BTHR GN 1/295/16 and 1/312/16.

Many reports do not even mention whether or not the system is to be used on particular lines. The most probable reason is that it was expensive, both in capital and in operating cost: though the cost might be offset by the increased capacity of the lines— a point made in a report to the L.N.W. as early as 1854.[1] A typical estimate for conversion to block working was £6,162 plus £3,700 per annum for fifty-six miles of line.[2] Companies would be more likely to challenge costly requirements than cheap ones.

The history of continuous brakes, communication devices, and block working has shown that three conditions were necessary for the Board to influence companies to the fullest extent. Its recommendations had to be based on law, restricted to what was technically possible, and not so costly that companies would find it cheaper to resist than to acquiesce. Many examples can be found in the Department's *Requirements* for the opening of new lines, the first edition of which appeared in 1858. Hitherto, inspectors had considered each new line on its merits. Now they had a standard code to guide them. Revised and enlarged editions appeared in 1859, 1860, 1862, and 1867.

Those documents are of considerable interest from the legal point of view, since they are examples of quasi-legislation— which is usually thought of as a twentieth-century development —as much as delegated legislation. The Department had power to postpone the opening of a line if such opening 'would be attended with danger to the public using the same, by reason of the incompleteness of the works or permanent way or the insufficiency of the establishment'.[3] It had no power to issue regulations under this Act. The *Requirements*, then, had a dubious basis in law, being no more than statements of the terms on which the Department proposed to exercise its discretion. For example, platforms were to terminate in ramps, not in steps.[4] No doubt steps were more dangerous, but it is hard to see how they could be brought under the heading of 'incompleteness of the works or permanent way' and they were clearly nothing to do with 'insufficiency of the establishment'.

The restriction of the Board's powers to new lines was less important than might at first sight appear. Not only was the

---

[1] BTHR HL 2/19/161/21.   [2] Ibid., GN 1/304/5.
[3] 5 & 6 Vict., c. 55, s. 6.   [4] Rolt, 219.

mileage opened during the period covered in this chapter very considerable—in round figures, 6,000 miles—but also the concept was capable of considerable enlargement. An additional track to an existing railway, for instance, was reckoned to be a new line. As already shown, telegraph working on the L. & Y. Burnley branch was introduced under pressure from the Department when the line was doubled.[1] Again, new lines were normally connected with old lines, and the Department could insist on modifications to the old line at the junction as a condition for opening the new.[2] In the last year of our period, the Department asserted a right to inspect new stations as well as new lines, by an ingenious construction of the 1844 Act. In 1867, the Midland Railway opened a new station at Stapleton on the twenty-five-year-old Bristol to Gloucester line. When it sought approval for its revised Parliamentary train arrangements, the Department replied that the station must first be inspected, since they could 'not approve of passengers being taken up and set down at a station unless it is provided with platforms and other necessary accommodation for the safety of passengers'.[3]

The *Requirements* derived from the Department's experience, and in some cases the connection is obvious. For example, an accident occurred at Stratford on the Eastern Counties Railways in 1855 as a result of points failing to act. The rod connecting them with the point lever was found to be defective. The company decided to fit double connecting rods in future, so that if one should fail, the other would act, and Yolland commended this plan. Hence the provision in the *Requirements* that all points were 'to be provided with double connecting rods'.[4] But in other cases, the connection is less straightforward. For instance, it was laid down that 'turntables for engines [were] to be erected at terminal stations'.[5] To grasp the significance of this, it is necessary to consider the development of the Department's ideas from as far back as 1841. In that year it had formulated one of its earliest doctrines of railway safety, namely, 'the impropriety of running tender foremost'. This practice

---

[1] See p. 180. [2] See p. 194 ff.
[3] BTHR MID 4/41/13, cf. LNW 1/90, 14 and 22 Jul. 1867, for a similar case. [4] P.P. 1854-5, xlviii, 506. *Requirements* (1858).
[5] Ibid.

had been a factor in accidents on the Sheffield & Rotherham and North Union lines.[1] It was still a factor in accidents in 1906,[2] and the practice will probably continue in occasional use so long as steam engines run, whatever law and regulations, boards of directors, and government inspectors may say to the contrary.

The problem was to reduce safe working practices to forms which the Department could enforce and check by inspection. In this case, the solution proved to be turn-tables, the provision of which made it much less likely that engines would run tender first. It seems to have been first brought to the notice of the Department in 1846, in connection with the Worthing branch of the London & Brighton Railway. In response to a complaint that it was running engines tender first there, the company undertook to erect a turn-table at the terminus.[3] For some years, the Department made only occasional use of this knowledge.[4] But in the period 1855–6, it held up the opening of the Bedale & Leyburn Railway for more than six months, pending the installation of a turn-table at Leyburn. This case also provides a striking illustration of the way in which the Department could, in the exercise of its powers over new lines, modify old ones also. The new line was an extension of the N.E.R. branch from Northallerton to Bedale. The Department secured the erection of a turn-table at Northallerton also—a point six miles from the line under inspection and on a line belonging to another company.[5]

Before the Bedale case was finally closed, the next development took place. The engineer of the Jedburgh Railway wrote to ask whether 'turntables . . . [were] required . . . at the terminal stations of short single lines of railway worked by tank engines'. All three inspectors gave their opinions on this case, and it was laid down that the Board would 'require turntables . . . at the terminal stations of all lines of railway, whether worked by tank engines, or engines with tenders, except in case of lines not exceeding two or three miles in length'.[6] Finally, as

---

[1] P.P. 1842, xli, 20. [2] Rolt, 102.
[3] MT 13/5, 18 Feb. 1846. [4] E.g. MT 11/20, 22 Nov. 1851.
[5] Henry Parris, 'Northallerton to Hawes: a study in branch line history', in *Journal of Transport History*, ii (1955–6), 240.
[6] MT 13/21, 26 Apr. 1856.

shown already, turn-tables at terminal stations appeared among the *Requirements* in 1858.

To postpone the opening of a line might, of course, entail serious loss to a company. But by the same token, the Department's most effective means of pressure was lost once a line was open. Companies would make promises in order to avoid postponement but their promises were not always to be trusted. For example, in November, 1865, the Department sanctioned the opening of a section of the Central Wales Railway, on condition that the company put up a turn-table at Craven Arms within eight weeks. It was not always possible for inspectors to pay subsequent visits to see whether such conditions had been fulfilled. But in this case, Yolland reported more than two months later that there was as yet no turn-table. When called on to explain, the company stated that the turn-table had been made, but not installed, because it was impossible to do so until other alterations at the station were complete. On a third visit, in August, 1866, Yolland found that there was still no turn-table.[1] The company blamed the Shrewsbury & Hereford Railway, which also had an interest in the station, for the delay, and enclosed a copy of correspondence which went some way towards bearing this out. At last the company was able to tell the Department, at the end of October, 1866, that the turn-table had been put up.[2] As the company completed succeeding sections of its line, the turn-table was moved on, stage by stage, so as to be always at the head of the line.[3] It had been promised within eight weeks; it had taken almost a year. But for the visits of the Inspector, would it ever have been put up at all?

Other provisions in the *Requirements* are explicable in a similar way. For example, time-tables and time-interval regulations were a mockery if railway servants had no means of knowing the time. But the Department could not force companies to provide them with watches, nor could the inspectors say of their own knowledge how many drivers, guards, and so on, were carrying watches at any given moment. As they travelled the railways of Britain, however, the inspectors could see whether or not stations had clocks where drivers and guards

[1] MT 6/37, 431/1866.   [2] MT 6/42, 2322/1866.
[3] G. P. Neele, *Railway Reminiscences*, London (1904), 152–3; for this reference I am indebted to Mr. R. M. Robbins.

could see them. They could, moreover, insist on such clocks as a condition of sanctioning the opening of new lines. Hence the provision that 'clocks [were] to be provided in a position where they are visible from the line'.[1] The Department used its powers of postponement to enforce this requirement where necessary.[2]

The *Requirements* of 1858 embodied the 'knowledge acquired from the results of the past working of railways'. Successive editions aimed to incorporate also 'progressive improvements made in appliances for better securing the safety of the travelling public'.[3] This process may be illustrated by describing the development of the Department's ideas on signalling.

Signalling by hand or flag was common on the early railways, and where fixed signals were installed, it was usual to work each by a separate lever at the base of the signal itself. Similarly, each set of points was normally worked by a separate lever at the side of the line. As late as 1863, a very important junction at Bristol was controlled in this way:[4]

> the Midland Railway, and the line from the G.W. engine shed, and the South Wales Union Railway, all meet the main line of the G.W.R. at 720 yards from [Bristol] station . . . the signalman is . . . on the ground, and the levers which he is required to work are scattered about, between different lines of rails, at various distances from him; and he is liable to be interrupted in his duties by passing trains, as well as to be prevented from making proper use of the telegraph instruments with which he has now been provided.

The inspectors made a few recommendations relating to signals in their early reports, and when occasionally they did so, confined themselves to the plane of common sense. But following the re-formation of the Department in 1851, a deeper interest in the subject developed. Inspectors noted first the advantages of concentrating levers so that two or more signals might be worked from one spot. At the bridge which carried the Y.N.M. Knottingley branch over the River Aire, for example, there were two distant signals. One was on each side of the bridge, and both were worked by a man 'in a central situation between them; he works both signals by means of one lever

---

[1] *Requirements* (1858). [2] E.g. MT 6/21, 1698/1860; 6/27, 1483/1863.
[3] MT 6/40, 1731/1866; for the case in which these words were used, see below, p. 194 ff. [4] MT 6/28, 2888/1863.

handle, and the principle is, that when he turns one signal off, the other is necessarily turned on'.[1] It was in fact the signal-box, as understood today, in embryo. Although the signal-box originated in or before 1839,[2] it did not become general for many years. Moreover, early examples were merely shelters for the signalmen, with the levers still scattered outside.

Cases such as these led the Department to lay it down as a general rule 'that it is highly important to bring the handles of the signals and switches as near together as possible'.[3] Inspectors were guided by this rule in reporting on new lines. An early case was the Arpley branch of the Warrington & Stockport Railway, which was ready to open in 1855. It was to form a junction with the L.N.W.R. close to an existing junction. Yolland stipulated[4]

> that the whole of the fixed signals for these two junctions should be brought together to a box, placed midway between the two junctions, and placed under the entire control of the pointsman, receiving his instructions from one of the companies.

Yolland's views were too advanced for the company's engineer, who could not[5]

> see how it is to be carried out, as the switches . . . are 101 yards apart: the man who turns the switches would be in each case 50 yards from his work. This would be highly objectionable . . . although machinery might be made to turn points 50 yards from the pointsman, I think it would be better to devise some other way of working.

Once it had become the practice to concentrate a number of levers in one place, the next development was to make the movement of the levers dependent on one another. The first step in this direction had been taken at Bricklayers Arms junction as early as 1843. There C. H. (later Sir Charles) Gregory had so arranged the controls as to prevent conflicting signals being given. Experimentation along these lines culminated in Saxby's patent of 1856, by which a single lever controlled the simultaneous motion of a set of points and the corresponding signal. In the following year, Yolland noted Saxby's apparatus at a new junction between the West End of London & Crystal

---

[1] P.P. 1852–3, lv, 249. For further details of this bridge, see p. 147 ff.
[2] Cf. Dendy Marshall, *History of the Southern Railway*, London (1936), 40.
[3] P.P. 1856, liv, 9. [4] Ibid., 50. [5] Ibid., 51.

Palace and L.B.S.C. Railways.[1] The 1858 *Requirements* specified the use of signals of this type in connection with facing points.

The next big step forward came in 1859. The opening of the Hampstead Junction Railway, which ran into the L.N.W. and North London Railways near the present Camden Road Station, had already been twice postponed. After the third inspection, Yolland reported:

> It was admitted by officers of the [three companies] 'that as the traffic on the North London Railway was very heavy it was desirable to alter the signals so that a signalman shall not have it in his power to give contradictory signals that might lead to a collision at the junction of the two lines' and a gentleman from the firm entrusted by the company with the erection of the signals stated that it should be done. I explained . . . where such signals could be seen in full operation on the L.B.S.C.R. I have now to state that the firm in question have failed in complying with that requirement.

The problem was solved by a North London employee, Austin Chambers. In so doing, he made a notable advance on Saxby's system. Abandoning simultaneous motion, he interlocked the lever controlling the signal with the lever controlling the points, so that the former could not be moved to 'all right' until the latter had been put in the correct position. Yolland reported on the new system, and pointed out an incidental advantage:

> when all the signals stand at 'danger', the points are left perfectly free to be used as required for shunting operations. In addition, the signalman is prevented from showing two signals at the same time, that if obeyed by engine drivers, would lead to a collision at the junction . . . these arrangements carry out in an effective and much more simple and inexpensive manner the improvements in junction signals first introduced by Messrs. Saxby & Co.

The line was permitted to open, and Chambers patented his invention. It seems clear that he would not have made it but for stimulus from the Department.[2]

---

[1] For the early history of signalling, see R. C. Rapier, 'On the Fixed Signals of Railways', in *Proceedings of the Institution of Civil Engineers*, xxxviii (1873–4); Westinghouse Brake & Signal Co., *John Saxby (1821–1913) and his part in the Development of Interlocking* (1956), 3–7. For Yolland's report, see P.P. 1857–8, li, 261–2.

[2] MT 6/20, 3849, 4317, 4427, 5025/1859. The last is missing from the P.R.O. set, but there is a copy at the Ministry of Transport. Chambers'

What appears to have been the first dispute with a company about interlocking occurred in 1861. A short line had been constructed to link the L. & Y. with the Midland Railway near Oakenshaw in the West Riding.[1] Even before it was inspected, Smithells, general manager of the L. & Y., warned the Midland that he had seen Tyler, and learnt from him that he could not approve the latter company's junction. The Midland did not, however, take the hint. After the inspection, Tyler reported that 'a raised stage has been erected at the L. & Y. junction of a superior description, and the points and signals have been placed conveniently under the hand of the signalman'. The Midland junction, on the other hand, was 'very inferior. The signalman's platform is on a level with the ground', the handles were poor, and the regulations objectionable. He recommended interlocking, and the L. & Y. agreed to install the necessary apparatus within six weeks. Smithells wrote to tell the general manager of the Midland, James Allport, that Tyler would recommend postponement and went on:

> For your own guidance, I may add that [he] made some strong remarks on the state of your permanent way, signals etc. It seems that a junction house like the one we have built . . . will have to be provided and other matters which he has pointed out but that he will allow us to have the use of the line on your giving an undertaking to do within a certain time what he has indicated. . . . Having issued our bills to the public and made all preparations . . . I trust you will not fail to comply with the requirements [so far as] may be necessary to enable us to commence on the 1st of July.

The Midland did not comply, the opening was postponed, and the L. & Y. was, of course, annoyed. Smithells wrote again to Allport:

> It is a great misfortune we were not able to open as announced to the public. I trust you will lose no time in seeing the Board of

own account of the incident may be compared with Yolland's. The Inspector's requirement put the company in a quandary, but 'Being appealed to for information as to how the object could be attained, Col. Yolland replied, "It is not my province to suggest but to approve." . . . During the [final] inspection Col. Yolland made this remark to the Manager. "You see I have not asked for more than could be done, as one of your own staff has provided it; you will some day thank me!" ' (*Proceedings of the Institution of Civil Engineers*, xxxviii (1873–4), 216–17).

[1] The account of this case is based on MT 6/23, 1942, 1999, 2053, 2159/1861; and BTHR MID 4/41/2.

Trade and inducing them to allow us to commence to use the junction. . . . I fear we shall for a time be a laughing stock to our competitors, and that my directors will be very much disappointed when I report to them tomorrow that the junction is not being used.

The directors were more than disappointed; after their meeting, the following telegram was sent to the Midland: 'Directors greatly disapprove of . . . junction not being opened . . . no time must be lost great outcry'.

The next day, the Midland told the Board that the required interlocking would be carried out within six weeks, though under strong protest. The company still refused, however, to accept some minor amendments in the regulations for the junction. Tyler was in Ireland, and so did not see the file before it went to Booth. Booth minuted that he regretted the company's attitude, 'but we cannot force [the regulations] on the company by refusing to allow the line to be opened'. Sanction to open was therefore given. Booth must have known that the Department forced many things on companies by refusing to allow lines to be opened. He meant, presumably, that he did not like exercising the Board's powers in this way. This interpretation is borne out by his remark in another case that 'there are always very strong objections to our insisting on any particular mode of construction . . . to which the engineers of the company object, as in the event of accident the responsibility is very likely to be removed from the company and thrown upon this Department'.[1] These statements suggest that Booth's personal influence may have been partly responsible for the comparatively slow progress made in enforcing, for example, telegraph working on new lines.

From this point onwards, signal boxes and interlocking were referred to with increasing frequency in the reports of inspectors on new lines. Where they were already installed, the inspectors commented favourably.[2] Where they had not been, they were prepared to recommend postponement, as a result of which companies were generally willing to comply.[3]

Three companies, however, were less co-operative. The

---

[1] MT 6/40, 1731/1866.
[2] E.g. MT 6/27, 239/1863; 6/31, 1141/1864; 6/35, 205/1865; 6/36, 2170/1865.   [3] E.g. MT 6/41, 1978/1866, and 6/42, 2174/1866.

Department's dealings with each raised important questions of principle. The first relates to the question of technical advance. In these early years of interlocking, it was clearly desirable that companies should experiment in order to bring the system nearer to perfection. Tyler found the North Staffordshire Railway doing so, when he inspected its Biddulph branch in 1863. Near the junction of the new line was the Congleton junction which had 'been constructed with a locking apparatus of a new form devised by a signal-fitter in the service of the company'. Tyler considered the new junction should be locked also, and advised postponement. Eventually the opening was held up for nine months pending the carrying out of Tyler's requirement. The company may have been perfectly reasonable in wishing to make a full test of its own apparatus before extending its use, or buying from one of the firms specialising in the manufacture of signalling equipment; though admittedly the view of its engineer that locking at the new junction was 'unnecessary for the public safety' makes this unlikely. However, had the unusually rigid attitude of the Department in this case become general, it might have had a discouraging effect on technical progress.[1]

A case involving the N.B.R. raised the question whether, by issuing the *Requirements*, the Department had limited the exercise of its own discretion. The first edition stated clearly that it contained only some of the requirements for new lines. A company might well feel a sense of grievance, however, if after meeting all the requirements specified, permission to open were refused on other grounds. When Tyler inspected the line from Peebles to Innerleithen, he stipulated interlocking at Peebles junction. The company agreed, and permission to open was given. The chairman of the company, Richard Hodgson, M.P., now wrote to say that, having discussed the case with MacGregor and Farrer, he felt it raised an important point of principle. In several instances, inspectors had objected to works constructed in accordance with the *Requirements* and similar to works previously approved.

Additional or altered works [had been] imposed as the condition or sanction to the opening of a new line. While on the one hand, I

[1] MT 6/28, 2549, 2769, 2837/1863; 31, 1031/1864; BTHR NS 1/6, 14 Oct. 1863.

quite admit that this sanction should be withheld where stated requirements have not been observed, I think it only reasonable that, as additional experience prompts further requirements, these should be embodied in the printed particulars and a copy furnished . . . to each company on presentation of their first notice of opening.[1]

In view of Hodgson's importance in railway politics, and the force of his argument, it is curious that the Department appears to have done no more than acknowledge his letter. Although he was wrong in his facts—interlocking had been one of the *Requirements* since 1860—the point he had raised was of some importance. Was the Department to make no new requirements for individual lines until they felt justified in making them for all? Clearly, such a rule would have tied their hands too much.

It is probable that Hodgson's letter influenced the Department's practice in one respect. The first two editions of the *Requirements* were sent out as a general circular to companies. The next two, on the other hand, went only to companies as they gave notice of opening of new lines, and Hodgson claimed that his company had not seen them. With the 1867 edition— the next after he wrote—the Department reverted to the earlier practice. The importance of the *Requirements* in the railway world was shown by the decision of the L.N.W.R. to refer them to the manager and engineer who were 'to advise if any objectionable stipulations had been introduced'.[2] They were also to be considered by general managers under the auspices of the United Railway Companies Association.[3]

The interest of these last two cases does not lie in any hostility to interlocking itself. That distinction was reserved for the Midland Railway, whose experience at Oakenshaw did not convince it of the value of the system. The Department sanctioned the opening of a few new Midland lines in the period 1862–3 without insisting on interlocking.[4] A further dispute arose, however, over the Morecambe branch, which was a short line built to link the L.N.W.R. with the Midland.[5] It was

[1] MT 6/32, 1973/1864.   [2] BTHR, LNW 1/90, 3 Oct. 1867.
[3] Ibid., 6 Nov. 1867.
[4] MT 6/25, 1142 and 2154/1862; 6/27, 1497/1863.
[5] This account is based on MT 6/28, 2815, 2993, 3080, 3213/1863; 6/40, 1731/1866; and BTHR MID 4/41/5.

first inspected by Yolland in 1861, who reported that inter-locking was needed and the opening was postponed. Both the companies and the Department now appear to have forgotten the existence of the branch for two years. The L.N.W.R. then agreed to the Department's suggestion and wrote to the Mid-land that 'the opening of the branch is a question of consider-able importance to this Company'. In spite of this appeal, the Midland persisted in its refusal. Allport now developed a rea-soned case, in which he appears sincerely to have believed, against interlocking. He had taken Yolland's advice to go and look at locking installations at Stratford (an important junction on the Great Eastern) and elsewhere, but believed they were more dangerous than the ordinary kind. Accidents of the kind interlocking was designed to prevent were rare, whereas

> the overrunning of junctions by drivers with signals against them is a far more prolific cause of accidents . . . [there had been six or eight cases] where two trains have been approaching a junction at the same time . . . at the last moment [it] became apparent to the pointsman . . . that the driver of No. 2 train would be unable to stop without fouling the junction, [and] he has by suddenly throwing over the points and turning No. 1 train along the straight line instead of across the junction prevented a collision.

Interlocking would have left no time for this operation, and so 'in endeavouring to prevent an imaginary evil, would give rise to real danger'. Yolland made the obvious rejoinder that All-port's remedy was necessary only because Midland drivers were so lacking in discipline as to overrun signals at danger; in any case, the extra time required to operate interlocked levers was so slight that such action would still be possible when required. Yolland had already suggested that permission to open be given, on the grounds that it was unfair to penalise the L.N.W. for the obstinacy of the Midland. Eventually, in 1864, this was done. Fane suggested that the Board should merely 'allow the month's postponement to expire without renewal'. Booth did not care for this plan and proposed the more straightforward course of withdrawing the objection hitherto made. Hutt con-curred in this.

The Morecambe case seems to have had an important in-fluence on the development of L.N.W. signal policy. Not long after Yolland's first requirement of interlocking, Saxby met the company's Traffic Committee and demonstrated the apparatus he had developed since Chambers' invention. Cawkwell, the general manager, was told to arrange a trial at an important junction in Birmingham. The following year the company made an agreement with Saxby for the general use of his patent equipment. In 1867, the directors resolved

> that the locking system be applied . . . to the L.N.W. company's junctions having facing points on the main lines and principal branches . . . [and] that . . . companies having junctions with the L.N.W. lines arranged on the old principle be called upon to improve them by adapting them to the locking plan.[1]

The Midland Railway too seems to have been affected by what had happened at Morecambe. Although its policy remained unchanged, its policy and its practice began to diverge. In 1864, it interlocked a new junction with the South Leicestershire Railway at Nuneaton on Saxby's principle;[2] while at its own new Whitacre junction, the levers were arranged on a new plan which sought to give some of the advantages of interlocking.[3] Tyler described similar apparatus on the Midland-N.E. joint Otley-Ilkley line in 1865:

> the levers of the junction points have been so placed that the points can only be moved when the signals are at danger. This is an important step towards the adoption of the locking apparatus.[4]

There were other Midland interlocked junctions at Peterborough and Kettering prior to 1866.[5]

It was in February of that year that the great trial of strength between the Department and the company arose. The Aston curve, a short new link between two older lines near Birmingham, was ready to open. Yolland recommended postponement on the ground that the junctions were not locked. The minute on his report states that all the inspectors agreed that interlocking was the safest course—a rare instance of a deliberate effort to secure a united front—and even MacGregor ventured a technical opinion:

> I think the time has arrived when this system should be *absolutely* insisted upon when the new line for which the signals are required

---

[1] BTHR LNW 1/170, 6 Dec. 1861; 1/82, 6 Mar. 1862; 1/90, 19 Jul. 1867.
[2] BTHR MID 4/41/6.　　[3] MT 6/32, 2097/1864. BTHR MID 4/41/8.
[4] MT 6/34, 1553/1865. BTHR MID 4/41/9.　　[5] MT 6/40, 1731/1866.

and the *old line* with which it forms a junction belong to the same company, as is the case in the present instance.

The file next went to Fane, who summarised the precedents, with the curious exception of the Oakenshaw case—the one instance in which the Midland had succumbed to pressure. He then gave a singularly clear statement of the Department's method of enforcing its recommendations. The company would probably refuse, and so

> in order to put continued pressure upon them, this Board will have to order a re-inspection and make an order of postponement every succeeding month, until the company make the change, or open in defiance of the prohibition, or incur a penalty for not opening within the prescribed time.

The case went to Milner-Gibson, and the opening was postponed.

After a second postponement, Milner-Gibson ordered an enquiry, in which nine major companies were asked to state whether it was their rule to provide interlocking at

        (a) new junctions, and
        (b) existing junctions.

Their answers may be summarised as follows:

G.E.R.   (a) yes
        (b) yes, when 'material alteration' was necessary anyway.

G.N.R.   (a) 'We now invariably adopt the plan.'
        (b) – –

G.W.R.   (a) 'At new junctions which have been opened lately the government inspectors have recommended locking apparatus . . . which the company have been willing to adopt and have applied.'
        (b) Yes, at eight in the last two years; work in progress at others.

L.N.W.   (a) Yes, 'whenever . . . practicable'.
        (b) Yes, 'in several cases'.

L.S.W.   (a) 'Recently we have adopted the system . . . in pursuance of the recommendation of the . . . Board of Trade; but in doing so, I am not prepared to say that the system affords greater safety.'

         (b) Yes, 'at several junctions . . . believing that there should not be two systems on the line, and as the locking apparatus has been considered a *sine qua non* for all new lines and junctions, the company is gradually introducing the system at the old junctions'.

L.B.S.C. (a) 'This company prefers to use the locking apparatus.'

         (b) Yes, at seven junctions.

L.C.D.   (a) Yes, for 'some time'; company 'satisfied' it was safer.

         (b) Yes, at several important junctions; both Stevens' and Saxby & Farmer's apparatus had been used; company had 'every reason to be satisfied'.

N.E.R.   (a) Yes, 'of late years'.

         (b) No.

S.E.R.   (a) Yes, 'most conducive to safety'.

         (b) Yes.

Milner-Gibson saw two representatives of the company, Price and Allport. They agreed to interlock the signals with one another, but still argued that interlocking of signals and points was a source of danger, and submitted a list of incidents in which signalmen had averted collisions by switching one of two approaching trains on to another line. Interlocking would leave no time for such action. Yolland put this argument to the test, and found it took one and a half seconds—a short enough time, he thought, to destroy the company's objection. He wrote:

> If the President could find half an hour to drive to Charing Cross or Victoria Station to go into one of the signal boxes it would probably do more . . . than . . . pages [from me] on the subject.

Accidents which interlocking would have prevented were more numerous. There had been twenty-seven in the period 1861–5, in which seven people had been killed and 257 injured. Some of them had occurred on the Midland, and, in 1858, there had been such an accident near the site of one of the new junctions.

The Midland argument was based, so Allport said, on experience. But the lessons of experience were of limited value as railway working became more complicated. Tyler made this point in a memorandum on the case:

when junctions become more complicated, with extra lines meeting and crossover roads, through crossings, and sidings, and with 20, 30 or even 60 levers worked from one box, then the signalman requires in a much greater degree the assistance that the locking apparatus affords to him to prevent his making mistakes daily.

Tyler suggested that the Midland should be challenged to name the companies which it alleged had been forced by the Department to adopt interlocking against their will. Companies might have fitted the apparatus in the first place at the suggestion of an inspector; but they were now convinced of its advantages:

> for instance, Mr. Scott, the General Manager of the L.S.W.R., was altogether opposed to it till lately. . . . But he has now adopted it on parts of the old line as well as on new lines—as may be seen at Nine Elms, and in the works in progress near Waterloo, and lately has expressed a desire to lock the distant signals as well as the main signals when I have met him on new lines.[1]

At last, in June, the Midland Traffic Committee resolved, since the Board now insisted on interlocking at all new junctions, that their

> requirements be complied with; but that the Board be informed that such requirements are against the convictions of the Midland directors and officers and that they must decline to be held responsible for their adoption.

Yolland reported in July that work was complete at one junction, and nearly finished at the other. The objection to opening was withdrawn—nearly six months after the first postponement.[2]

The Department's dealings with the Midland Railway in 1867 suggest that the company had more or less accepted the new principle. Permission to open the Evesham-Redditch line was given, on an undertaking by the engineer to complete the interlocking.[3] The Keighley & North Valley line, which the Midland was to work, was allowed to open, after postponement, on receipt of the Midland's agreement to supply locking apparatus.[4] The opening of the Stonehouse & Nailsworth

---

[1] The partial contradiction between this and the view of the L.S.W. quoted above is probably to be explained by the fact that the latter was written by a different officer, namely, the Secretary.

[2] The entire account of the Aston case is based on MT 6/40, 1731/1866; and BTHR MID 4/41/11. [3] MT 6/44, 109/1867.

[4] Ibid., 667/1867. BTHR MID 4/41/16A.

Railway, which formed a junction with the Midland, was held up for a time. But the dispute related to the provision of a turn-table, and the documents do not make it clear whether the junction was locked or not.[1] The Department sanctioned the opening of the line from Derby to Spondon, after postponement, on learning that the required interlocking had been carried out.[2] Reporting on the line between Duffield and Wirksworth, the Inspector stated that 'the points and signals at the [Duffield] junction are arranged on the locking principle'; it was allowed to open.[3] It appears that under pressure the company had given up its opposition to interlocking.

A case relating to three short branches on the Caledonian Railway shows that the attitude of the Department was still fundamentally empirical. On the Cleland branch, Rich found the locking and signals imperfect, and the opening was postponed. At a subsequent inspection, the company promised to adopt his suggestions. When it later wrote to say that some had been carried out, and the others would be attended to, permission to open was given. Rich found the junction between the main line and the Dolphinton branch locked, but suggested improvements to the signals; he thought the line might open, however, and permission was given without waiting to see whether the company would carry out the improvements suggested. The Wilsontown branch had been open for some time as a mineral line, and the company now wished to use it for passengers. There were mineral sidings from it, over which the Department had no jurisdiction. The Inspector may have felt some uncertainty as to his powers. Nevertheless, it is surprising to find him recommending that the line should open for passengers, although the junctions with the sidings were not only not locked, but were not even provided with signals. His recommendation was followed.[4]

The Aston curve case did not, then, settle the question once for all. Nevertheless, interlocking was general, though not universal, on the new lines inspected in 1867. In a number of cases, suitable apparatus was found at the first inspection.[5] Other lines were allowed to open, on the companies promising

---

[1] MT 6/46, 1057/1867.   [2] Ibid., 1302/1867. BTHR MID 4/41/17.
[3] MT 6/48, 2019/1867. BTHR MID 4/41/19.   [4] MT 6/46, 1084/1867.
[5] E.g. MT 6/45, 835, 873, and 1021/1867; MT 6/47, 1532/1867.

to fit such apparatus.[1] Others again were permitted to open after postponement, the required gear having been installed.[2] A difficulty in interpreting some of the evidence is that the inspectors seem to have reached the stage of taking interlocking so much for granted that they did not invariably report its presence, but only drew attention to its absence. Hutchinson reported of one line, for instance, that 'the junction arrangements are of a perfect character'; and of another, three days later, 'the signal arrangements are all of a complete character'. Though this does not prove that the lines were interlocked, it gives the impression that they were; an impression that is deepened by the addition of the significant words 'put up by Stevens & Co.' to the second description.[3]

Interlocking was the most important example in the technical field of the Department's influence on railways. Invented under a stimulus from an inspector in 1859, it became within eight years universal in theory, and general in practice, on new lines.[4] Comparison with the other devices discussed above suggests why the Department's efforts should have been more successful in this case. The difficulty with continuous brakes was that it had no legal power between 1889 to enforce their use. In the case of communication between passengers, guards, and drivers, the technical problems had not been solved. As for telegraph working, it appears that the cost was the main obstacle to the Department's pressing for its more general introduction.[5]

The case of interlocking was different from any of these. The Department used its power of postponement to enforce its adoption on new lines. Although improvements continued to be made, the fundamental technical problem had been solved at the first attempt. And it was comparatively cheap. Saxby estimated £850 to fit up the junctions north and south of the

[1] E.g. MT 6/44, 31/1867; 6/45, 741 and 771/1867; and 6/47 1642/1857.
[2] E.g. MT 6/44, 325, 357, and 425/1867; and 6/46, 1287/1867.
[3] Ibid., 1309 and 1359/1867.
[4] Signal manufacturers advertised their products as fulfilling 'all the requirements of the Board of Trade'. Cf. *Engineering*, 4 Oct. 1867. For this reference I am indebted to the late Mr. T. S. Lascelles.
[5] Block working for tunnels, etc., first appeared in *Requirements* (1862); and for general use in *Requirements* (1874); the wording is deceptively simple: 'The requisite apparatus to be provided at the period of inspection for ensuring an adequate interval of space between following trains'.

L.N.W. station at Birmingham in 1861. To improve the signal system on the Cornwall Railway in 1868, on the other hand, including the locking of twenty-four junctions, was expected to cost only £515. According to this estimate, it was possible to lock points and signals for as little as £5. In all probability, these were extreme figures, applicable to circumstances respectively much more complex and much more simple than the average. Immediately after the end of our period, however, the G.N.R. accepted Saxby & Farmer's tender to interlock Grantham North Junction at a cost of £175. The layout was fairly complicated with five point levers and eight signals. It seems reasonable to suppose that it was representative of the cost of such conversions.[1] Moreover, concentration of levers brought some saving in running costs.[2]

Yolland suggested that the extra cost to the Midland Company of interlocking the two junctions in the Aston case would be £100–150.[3] Comparison with the Grantham estimate suggests that this was not unreasonable. It appears, therefore, that Allport's opposition was sincere, and not merely an excuse for parsimony. Confronted with a novel demand from the Department on one occasion, the L.N.W. solicitor advised his directors that, though there might well be grounds in law for resisting, they should consider whether it was expedient to do so.[4] When knowledge and power were on the side of the Department, companies had to compare the cost of acquiescence with the cost of resistance. The *Requirements* are full of items—tests for the strength of bridges,[5] clocks in junction signal boxes,[6] mile and gradient posts,[7] signals weighed to fly to 'danger' in case of a

---

[1] BTHR LNW 1/82, 12 Dec. 1861. COR 1/31, GN 1/299/16. The Grantham figure compares closely with the estimate of £15 per lever and connections given in Rapier, loc. cit., 186. The remainder of Rapier's discussion relates mainly to interlocking combined with the block system, and so is not comparable.

[2] Rapier, loc. cit., 187.

[3] BTHR MID 4/41/11.

[4] BTHR LNW 1/90, 14 and 22 Aug. 1867.

[5] *Requirements* (1859). [6] Ibid.

[7] *Requirements* (1860). Cf. above, p. 62. This edition also contains several new features: e.g., specifications for Parliamentary carriages (20 cu. ft., 60 sq. in. of glass window, and 16 in. width of seat per passenger, etc.); and regulations for single-line working; these appeared also in subsequent editions.

broken wire[1]—in regard to which it was normally cheaper to acquiesce. Such requirements, introduced gradually, and enforced company by company, and line by line, were, considered separately, of little moment; cumulatively, however, they had a profound influence on the development of British railways.

[1] *Requirements* (1862). This edition contained a new section, namely, precautions recommended as a result of accident enquiries: they included communication between guard and driver and continuous brakes.

7

RAILWAYS IN THE THEORY OF GOVERNMENT

THE period covered in this book seems in retrospect to many the very heyday of *laissez-faire*. Was public regulation of railways, then, in contradiction to the dominant opinion of the age?—Benthamism and Classical Economics? The central principle of the former was the doctrine of utility—that the prime object of legislation should be to secure the greatest happiness of the greatest number. While the latter placed so great an emphasis on the value of free enterprise that many people, then and since, have taken it to be its basic idea. Was there not, however, a contradiction between these two principles? Might not some restriction of free enterprise be necessary in order to secure the greatest happiness of the greatest number?

That there was such a contradiction is one of the main themes of Halévy's classic study of Benthamism; for a time it remained latent but eventually it led to the triumph of free enterprise over utility.[1] Sir Cecil Carr has said that the problem, 'How the Benthamites could reconcile [their theory of law] with their natural addiction to the doctrines of *laissez-faire* is one of the puzzles of political science'.[2] Lord Robbins, on the other hand, sees[3]

no evidence whatever for the view that the Classical Economists ever made the distinction which [Halévy] attributes to them. . . .

[1] E. Halévy, *Growth of Philosophic Radicalism*, Faber (Eng. ed., 1928), 490, 514.
[2] C. T. Carr, *Concerning English Administrative Law*, O.U.P. (1941), 8–9.
[3] L. Robbins, *Theory of Economic Policy*, Macmillan (1952), 191.

If they assumed anywhere a harmony, it was never a harmony arising in a vacuum but always very definitely within a framework of law. . . . If no other proof were available, their willingness to apply special rules and regulations where, for technical reasons, competition was not possible, should be a sufficient indication of the extent to which they regarded the appropriate legal framework and the system of economic freedom as two aspects of one and the same social process.

He shows how the apparent contradiction was reconciled. What is the purpose of production? Adam Smith's answer was: 'Consumption is the sole end and purpose of all production; and the interest of the producer ought to be attended to, only so far as it is necessary for promoting that of the consumer'. Producers should indeed enjoy free enterprise, but for the benefit of consumers, not themselves. This argument was elaborated by Bentham. Natural right is a fallacy, and therefore business men have no natural right not to be interfered with by the state. Free enterprise must be justified by utility, as must any proposed abrogation of it by the state. 'According to the principle of utility, as distinct from the *Naturrecht*, the expediency of any act of government must be judged solely by its consequence and not regarded as ruled out in advance by some metaphysical system of rights.' Bentham himself gives 'the most surprising examples of state action which is said to be beneficial—from accumulation, for instance, of large stocks of food against famine, in circumstances where the private market does not function adequately in this respect, to intervention to prevent over-speculation in stock markets'.[1]

In most cases, free enterprise is justified on grounds of utility, because competition will safeguard the consumer—will, indeed, do much more; it will ensure him the most abundant supply of the best quality goods at the lowest possible prices. The Classical Economists, therefore, were in general opposed to price-fixing; 'but, if there was no competition, this prohibition did not necessarily hold'. Adam Smith had argued that if bread were a monopoly, its price should be controlled. McCulloch favoured dividend limitation for public utility companies.[2] Arguing more generally from the principle of utility, Nassau Senior held that 'a government . . . must do whatever conduces to the welfare of

---

[1] Robbins, op. cit., 7, 14–15, and 40–1.   [2] Ibid., 38, 58–9.

the governed ... it will make mistakes, but non-interference may be an error too; one can be passively wrong as well as actively wrong'.[1] It was, then, widely recognised in the thought of the age that in certain circumstances the state should intervene in economic matters. Among the cases calling for such interference was that in which a group of producers (e.g. railway companies) enjoyed a monopoly.

The 1830's were, in fact, a period of rapid extension of government intervention in the life of the community. Sir Cecil Carr sums it up as follows:

> There they were, in full view, a century ago—a central government replacing a loose local administration, the paid professional official superseding the unpaid amateur, delegation of the legislative power, the possibility of appeal from administrative decision, the strictness of judicial interpretation, the well-intentioned bureaucrat's outpacing of public opinion, and so on. Most of the modern criticisms of bureaucratic encroachment were audible in the eighteen-thirties. How modern it all is![2]

Of the new activities of government, three were of particular importance from the present point of view—factory inspection, education, and poor law.

The story of the Factory Acts is, of course, well known, as is the part played by Southey and Oastler, Sadler and Lord Shaftesbury. It is also generally acknowledged that what made the Act of 1833 more effective than its forerunners was the appointment of inspectors with wide powers. This innovation was suggested, not by any of the well-known figures mentioned above, but by Edwin Chadwick.[3] He was then at the outset of his official career, having been private secretary to Bentham until the latter's death in the previous year.

The men appointed under the Factory Act of 1833 were the first government inspectors. At first there were only four, responsible to the Home Office for about 4,000 factories. There were no precedents to guide them; everything had to be worked out from scratch. Within his division

> the inspector possessed tremendous powers; he made rules and regulations to carry out the Act; he performed the judicial

[1] M. Bowley, *Nassau Senior & The Classical Economists*, Allen & Unwin (1937), 265.　　　　　　　　　　　　　[2] Carr, op. cit., 8.
[3] M. W. Thomas, op. cit., Thames Bank, 55.

function of deciding factory cases when they were brought before him; he had to see that enough good schools were established and maintained in his division for the education of factory children. He reported to the Home Secretary twice a year; and met twice a year in London with his colleagues to discuss common policy. ... What is stressed here is the fact that the four original inspectors wielded in their hands overwhelming powers, administrative, legislative and judicial.[1]

The Poor Law Commissioners set up under the Act of 1834 extended to local authorities a kind of central control similar to that which the Home Office was exerting over factories. They exercised extensive delegated powers, working through Assistant Commissioners, who corresponded to inspectors. Without their work in the field, the principles of 1834 would have been introduced more slowly and less widely. On them fell the brunt of organising the parishes into unions, and of banning out-relief. Often they had to face the most bitter and violent local opposition, especially in the north. Other features of their work were the inspection of pauper schools, and the promotion of schemes of migration from areas such as East Anglia to the industrial north.[2] The setting up of the department was, of course, the work of Chadwick, and he supplied the drive in the early years.

In 1839, an education department was set up. The first official head was Kay-Shuttleworth who had previously been an Assistant Commissioner of Poor Law.[3] The department administered the Exchequer grants first voted six years before to the voluntary bodies engaged in education. An elaborate code of regulations was built up, and a system of inspection founded—even today the initials H.M.I. mean, primarily, Her Majesty's Inspector *of Schools*. It is not easy to say how far Kay-Shuttleworth was influenced directly by Bentham, but he was certainly influenced very greatly by having worked with Chadwick under the Poor Law Commissioners.

Against this background, it becomes clear that the setting up of the Railway Department of the Board of Trade in 1840 was not an isolated incident, but part of a general trend towards the

---

[1] T. K. Djang, *Factory Inspection in Great Britain*, Allen & Unwin (1942), 33–4.
[2] F. Smith, *Life of Sir J. Kay-Shuttleworth*, Murray (1923), 37–8.
[3] Ibid., 35 ff.

intervention of government in more and more branches of national life. Like the other departments described, the Railway Department exercised delegated powers, and worked largely through inspectors, who were its representatives in the field. Many of the problems which arose were common to the Railway Department and the other services. An important aspect of the growth of a professional code in the inspectorate, for example, was the problem of social relations between inspectors and inspected. Could a man maintain his impartiality after accepting an invitation to dinner? This problem had caused some difficulty in the early days of the factory inspectorate. Similarly, how could equal and independent inspectors achieve a common policy? Should there not be an Inspector-General of Factories? Should inspectors have power to publish reports before they had the approval of the minister.[1] Each of these problems has been discussed above in relation to railways.[2]

It would be natural to expect that as time went on this activity of government would increase. Indeed, studies of factory legislation have emphasised the extension of the code to more and more sections of industry as the century progressed. From the administrative point of view, on the other hand, it appears that inspectorial control actually declined, since, until 1878, the number of inspectors failed to keep pace with the number of factories to be inspected.[3] Moreover, in 1844 the inspectors lost their power to make regulations and to act as magistrates.[4] In Poor Law, Chadwick fell out with his chiefs, and his influence had ceased to count for some years before he was finally forced out in 1847. There seems to have been a lessening rather than an increase in activity after the middle 'forties. In 1834, for example, no part of the new reforms seemed more important than the banning of outdoor relief; in fact, it never was completely banned over the entire country. The pattern in education was similar. Kay-Shuttleworth resigned in 1849, and in later years, the 'payment-by-results' system entirely transformed the education service. The grant was administered by formula, and very little scope remained for creative administration. The inspector of schools became an

---

[1] Thomas, op. cit., 76, 96, 245–7, 254–8, and 261–3.
[2] See above, pp. 32–4, 66 and 92–3.
[3] Djang, op. cit., 34.   [4] Thomas, op. cit., 251.

examiner of children and forfeited much of his influence. A similar trend is discernible in railway regulation. From its foundation in 1840, it developed rapidly at first; but from 1844 until 1868 there was no significant development of the Board's legal powers. Its influence on the companies increased, however, because the Board's officers learnt how to exercise those powers more and more effectively.

Though the current towards more state intervention may have moved more slowly for a time, its direction was never in doubt. The central government acquired powers to supervise prison authorities, to promote public health, and to inspect coal-mines, emigrant traffic, and merchant shipping. In 1854, the Railway Department was only one of sixteen Departments endowed with comparable powers.[1] The Board of Trade was at the centre of this development. A report of 1853 stated:

> There is probably no department of the Government to whose functions so many and such important additions have recently been made as the Board of Trade. While, however, these additions have been of such a nature as almost entirely to change the character of the Department, its constitution has not as yet been revised with a view to the efficient discharge of its new duties. . . . As each of these subjects has been successively assigned to the Board of Trade, some provision has been made for supplying the machinery required to deal with it; but this has generally been done by adding to the Department either some new officer, or some subordinate Board, specially charged with the management of the new business, and not by any such general recasting of the office as would render it efficient as a whole for the discharge of its functions.[2]

This process—what a recent writer has called 'the transformation of the Board of Trade'[3]—had been going on since 1833. Before that, there had been no departments within the Board; but with the appointment in that year of G. R. Porter, as head of the new Statistical Department, the remainder came to be called the Commercial Department for the sake of distinction. No more elaborate organisation was necessary, for in 1840 the entire staff was only thirty.[4]

[1] D. Roberts, *Victorian Origins of the British Welfare State*, Oxford (1960), 106 n. [2] P.P. 1854, xxvii, 161.
[3] R. Prouty, *The Transformation of the Board of Trade, 1830–55*, Heinemann (1957). [4] Sir H. Llewellyn Smith, op. cit., 52.

The Board was in origin a committee of the Privy Council, headed by a President and Vice-President, who were its Parliamentary heads. Even in 1845 'the tradition of weekly or semi-weekly meetings of the Board was kept up, but no one attended—probably no one was summoned—except the President and Vice-President and the minutes merely recorded the President's decision as the result of their consultations'.[1] Before 1840, the Board was mainly concerned with trade as distinct from industry. Already, however, it had a vague responsibility for factory inspection, in partnership with the Home Office,[2] and a more definite interest in industrial design.[3] Nevertheless, the setting up of the Railway Department was a turning-point for the Board of Trade, establishing its claim as an embryo ministry of industry.

The new members of the staff were recruited by patronage and this study has shown how that system worked in practice. 'The government patronage', wrote Trevelyan to Gladstone in 1853,

> is habitually employed in influencing, or according to a stricter morality, corrupting representatives and electors at the expense both of their independence and of the public interests. Even the establishment at the Board of Trade for protecting our lives and limbs when travelling by railway is not exempt from the blight of this system.[4]

The evidence does not bear out the implication of this passage. The officers of the Department were models of ability, industry, and integrity. They exemplified in a notable degree the conclusion to which Trevelyan subscribed on another occasion that civil servants were 'much better than we have any right to expect from the system under which they are appointed and promoted'.[5]

Another point to note in connection with Trevelyan is that the division which he, with Northcote, advocated between intellectual and mechanical work[6] was a feature of the Railway Department's work from the beginning. There were at all times

---

[1] Sir H. Llewellyn Smith, op. cit., 51.
[2] Thomas, op. cit., 115. [3] Prouty, op. cit., 20 ff.
[4] q. E. Hughes, 'Sir Charles Trevelyan & Civil Service Reform, 1853–1855', in *English Historical Review*, lxiv (1949), 68.
[5] P.P. 1854, xxvii, 5. [6] Ibid., 163.

two distinct classes of officers. The higher consisted of well-educated, and normally professionally qualified, men whose time was fully occupied with work of a highly skilled and responsible character. The lower consisted of men recruited for routine clerical duties, though some of them eventually gained promotion to more responsible posts.

As a result of this division, the higher civil servants in the Department influenced the formation of policy from its earliest days. This is not to say there was no development in the process of decision-making. Quite apart from the two unfortunate experiments with board administration (the Railway Board and the Commissioners of Railways), there was a profound contrast between the beginning and the end of the period in this respect. At the beginning, the President and Vice-President were so much involved in the Department's work, that its decisions were in a real sense, their decisions. By the end, however, the Department was administered on the modern pattern. The majority of the decisions were taken by permanent officials. The President and Vice-President took responsibility for all decisions, but were personally involved in only a small proportion of them. Ministerial responsibility had become a political fiction. In this development, the Department was a microcosm of British central administration in the nineteenth century.

The Department influenced the course of legislation at a number of points. Many provisions in public general Acts relating to railways derive directly from its administrative experience. Bills which it promoted were drafted by qualified specialists, while Bills relating to railways promoted by private Members came to depend for their success very largely on the attitude of the Department towards them. The Department, by issue of certificates, conferred powers on companies of a kind which would formerly have required private Acts. All these activities were part of a general process whereby in the nineteenth century the executive came to play an increasingly important rôle in legislation. Nor was this rôle confined to drafting Bills; it extended also to the process of amendment. The Department was able to modify measures promoted by railway companies. Its own measures were subject to pressure from the railway interest, and were often radically altered by direct consultation, instead of in Parliamentary committees.

During the Department's early years, its powers grew as a result of the passing of public general Acts. But after 1844, this trend was checked until the close of the period. The check was more apparent than real, since the Department came to intervene more effectively in the interests of public safety without any formal increase in powers. It did so by developing a system many of whose features—delegated legislation, administrative tribunals, appeal to the minister, and quasi-legislation, for example—have proved highly controversial in our own day. Such developments were not consciously intended. No statute within the period empowered the Department to act as a tribunal, for example; it did so as a result of the truth perceived by Dicey late in life that 'the imposition upon the government of new duties . . . almost implies, and certainly has in fact promoted, the transference to departments of the central government . . . of judicial or quasi-judicial functions'.[1] Because this body of administrative law grew up in such a way, its existence was little known. 'The new laws were not lawyer's law; lawyers did not study them.'[2] Hence even today the nineteenth-century origins of modern administrative law are not generally recognised.

In a recent discussion of quasi-legislation, for instance, Professor Keeton spoke of the process whereby 'departmental . . . circulars and explanatory memoranda can acquire compulsive force'[3]—words which describe to perfection the effect on railways of the Department's *Requirements*. And in the note where Mr. Megarry first used the expression, he expressed lucidly the motive which made companies submit; although departmental circulars are open to challenge in the courts, they

> can be said to have the practical effect of legislation . . . to the extent that the expense, delays and uncertainties of litigation in general, and of opposing the unlimited resources of the administration in particular, make those affected prefer to be submissive rather than stiff-necked.[4]

[1] A. V. Dicey, 'Development of Administrative Law in England', in *Law Quarterly Review*, xxxi (1915), 149.

[2] C. T. Carr, *Concerning English Administrative Law*, O.U.P. (1941), 21.

[3] G. W. Keeton, *The Passing of Parliament*, E. Benn (1952), 200.

[4] R. E. Megarry, 'Administrative Quasi-Legislation', in *Law Quarterly Review*, lx (1944), 126.

But although their remarks apply so well to the methods employed in the regulation of railways from 1858 onwards, the assumption underlying their discussion of the subject is that quasi-legislation originated only during the Second World War. In fact, the Railway Department was quietly developing the technique more than eighty years earlier.

EPILOGUE: 1868–1914

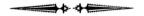

1867 was a turning-point in relations between railways and the state. For more than two decades before that date there had been no significant increase in the government's powers. The Royal Commission that reported in that year recommended no fundamental change. But from 1868 onwards the tendency towards greater state intervention resumed. In the field of safety, specific devices, such as interlocking, block working, and continuous brakes, were made compulsory. The state reduced and restricted the rates charged by the companies. Railwaymen's hours of work were cut by Act of Parliament and fixed at levels to be determined by the Board of Trade. It is tempting to ascribe the changes to a change in the *Zeitgeist*; to see a spirit of collectivism succeeding to one of *laissez-faire* as the dominant legislative opinion. But on closer inspection, the contrast is less profound than at first appears. Precedents for each class of intervention are to be found as far back as the early 1840's, and at least part of the explanation is that it was not until after 1867 that the political conditions of the early 1840's returned. For some years before 1846, and again after 1867, the House of Commons was dominated by parties—normally, by two parties. Hence the government of the day relied on a majority large enough to enable it to carry most of its Bills; although the proportion which foundered seems high by mid-twentieth century standards. In the period, 1846–67, on the other hand, as a result of the Conservative split following the repeal of the Corn Laws, there was a reversion to a situation more closely resembling the eighteenth century, in which the House of Commons had been dominated by groups rather than by parties.

So long as such conditions prevailed, no government found it easy to carry a measure against the opposition of a determined group, no matter what its nominal majority might be.

Most contentious measures did run up against such opposition, and so the period, 1846–67, was not memorable for great re- forms, as compared with the preceding or the following periods. Railway Bills, in particular, had to encounter the opposition of the railway interest—a numerous group of members of both Houses, though stronger in the Commons, and cutting com- pletely across party lines. Today, party loyalty is so strong as to predominate almost invariably over all other interests of an M.P. This is because the M.P. who defies his party is likely to find support withdrawn at constituency level—an event which is virtually certain to lead to the loss of his seat and very likely to mean the end of his political career. In the mid-nineteenth century, on the other hand, many—perhaps most—M.P.'s were so strongly entrenched in their constituencies that they could snap their fingers at the party whips with impunity. Though they called themselves Whigs or Tories, Liberals or Radicals, their behaviour was independent. Hence, a Liberal railway director M.P., giving his general support to a Liberal government, could cheerfully join with a railway director on the other side of the House in opposing a government railway Bill. Of course, such action was not likely to advance a man to the front bench. But many nineteenth-century M.P.'s did not actively aspire to high office. Sir Daniel Gooch, Chairman of the G.W.R., was not untypical when he wrote in his diary on leaving Parliament: 'The House of Commons has been a pleas- ant club. I have taken no part in any of the debates, and have been a silent member. It would be a great advantage to business if there were a greater number who followed my example.'[1] Many motives sent men into Parliament besides straightforward political ambition. They went to serve local communities, to maintain family tradition, to secure higher social status, or to advance industrial or commercial interests. All of these ends could be served by an M.P. who incurred the disfavour of his nominal leaders. Hence many of them did not hesitate to do so.

After the 1867 Reform Act, conditions gradually changed. A party system once more emerged at Westminster, though it was not always a two-party system. The minor parties did not, however, complicate the issue so far as railway measures were

---

[1] *Diaries of Sir Daniel Gooch Bart*, London (1892), 248.

concerned. As the power of the parties grew, so did that of the groups—including the railway interest—decline. M.P.'s became more dependent on their constituencies, and as the franchise spread, the number interested in lower rail charges, for example, came to exceed the number of those interested in high rail profits. None of these changes took place instantaneously. Indeed, they were not complete by the end of the century. Nevertheless, it is worth bearing in mind that the railway legislation of 1867–1914 took place against a changing political background, and that the government was increasingly expected to intervene on behalf of the public at large, and was increasingly able to do so even in restraint of powerful sectional interests— whether the church (Irish disestablishment), the Army (abolition of purchase of commissions), or the railways.

Before discussing new departures, it is worth emphasising that the kind of influence on companies already exercised by the Railway Department continued to grow. Judicial decisions continued to extend the category of 'new lines', power to postpone the opening of which remained the Board's heaviest weapon. In 1872, the court of Chancery upheld the Board's right to inspect a line built on land already belonging to a company[1]—a very important step at a period when the multiplication of existing facilities was becoming more important than the building of new routes. Thus railway companies were penalised as compared with other landlords. Not that private landowners always took advantage of the privilege, however, The Snowdon mountain railway, for example, being entirely built on the estate of a single owner, was not a statutory undertaking, and so not liable to Board of Trade inspection. Nor was the Board anxious to inspect it. At last, however, in 1896, one of the inspectors did look over it unofficially and reported favourably. He recommended that anemometers should be placed at the most exposed places, and train working made subject to a maximum wind force.[2] The L.S.W. introduced in 1897 the first of a new series of engines, the largest and most powerful 0–4–4 tanks ever built. They were originally intended for working express trains over the difficult Dartmoor line west of

[1] *Law Reports (Chancery)*, vii (1871–2), 767; and see above, p. 91.
[2] C. H. Ellis, *British Railway History, 1877–1947*, Allen & Unwin (1959), 143.

Exeter. As a result of criticism by an inspector from the Department following a derailment near Tavistock, the whole class of
engines was transferred to suburban traffic in the London
area.[1] The design of the original locomotives of the Central
London Railway was modified, under the influence of the Board
of Trade, even before a prototype was built. The original proposal was that there should be two electric locomotives to each
train, one at each end, and working together from one controller. But the Railway Department objected, on the ground
that it was undesirable to have power cables running through
the coaches. Instead, locomotives of a different type were designed for working singly at the heads of the trains.[2] The occasional hearing in which the Board of Trade appeared before the
Railway and Canal Commission as a plaintiff is a very incomplete indication of the influence given to it by the legislation
setting up the Commission.

> The informal discussion of grievances between the Board of
> Trade, in accordance with the provisions of section 31 of the
> Railway & Canal Traffic Act, 1888, is a method of conciliation
> which has accomplished much good; 1,577 complaints have been
> dealt with by the Board of Trade under this procedure between
> 1889 and 1907, and in 1,000 instances settlements more or less to
> the satisfaction of the complainants have been obtained or the
> explanations of the railway companies have been accepted. . . .
> We understand that no representation with regard to the condi-
> tions or charges relating to goods traffic made to the Board of
> Trade under these provisions is rejected by them on the ground
> that it does not fall within the scope of the section.[3]

State intervention in the railway sphere went further in three
main directions:

(a) additional measures for the safety of the travelling public.
(b) regulation of charges.
(c) settlement of labour disputes.

The first safety measure in the period was the Railway
Regulation Act,[4] which required companies to provide means

---

[1] Ibid., 188.
[2] Ellis, *British Railway History, 1877–1949*, 163.
[3] *Report of the Departmental Committee on Railway Agreements & Amalgama-
tions* (1911), Cd. 5631, 26.
[4] See above, p. 156.

whereby passengers could communicate with the driver and/or guard in case of emergency. The history of the subject to 1868 reads like a long series of attempts to impose a requirement by law, and of the resistance offered by the companies to those attempts. Events after 1868 suggest that the problem was less simple than that. At the suggestion of the companies, the Board approved the bell and cord system for general use. Access to the cord for passengers was normally provided through the windows. The Board allowed two companies, the S.E.R. and the L.S.W., to continue to use electrical systems. So unsatisfactory did the bell and cord system prove, however, that the Board revoked its approval in 1873.

Why was the 1868 Act not more immediately effective? The Board might have done better to support Tyler's recommendation of an electrical system,[1] by imposing it on companies instead of the bell and cord. No doubt other companies like the G.N.[2] preferred the latter because it was cheaper. Cave had warned the Commons in 1867 against the danger of premature decision: 'if the House compelled the railways to adopt at heavy expense one of the present confessedly imperfect means of communication, they would do great mischief by retarding something better'.[3] The 1868 Act may well have had the effect he foretold. What emerges clearly is that merely to legislate on a railway problem settled nothing, if the technical problems remained unsolved.

In the end, the problem of communication was not so much solved as circumvented. Following the Railway Regulation Act of 1889, it became compulsory for all trains to be fitted with continuous brakes. The next step was to provide means whereby passengers could themselves apply the brakes in case of emergency—the chain in a tube still familiar today as the 'communication cord'. The G.W.R. were the pioneers of the device in 1891. It is a curious instance of conservatism in language that after more than sixty years the chain is still called a cord, and that it is known as a communication cord although its purpose is primarily action and only incidentally communication. The Board approved the new device as complying with the requirements of the 1868 Act, and other companies adopted it

[1] P.P. 1865, l, 26. [2] BTHR GN 1/299/14.
[3] Hansard, clxxxvi, 1831.

216

from the G.W.R. By the early years of the twentieth century, it had become standard throughout the railways of Britain.

An Act of 1871[1] cleared up a curious anomaly. As noted above,[2] the legal basis for the accident enquiries conducted by the Railway Department had been dubious ever since its foundation. Now a procedure was prescribed by which the Board of Trade might appoint a tribunal of three members to investigate accidents. It is interesting to note that in almost a hundred years, the form laid down has in fact scarcely ever been used. The enquiry into the Tay Bridge disaster in 1879 is one of the rare examples. As a general rule, the older, more flexible, pattern of investigation has been preferred. That is not to say, however, that the Act has had no value. Since 1871, as before, the voluntary co-operation of the companies has, in general, been enough to secure for the Board's Inspecting Officers all the facilities they have required. But since 1871 they have had statutory powers in reserve—a big stick to carry, though they have not for that reason ceased to walk softly.

Before 1867 three devices had emerged as paramount in importance for the safety of passengers—interlocking signals, block telegraph working, and continuous brakes. By 1872, the two former were required as a condition for Board of Trade approval of new lines. In 1875, the L.C.D. installed the first lock-and-block working in the world, by which the operation of the signals was interlocked with the telegraph instruments, at Cambria Junction, Brixton. Within a few years, this important advance was extended to the whole of the company's main line. Meanwhile, an Act of 1873[3] had required companies to make annual returns showing what progress they were making with interlocking of signals and the introduction of block working. It was hoped that the resulting publicity would encourage the progressive and shame the recalcitrant.

The importance of these devices was demonstrated in a series of disastrous accidents in the early 'seventies, which led to a Royal Commission on Railway Accidents. One result of the Commission was a series of trials of continuous brakes in 1875,

[1] Regulation of Railways Act, 34 & 35 Vict., c. 78.
[2] See above, p. 43.
[3] Railway Regulation Act (Returns of Signal Arrangements, Workings, etc.), 36 & 37 Vict., c. 76.

from which two—the automatic vacuum and the Westinghouse air—emerged triumphant. Both were automatic as well as continuous. The findings of the Commission did not immediately lead to the imposition by law of any of these devices on the railways. But an Act of 1878,[1] similar in motive to that of 1873, did require the companies to make periodical returns detailing their progress—or lack of it—in introducing continuous brakes on their networks. After a decade, it became apparent that voluntary action had done a good deal. It also became clear that such action alone was unlikely ever to achieve the goal. A tragic accident at Armagh in 1888 settled the issue. It resulted from the train not having automatic brakes. In the following year, an Act[2] required companies to fit automatic brakes to all trains, and to complete the process of interlocking and blocking their entire systems. They were given thee years to fulfil the terms of the Act, and the Board of Trade was entrusted with the power of approving the various types of brake which the companies were using or wished to adopt. The Board was widely criticised for the use it made of its power. Easy co-operation between companies called for interchangeability of rolling stock. Hence it was obviously desirable to standardise brakes. As pointed out above in connection with passenger communications,[3] premature standardisation may inhibit technical progress. But engineers had been developing continuous brakes for more than thirty years and two types—the automatic vacuum the Westinghouse air—were generally accepted as pre-eminent. There can be little doubt that the public interest—and that of the railways themselves—would have been better served had the opportunity been taken to impose one or other of these brakes on all companies. Lack of standardisation remained a problem as late as the 1920's.[4]

The 1889 Act remained the keystone of public safety on the railways down to 1914. Companies continued to experiment with new devices—for example, automatic train control on the G.W.R.—and the Board of Trade to take an interest in the

---

[1] Railway Returns (Continuous Brakes) Act, 41 & 42 Vict., c. 20.
[2] Regulation of Railways Act, 52 & 53 Vict., c. 57.
[3] See above, p. 216.
[4] C. E. R. Sherrington, *Economics of Rail Transport in Great Britain*, E. Arnold (1928), i, 249.

progress that was made. But so far as concerns relations between government and the railways, nothing more need be said here.

As late as 1867, the Royal Commission on Railways was strongly against increasing public control of railways. Not only did it advise against exercising the purchase powers of the 1844 Act, it did not even 'consider it would be expedient, even if it was practicable, to adopt any legislation which would abolish the freedom the railway companies enjoyed of charging what sum they deemed expedient within the maximum rates'.[1] Attitudes began to change, however, in the early 'seventies as a result of a new crop of amalgamation proposals. Once more the cry went up that absolute monopoly was about to be established, and that therefore new measures of state intervention were needed. Whether or not that conclusion was justified, there was considerable misunderstanding of the facts. Far from dying out, competition was increasing, although, paradoxically, monopoly remained strong also. The paradox can be at once illustrated and resolved by reference to three kinds of traffic: main-line expresses; holiday-makers; and imported goods.

As owners of the line between York and Darlington, the N.E.R. was a monopoly and could make a large gross profit from each passenger who joined a train at one of those places and left it at the other. But such local passengers were comparatively unimportant. The main importance of the line was as a stage in the East Coast route, and one partner in that route, the N.E.R., was in competition with the L.N.W.R. and its associated companies for the traffic from London to Scotland. Rivalry became more acute after 1878 when the Midland Railway opened its Settle-Carlisle line, thus providing travellers with a third alternative route. Competition increased still further as the bridging of the Tay and the Forth carried improved communication farther north and culminated in the railway races of 1888 and 1895—perhaps the most flamboyant demonstration of competition ever seen on British railways. Similar examples might be given from other parts of the country. Monopolies, where they existed at all, were local. In spite of all the price-fixing agreements and pooling arrangements, long-distance traffic was competitive.

Most railway companies stood in the relation of sole provider

[1] *Report of the Royal Commission on Railways* (1867), lxxxviii.

to one or more holiday resorts, to whose development they had often contributed much. The N.E.R. had Scarborough, the M.S.L., Cleethorpes, and the L.B.S.C., Brighton. The Londoner who wished to travel to Brighton, and nowhere else, was very much at the mercy of the company. But holiday-makers were not so restricted. In choosing where to spend a holiday, the fare is one of the main considerations. If the company abused its power, the trippers would go elsewhere. Hence the spread of posters boosting the claims of rival resorts. Even where a company owned the sole line to a resort, its monopoly was limited; it was still in competition with other companies for the traffic of uncommitted holiday-makers.

Competition between companies for the traffic in imports can be illustrated by reference to the L.S.W. line from London to Southampton. So far as passengers were concerned, few companies enjoyed so complete a monopoly over so important a line. But the line was in competition for goods traffic both with other railways and with shipping. In deciding at which port to land their cargoes, shipping companies were influenced among other things by the railway rates between the various ports and the ultimate destination of the goods. Moreover, a very high proportion of goods landed at Southampton went on by rail to London; hence the shipping lines had the alternative of landing their cargoes actually in London. L.S.W. goods rates, therefore, had to be competitive both with the rates charged by other companies on lines connecting ports with inland markets, and also with rates by sea. It was reckoned that, in 1872, three-fifths of the stations in the country were affected by the competition of transport by sea. British manufacturers and farmers found it very hard to understand the policy of the companies, and accused the railways of favouring foreigners and ruining native industry and agriculture by flooding the country with cheap imports. As Clapham put it, they 'attributed to railway vice what should have been attributed to Britain's good fortune in being an island with a much indented coast-line'.[1]

Thus competition continued right down till the eve of the First World War. Its cruder manifestations, such as price wars, were avoided by agreements between the companies. But in

[1] J. H. Clapham, *Economic History of Modern Britain: Free Trade & Steel, 1850–1886*, Cambridge (1932), 193.

other ways, it remained vigorous. Take, for example, the succession of innovations made by the Midland in the 'seventies; in 1872 the inclusion of third-class carriages in all passenger trains; in 1874 the introduction of the first Pullman cars to run in Britain; in 1875, the abolition of second class; all of these moves were animated by the desire—which was largely successful—of securing from its rivals a larger share of the North-South passenger traffic. Nor was competition in facilities confined to passenger services. Goods agents could outbid one another in a score of ways: favourable warehouse charges; turning a blind eye to traders' full trucks left on sidings; free weighing; or complaisance in settling claims for delay and damage. The increasing standardisation of rates and fares tended to stimulate competition in facilities. Long before its force was spent, competition from other forms of inland transport—almost dead since 1840—had begun to revive. By 1914, electric trams and the motor car had proved themselves serious rivals to the steam locomotive.

These considerations, however, carried little weight with the public when faced with a crop of amalgamation proposals. The Joint Committee on Railways, 1872, put paid to the schemes then under consideration, and without calling for immediate regulation of charges, made a recommendation which turned out to be an important step in that direction. This was that a new tribunal should be set up to deal with the complaints of the public and to exercise the jurisdiction created by Cardwell's 1854 Act. An Act of 1873[1] implemented this recommendation by setting up the Railway Commission, at first for five years, but renewed thereafter year by year. As shown above,[2] Cardwell's Act had not in itself had significant results, but with the provision of new machinery, more use began to be made of its provisions. Within three years, the Commission had dealt with as many cases as there had been during the whole of the period 1854–73. By 1882, the total number of cases decided had risen to 110.

The Commission and the Department were both central government agencies concerned with railways, but beyond that, they had little in common. The contrast between the two is illuminating, especially since the setting-up of the

[1] 36 & 37 Vict., c. 48.   [2] See above, p. 154.

Commission would have been unnecessary, in all probability, had the Department been able to persevere with the policy of 'equivalents' initiated by Gladstone.[1] Gladstone's idea was to regulate rail charges by administrative means; to persuade the companies to reduce their rates in return for protection against the competition of new lines. Had such a pattern become established, it is likely that rail users would have got into the habit of addressing all their complaints to the Board of Trade, and would not have felt the need of a special tribunal. Pressure on the companies would have been likely to succeed as a rule, because they were not to be asked to do something for nothing; for each concession, they were to get an equivalent. The Commission, on the other hand, was a judicial body, and so had nothing to offer companies in return for the concessions it exacted. Proceedings in almost all cases were opened by traders, and took the form of complaints against companies. The Commission's judgments tended to take the form of compromises between what the complainants sought and the previous practice of the companies. Those who complained rarely got all they wanted, but they stood a fair chance of getting something. Companies, on the other hand, except occasionally when they used its procedure against another company,[2] got nothing out of the Commission. However impartial it might be, it was bound to confer more benefits on traders than on companies, since it was difficult for it to confer any on the latter at all.

With the onset of the Great Depression, the vague belief of the man in the street that rail charges were oppressive became a profound grievance. 'General prices had been falling for years. Looking about in its malaise, the trading community saw some real abuses on the railways; a great many things which it did not understand that looked like abuses; and a government mechanism for checking abuses—real or potential —which was unmistakably inadequate. At all costs traders wanted lower rates or better facilities, or a combination of the two, to meet the needs of the time. They alleged that they got neither, or that the wrong people—importers of foreign goods in bulk, perhaps—got both.'[3] Manufacturers, farmers, and

[1] See above, pp. 77 ff.
[2] For an example, see Ellis, *British Railway History, 1877–1947*, 54.
[3] J. H. Clapham, 1932, op. cit., 196.

traders felt that rail charges should fall in sympathy with the general fall in prices, and that such a reduction in costs would tend to offset the general decline in profits which rail users were experiencing. Symptomatic of this new mood was the appointment of a Parliamentary committee in 1881 to discuss, quite simply, rates and fares.

Joseph Chamberlain, as President of the Board of Trade, made, in 1884, the first attempt to legislate on the Committee's recommendations by extending the powers of the Railway Commission. He failed. As a counter-move, the companies prepared Bills on railway charges for the session of 1885, the progress of which was cut short by Gladstone's defeat in June of that year. Salisbury's first Cabinet got as far as considering the sixth and final draft of a Bill on the same subject. Mundella found it on his desk when he went to the Board of Trade in 1886, and took it as the base of a measure which he introduced himself. It had no more success than previous attempts, but it is a nice point whether it contributed to the defeat of the first Home Rule Bill, or whether it was the defeat of the latter which engulfed a proposal for the railways which would otherwise have passed. Salisbury's second government made yet one more attempt in 1887 with a Bill closely resembling Mundella's. *The Economist* commented: 'To introduce a new measure which retains all the objectionable features of the old one is simply to court defeat. It is a proceeding which can only be explained on the assumption that the permanent officials of the Board of Trade have succeeded in dominating their successive Presidents.'[1]

Eventually, in 1888, the Railway & Canal Traffic Act[2] settled the question. It made permanent the tribunal set up in 1873, under the extended style of the Railway and Canal Commission. Each company was to submit a revised classification of merchandise traffic, in place of the crude and conflicting scales contained in the original Acts. This was not too difficult, since the Railway Clearing House had, in fact, used such a classification for many years. Suitably amended, it now acquired

---

[1] q. in W. H. G. Armytage, 'The Railway Rates Question & the Fall of the Third Gladstone Ministry', *English Historical Review*, lxv (1950), 45–6; see also, P. M. Williams, 'Public Opinion & the Railway Rates Question in 1886', ibid., lxvii (1952), 37–73.   [2] 51 & 52 Vict., c. 25.

the force of law. Companies had also to submit revised schedules of rates and charges—a task which was very much more difficult. In the first place, millions of distinct rates were involved. In the second, the new scales had to blend together three distinct elements: toll, haulage charge, and terminal charge. The earliest Railway Acts had assumed that rail traffic would be, like canal traffic, largely carried on by independent carriers, subject to the payment of toll to the company. The main stress in the Acts had, therefore, been on the fixing of maximum tolls. As soon as it became apparent that the companies would, in practice, be sole carriers on their lines, maximum rates for haulage were also laid down in their Acts. The very cheapness of the railway as compared with all preceding forms of transport soon made these ineffective, however. Companies could make large profits while charging much less than the sums permitted by law. The third element—the terminal charge—differed from the first two in that it did not derive from the Acts of the companies. A terminal was the payment demanded for services rendered at either end of the haul; e.g. loading and unloading, use of the stations, etc. The companies had made three attempts during the 'sixties to secure Parliamentary recognition for the principle in return for statutory limitation on the sums that might be charged. Each had failed, because public opinion was not willing to concede any justification for such charges at all—a good example, incidentally, of the weakness of the railway interest when it tried to do something positive, as contrasted with its strength in opposing measures originating elsewhere. What Parliament had denied, the courts eventually granted; in *Hall* v. *L.B.S.C.R.* (1885) the legality of terminals was upheld.

When the companies' schemes began to come in it became apparent that they and the Board of Trade did not agree. During 1889 and 1890 two special commissioners sat for eighty-five days to consider the companies' proposals, to which more than 4,000 objections had been tabled. The Board then submitted to Parliament thirty-five Provisional Orders with Schedules of maximum rates. After some further revision by a Joint Committee, the upshot was a series of Confirmation Acts, under which the day appointed for the new rates to come into force was 1 January, 1893.

But the new statutory rates were maxima. The rates hitherto charged in an immense number of cases had been special rates. The companies were not unwilling to let special rates continue, but had not had time to work them out afresh to come into effect simultaneously with the new maxima. Instead of continuing to charge the old rates, pending the calculation of new ones, the companies began demanding the new maxima, without making it clear to the public that their policy was only provisional. A great many traders found, therefore, that the outcome of the long agitation to reduce railway rates by state intervention was that they were actually having to pay more. Understandably, there was a great outcry. The result was yet another Act,[1] passed in 1894. It had the effect of freezing rates at the levels ruling on 31 December, 1892, and preventing companies from raising their charges, even to the legal maxima, unless they could satisfy the Commission that they had reasonable grounds for doing so. The consequences for the national economy were serious. Companies hesitated to reduce their charges, even experimentally, because they knew that if they wished to raise a rate again, the Commission might not let them do so. Hence the structure of charges became more and more rigid as years went by.

This rigidity was one of the main factors in the labour trouble on the railways in the late nineteenth and early twentieth centuries. Once the companies found their charges restricted by law, they naturally tried to stabilise their costs wherever they could, and notably their labour costs. Their traditional reluctance to meet the demands of their employees became even more marked, in regard both to wages and hours. As shown above,[2] the Railway Department in its early years took an interest in the question of railwaymen's hours, not so much on philanthropic grounds, as because excessive hours would, by causing fatigue, endanger the safety of passengers. Inspectors returned to this theme again and again over the years in their reports on accidents. In the Clayton Tunnel accident on the L.B.S.C. in 1861—the most serious on a British line up to that time—it came out that the two signalmen involved worked a twenty-four hour shift alternate Sundays.[3] Tyler said of another

[1] 57 & 58 Vict., c. 54.   [2] See above, p. 48.
[3] C. H. Ellis, *British Railway History, 1830–1876*, Allen & Unwin (1954), 281.

tunnel collision, at Blackheath on the S.E.R. in 1864, that it was at least in part due to the men's excessive hours. Yolland, reporting on an accident on the L.N.W. in the following year, remarked that signalmen who came on duty at 5.30 a.m. frequently worked through until 9 p.m. or later.[1]

In other industries, such grievances would have been taken up by Trade Unions. But on the railways, the employers with rare exceptions refused to recognise organised labour. The workers naturally looked instead to Parliament for help. A Liberal M.P., F. A. Channing, took up their cause and secured in 1891 the appointment of a Select Committee. It found that overwork was widespread, and systematic rather than exceptional. Railways were state-granted monopolies and the state had the right and the duty to insist on safe working and just conditions of labour, including reasonable hours. The varied conditions of railway service made it advisable to deal with each case on its merits. It was therefore better to delegate to the Board of Trade power to fix the hours to be worked than to limit them by statute. Disputes about hours between the companies and the Board should be dealt with by the Railway and Canal Commission. An Act substantially embodying these recommendations was passed in 1893.[2]

Intervention in conditions of work followed intervention in hours. The Railway Employment (Prevention of Accidents) Act, 1900,[3] sought to reduce the human costs of rail transport. It gave power to the Board of Trade to make such rules as would reduce as far as possible the dangers inherent in railway work. The companies were allowed a right of appeal to the Railway and Canal Commission. A series of rules made under the Act came into force in 1903 relative to the protection of permanent-way staff engaged on re-laying work; the protection of points and rodding; the labelling of wagons; and the lighting of sidings and stations. The Factory & Workshop Act, 1901,[4] was used in a similar way. Regulations made under it concerning the safety of men working in connection with shunting yards and train operation came into force at the beginning of 1907.

It has been shown above[5] how rail charges came to be

---

[1] C. H. Ellis, *British Railway History, 1877–1947*, Allen & Unwin (1959), 205–6.　　　[2] 63 & 64 Vict., c. 27.

[3] Ibid.　　　[4] 1 Edw. VII, c. 22.　　　[5] See above, p. 225.

stabilised by the Act of 1894. Two years later there was a reversal in the long trend of falling prices, and from then until 1914 prices tended generally to rise. The rigidity of rail charges naturally made companies reluctant to grant their workers higher pay, and was therefore an important—possibly the most important—cause of stagnant railway wages and so of the labour troubles that began with the Taff Vale strike of 1900 and culminated in the national strike of 1911.

The first threat of a national strike had come in 1907. Its aims would have been better wages and hours, but above all recognition. Lloyd George, then at the Board of Trade, stepped in at the last moment and averted the threat by prevailing on both sides to accept a system of Conciliation Boards. This was not quite what the men wanted, but it was a step towards recognition. The new machinery did not work well, however, and in fact constituted one of the grievances in the national strike of 1911. It was the period of the Agadir crisis. If war had come, the railways would of course have had a vital part to play, as they had in fact in 1914. Hence Asquith saw the leaders on both sides, and told them that the government could not allow the transport of the country to be paralysed. The government had power to take over the railways in time of national emergency under an Act of 1871,[1] passed at a time when the Franco-German war had brought home the rôle of railways in war. The Prime Minister's intervention, though significant of the stage which government intervention in railway affairs had reached, did not avert the strike. But Lloyd George soon settled it. He promised that the 1907 machinery should be speeded up and that a Royal Commission should review the whole procedure. The companies did not explicitly concede recognition; but it was almost impossible any longer to ignore the unions, once the Prime Minister had conferred with them. The government allowed the companies to pass on to the public the cost of meeting some of their claims. The Railway & Canal Traffic Act, 1913,[2] authorised higher rates and fares where it could be shown, to the satisfaction of the Railway Commissioners, that costs had risen in consequence of improved conditions of labour. The Commissioners had long recognised such increases as valid

---

[1] Regulation of the Forces Act, 34 & 35 Vict., c. 86.
[2] 2 & 3 Geo. 5, c. 29.

grounds for higher charges. But companies had generally preferred to risk discontent among their workers by keeping wages down than to antagonise their customers by seeking to raise rates. Now, with the blessing of the government, a general rise of 4 per cent ensued.

In 1872, Tyler had prophesied that the tendency towards consolidation would bring up the question 'whether the State shall manage the railways, or whether the railways shall manage the State'.[1] By 1913, when an Act of Parliament was needed, in a country whose business men boasted of free enterprise and individual initiative, before any railway company could put up its charges even by 4 per cent, Tyler's question seemed to have been answered by events. Any lingering doubts must, it would seem, have been dispelled by the events of the following year. When war broke out, the government, exercising its powers under the 1871 Act, took over the railways. Mobilisation went like clockwork. More than 1,400 special trains carried over 330,000 troops with their guns, horses, vehicles, and stores. The B.E.F. was landed in France in sixteen days without accident of any kind. The railways earned a tribute from Kitchener, speaking in the House of Lords. The government's Railway Executive Committee was managing more than 21,000 miles of route, the property of 130 companies or joint committees. The ascendancy of the state over the railways seemed complete.

But a look at the men who were exercising these powers on the state's behalf gives rather a different impression. They were not politicians, servicemen, or civil servants, but railway officers. The President of the Board of Trade was nominally head of the Railway Executive Committee but its effective chief was Herbert Walker, General Manager of the L.S.W. The members of the Committee were his opposite numbers from other leading companies. The government's Director-General of Movements and Railways was Guy Granet, General Manager of the Midland. All this was sensible enough, and largely a condition for the successful results achieved. At the same time it remains true that the state was managing the railways by delegating to railway officers very extensive powers, and that therefore those officers had acquired an important share in managing the state.

[1] Cleveland-Stevens, 260.

The events of 1914 make it clear that Tyler's distinction had been a false one. To think of the individual versus society, man versus the state—to quote the title of Herbert Spencer's famous pamphlet—or railways versus the government was in harmony with the general trend of thought in nineteenth-century Britain, but fallacious nevertheless. The individual is the product of society just as society is what individuals have made it. Had there been no government there would have been no railways; the capital could not have been raised, the land could not have been held, the passage of trains from place to place could not have been guaranteed. Equally, had there been no railways, government would have been very different from what it was. At the time, hostility was often thought of as the keynote of dealings between the government and the railways in the nineteenth century. In retrospect, it can be seen that the hostility was only superficial, and that the more fundamental pattern was one of emerging partnership.

APPENDIX A

Presidents and Vice-Presidents of the Board of Trade, 1840–67, with their dates of appointment

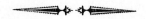

Date	President	Vice-President
27 Aug. 1839	H. Labouchere	R. L. Sheil
21 Jun. 1841		F. Maule
6 Sept. 1841	1st Earl of Ripon	W. E. Gladstone
16 May, 1843	W. E. Gladstone	10th Earl of Dalhousie
3 Feb. 1845	10th Earl of Dalhousie	Sir George Clerk
6 Jul. 1846	4th Earl of Clarendon	T. Milner-Gibson
22 Jul. 1847	H. Labouchere	
6 May, 1848		2nd Earl Granville
6 Feb. 1852		2nd Baron Stanley of Alderley
27 Feb. 1852	J. W. Henley	
28 Dec. 1852	E. Cardwell	2nd Baron Stanley of Alderley
31 Mar. 1855	2nd Baron Stanley of Alderley	E. P. Bouverie
30 Jul. 1855		R. Lowe
6 Apr. 1858	J. W. Henley	4th Earl of Donoughmore
3 Mar. 1859	4th Earl of Donoughmore	Lord Lovaine
18 Jun. 1859		J. Wilson
1 Jul. 1859	T. Milner-Gibson	
12 Aug. 1859		W. F. Cowper
22 Feb. 1860		Sir William Hutt
29 Nov. 1865		G. J. Goschen
6 Feb. 1866		W. Monsell
6 Jul. 1866	Sir Stafford Northcote	Sir Stephen Cave
6 Jul. 1867	6th Duke of Richmond	

APPENDIX B

The Commissioners of Railways

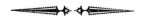

Col. R. C. Alderson, R.E. (died 1849). Commissioner of Railways, 1848. Secretary, Chelsea Hospital, 1849.

Col. Brandreth, R.E. (died 1848). Commissioner of Railways, 1846–8.

Henry Labouchere, 1st Baron Taunton (1798–1869). President of the Commissioners of Railways, 1848–51. M.P. (Whig), 1826–59. Held various ministerial and Cabinet posts, 1832–58, including Vice-Presidency (1835–9) and Presidency (1839–41 and 1847–52) of the Board of Trade. Raised to the peerage, 1859.

Granville G. Leveson-Gower, 2nd Earl Granville (1815–91). Commissioner of Railways, 1847–51. M.P. (Whig), 1836–46. Succeeded to the peerage, 1846. Held various ministerial and Cabinet posts, including Vice-Presidency of the Board of Trade (1848–51). Later Foreign Secretary and Leader of the Whig and Liberal peers in the House of Lords.

Sir Edward Ryan (1793–1875). Commissioner of Railways, 1846–51. Called to the Bar, 1817. Kt. 1826. Indian Judge and later Chief Justice of Bengal, 1826–43. Judicial Committee of the Privy Council, from 1843. Assistant Controller of the Exchequer, 1851–62. Chairman, Civil Service Commissioners, from 1855.

Edward Strutt, 1st Baron Belper, (1801–80). President of Commissioners of Railways, 1846–8. M.P. (Liberal), 1830–47 and 1851–1856. His election in 1847 was declared void on account of bribery; see Hansard, xcviii, 402. Raised to the peerage, 1856.

APPENDIX C

Higher Civil Servants with Responsibility for Regulation of Railways, 1840–67

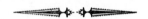

Arthur Barron. Legal Assistant, 1847–65 (6?).

James Booth (1796–1880). Joint Secretary of the Board of Trade, 1850–65. Educated at Cambridge. Called to the Bar, 1824. Served on Royal Commission on Municipal Corporations, 1833. Counsel to the Speaker, 1839–50.

Hon. W. F. Bruce. Secretary to the Railway Commissioners, 1846–7.

Capt. Joshua Coddington, R.E. Assistant Inspector, 1844–6; Inspector, 1846–7. Secretary, Caledonian Railway Company, from 1847.

W. D. Fane (1816–1912). Legal Assistant, 1855 (6?)–66 (7?), and Assistant Secretary, Railway Department, 1865–6. Educated at Cambridge. Called to the Bar, 1841.

T. H. Farrer, 1st Baron Farrer (1819–99). Joint Secretary of the Board of Trade, 1865–7, and Permanent Secretary, 1867–86. Educated at Eton and Oxford. Called to Bar, 1844. Legal Assistant, 1848–1850. Served in the Marine Department from 1850, and became its head in 1854. Baronet, 1883. Raised to the peerage, 1893.

Capt. Sir Douglas Galton, R.E. (1822–99). Held various positions under Commissioners of Railways and in the Railway Department, 1847–54; in charge of Railway Department, 1854–9. Educated at Birmingham, Geneva, Rugby, and R.M.A., Woolwich. First commissioned, 1840. Ordnance Survey, 1846–7. Held various posts under the War Office, 1860–9. Director of Works and Buildings in the Office of Works, 1869–75.

Gen. Sir Henry Harness, R.E. (1804–83). Joined the staff of the Commissioners of Railways in 1846, and served as their Secretary, 1847–50. Educated at R.M.A., Woolwich. First commissioned, 1827. Instructor at Woolwich and at R.E. Establishment, Chatham, 1834–45. Inspector of Welsh Roads under the Home Office,

1845–6. Deputy-Master of the Mint, 1850–2. Commissioner of Public Works, Ireland, 1852–4. Various military posts, 1854–60. Director, R.E. Establishment, Chatham, 1860–5.

Sir Robert Herbert (1831–1905). Became head of Railway Department, 1867. Educated at Eton and Oxford. Private secretary to Gladstone. Called to the Bar, 1858. Colonial Secretary to the Governor of Queensland, 1859. First Premier of Queensland, 1860–5. Transferred from Board of Trade to Colonial Office, 1870, and served as its Permanent Under-Secretary, 1871–92.

Maj.-Gen. C. S. Hutchinson, R.E. (1826–1912). Inspector, 1867–95. First commissioned, 1843. Promoted Maj.-Gen., 1876.

Lt.-Gen. Sir Robert Laffan, R.E. (1821–82). Inspector, 1847–52. Educated in France and R.M.A., Woolwich. First commissioned, 1837. Served in Africa, Mauritius, and Ireland, 1839–47. M.P. (Con.) for St. Ives, 1852–7. Held various military appointments, 1854–77. Governor of Bermuda, 1877–82.

Samuel Laing (1812–97). Served in Railway Department, 1840–5. Educated at Houghton-le-Spring Grammar School and Cambridge. Called to the Bar, 1837. Private Secretary to H. Labouchere. Chairman, L.B.S.C.R., 1848–55, and 1867–94. M.P. (Lib.), 1852–7, 1859–60, 1865–8, and 1872–85. Financial Secretary to the Treasury, 1859–60; Finance Member, Government of India, 1860–5.

Duncan MacGregor. Joined Railway Department as clerk in 1842. Registrar, 1844–53 (4?). Senior Clerk, 1853 (4?)–9. Head of Railway Department, 1859–65. Assistant to Fane (*q.v.*), 1865–6, and to Herbert, (1867–). Probably a brother of John MacGregor, Joint Permanent Secretary of the Board of Trade, 1840–7.

Major Morland. Assistant in Railway Department, 1854.

Capt. Donatus O'Brien. General Secretary, 1844–6. Prior to 1844, served in Army, as private secretary to Sir James Graham, and as secretary to the G.N.E.R. Later an Inspector of Prisons.

General Sir Charles Pasley, R.E. (1780–1861). Inspector-General, 1841–6. Educated at R.M.A., Woolwich. First commissioned, 1797. On active service from 1799. First Director, R.E. Establishment, Chatham, 1812–41. Public Examiner, East India Company's School, Addiscombe, 1839–55.

G. R. Porter (1792–1852). Superintendent of Railway Department, 1840–4. Senior Member of Railway Board, 1844–5. After failing in business as a sugar-broker, Porter was recommended to Lord Auckland (then President of the Board of Trade) as a statistician. First head of Statistical Department from 1833. Joint Secretary of the Board of Trade, 1847–52.

Col. F. H. Rich, R.E. (*1824–?*). Inspector from 1861.

Capt. G. Ross, R.E. Inspector, 1858–61.

Field-Marshal Sir John Simmons, R.E. (*1821–1903*). Inspector 1847–50. Secretary, 1850–4. Educated Elizabeth College, Guernsey, and R.M.A., Woolwich. First commissioned, 1837. Served in Canada, 1839–45; Turkey and the Crimea, 1853–7. Consul-General at Warsaw, 1858–60. C.R.E., Aldershot, 1860–5. Director, R.E. Establishment, Chatham, 1865–8. Lieutenant-Governor, R.M.A., Woolwich, 1869–75. Inspector-General of Fortifications under the War Office, 1875–80. Governor of Malta, 1884–8.

Gen. Sir Frederic Smith, R.E. (*1790–1874*). Inspector-General, 1840–1. Educated at a military school at Gt. Marlow and at R.M.A., Woolwich. First commissioned, 1805. On active service, 1807–12. Various military appointments, 1812–41. Kt., 1830. Gentleman-Usher, 1834–74. Commissioner under the Treasury for reporting on railway communication with Scotland, 1839–41. Director, R.E. Establishment, Chatham, 1842–51. Served on Royal Commissions on Railway Gauges and on Metropolitan Termini. Various military appointments from 1851. M.P. (Con.), 1852–3, when he was unseated on petition; 1857–68. Public Examiner and Inspector, East India Company School, Addiscombe, from 1856.

Capt. Sir Henry Tyler, R.E. (*1827–1908*). Inspector, 1853–70; Chief Inspecting Officer, 1870–7. Educated at R.M.A., Woolwich. Director, Grand Trunk Railway of Canada from 1867; later became Vice-President; and finally, President, 1877–95. Chairman, Westinghouse Brake Company, Peruvian Corporation and Rhymney Iron Company; Deputy Chairman, G.E.R., M.P., (Con.), 1880–92.

Col. G. Wynne, R.E. Inspector, 1847–58.

Lt.-Col. W. Yolland, R.E. (*1810–85*). Inspector, 1854–77; Chief Inspecting Officer, 1877–85. Educated at Exeter, Plymouth, and R.M.A., Woolwich. First commissioned, 1828. Served in Canada, 1831–5. Ordnance Survey, 1838–53. Director, London and St. Katherine Dock Co.

BIBLIOGRAPHY

A. UNPUBLISHED SOURCES

Public Record Office

The most important classes used are:

MT 6 Board of Trade Railway Department: Correspondence &
Papers (Transport): 49 boxes.

MT 11 Board of Trade Railway Department: Out-letter Books,
1840–1855; 30 volumes.

MT 13 Board of Trade Railway Department: Minute Books,
1844–1856; 21 volumes.

BT 6 Board of Trade Miscellaneous: 280 is a box of correspondence and papers of the Railway Department dating from
1842.

(From the point of view of records, the period falls into two parts.
Prior to 1855, there survive only a small proportion of all the papers
received, but minutes and out-letters on the great majority of all the
cases dealt with. From 1855, the surviving records are brought
together in files relating to particular cases. The surviving files are
only a small proportion of the whole; but each normally contains all
the papers—in- and out-letters, reports, minutes, and memoranda
—on the case.)

Private Papers

Melbourne Papers (Windsor Castle)
Clarendon Papers (Bodleian Library)
Ripon Papers (British Museum)
Peel Papers (British Museum)
Gladstone Papers (British Museum)
Pasley Papers (British Museum)
Aberdeen Papers (British Museum)
Russell Papers (Public Record Office)
Cardwell Papers (Public Record Office)
Dalhousie Papers (Scottish Record Office)
Disraeli Papers (Hughenden Manor)

N.B.—The National Register of Archives kindly let me see a list
of the papers of Sir Stafford Northcote, 1st Earl Iddesleigh, at a

time when the papers themselves were not available for study; it became apparent that there was nothing in this collection of importance for this subject. I am informed by Miss Nancy Mitford, who has worked on them, that the Stanley of Alderley papers were lost during the war of 1939–45. Search was also made for the papers of all those who held office as President or Vice-President (with the exception of a few who did so only for a few months): but in the remaining cases, neither relevant material, nor clear proof that none survives, came to light.

British Transport Historical Records

Records of the following railway companies:

> Bedale & Leyburn
> Cornwall
> Eastern Counties
> Great North of England
> Great Northern
> Hawes & Melmerby
> Lancashire & Yorkshire
> Leeds & Thirsk (later Leeds Northern)
> London & Brighton
> London, Brighton & South Coast
> London & North Western
> Mid Wales
> Midland
> North Eastern
> North London
> North Staffordshire
> Oxford, Worcester & Wolverhampton
> Stockton & Darlington
> York & Newcastle
> York, Newcastle & Berwick
> York & North Midland

N.B.—Communications from the Board of Trade to a company were normally referred by the Board of Directors, or appropriate Committee, to one of their officers (e.g. General Manager or Engineer) for a report, in the light of which the company's reply would be drafted. In searching a company's records, we may therefore expect to find traces of its dealings with the Board of Trade mainly in its correspondence, officers' reports, and minutes. Unfortunately, except for certain companies, notably the G.N. and the Midland, comparatively little survives under the first two of these headings. Companies' records have not, therefore, proved so useful in this study as was hoped.

BIBLIOGRAPHY

House of Lords Record Office

Proceedings on Railway Bills.

Ministry of Transport

Copies of Inspectors' Reports.
Requirements for new lines.

B. PUBLISHED SOURCES

Official

Hansard's Parliamentary Debates.
Journals of the House of Lords.
Journals of the House of Commons.
Parliamentary Papers.
Acts of Parliament: (i) Public General. (ii) Local & Personal.

Newspapers and Periodicals

Herapath's Railway Magazine.
Law Journal.
Railway Times.
The Times.

Books and Articles

A great number of books and articles, dealing especially with the
history of individual companies and with statesmen who held
office at the Board of Trade, have been examined for the purposes
of this study. Most of them yielded nothing of value. Few railway
historians have been interested in government regulation and few
political biographers have concerned themselves with day-to-day
administration. Books and articles which have been found useful
have already been fully cited in footnotes to the text.

INDEX

INDEX

239

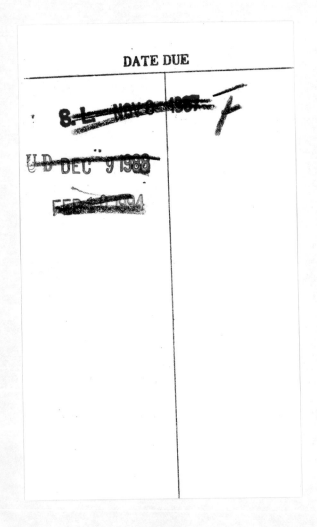